TEACHING
for a Culturally Diverse and Racially Just World

TEACHING
for a Culturally Diverse
and Racially Just World

edited by

ELEAZAR S. FERNANDEZ

 CASCADE *Books* • Eugene, Oregon

TEACHING FOR A CULTURALLY DIVERSE AND RACIALLY JUST WORLD

Copyright © 2014 Wipf and Stock Publishers. All rights reserved. Except for brief quotations in critical publications or reviews, no part of this book may be reproduced in any manner without prior written permission from the publisher. Write: Permissions. Wipf and Stock Publishers, 199 W. 8th Ave., Suite 3, Eugene, OR 97401.

Cascade Books
An Imprint of Wipf and Stock Publishers
199 W. 8th Ave., Suite 3
Eugene, OR 97401

www.wipfandstock.com

ISBN 13: 978-1-62032-110-2

Cataloguing-in-Publication Data

Teaching for a culturally diverse and racially just world / edited by Eleazar S. Fernandez.

xiv + 266 p. ; 23 cm. Includes bibliographical references.

ISBN 13: 978-1-62032-110-2

1. Theology—Study and teaching. 2. Clergy—Training of. 3. Multicultural education. I. Fernandez, Eleazar S. II. Title.

BV4020 T45 2014

Manufactured in the U.S.A.

Contents

Essay Contributors • vii
Acknowledgements • xiii

Introduction: Birthing Culturally Diverse and Racially Just Educational Institutions: Teaching to Transgress and Transform • 1
—Eleazar S. Fernandez

1 Theological Education of Not Yet • 21
   —Fumitaka Matsuoka

2 When *Subjects* Matter: The Bodies We Teach By • 31
   —Mai-Anh Le Tran

3 From Foreign Bodies in Teacher Space to Embodied Spirit in *Personas Educadas*: or, How to Prevent "Tourists of Diversity" in Education • 52
   —Loida I. Martell-Otero

4 Racial/Ethnic Diversity and Student Formation • 69
   —Peter T. Cha

5 You Cannot Teach What You Do Not Know: You Cannot Lead Where You Have Not Been • 88
   —Archie Smith Jr.

6 What Shall We Teach? The Content of Theological Education • 109
   —Willie James Jennings

7   Thoughts on Curriculum as Formational Praxis for
Faculty, Students, and their Communities · 126
—Elizabeth Conde-Frazier

8   Teaching Disruptively: Pedagogical Strategies to Teach
Cultural Diversity and Race · 147
—Boyung Lee

9   A Pedagogy of the Unmasked: "Unheard but Not Unvoiced, Unseen but Not Invisible" · 167
—Julia M. Speller

10   The Vocational Cycle to Support Institutional Justice:
A Pathway for Scholars of Color to Transform Institu-
tional Life and Governance · 184
—Mary Hinton

11   Institutional Life and Governance: Realities and Chal-
lenges for Racial-Ethnic Leadership within Historically
White Theological Schools · 202
—David Maldonado Jr.

12   Angle of Vision from a Companion/Ally in Teaching for
a Culturally Diverse and Racially Just World · 219
—Paul O. Myhre

13   Faculty Colleagues as Allies in Resisting Racism · 238
—Nancy Ramsay

Bibliography · 253

Essay Contributors

Peter T. Cha is Associate Professor of Pastoral Theology at Trinity Evangelical Divinity School, where he has taught since 1997. Trained at the University of Chicago (BA in sociology), Trinity Evangelical Divinity School (MDiv and ThM) and Northwestern University (PhD in Social Ethics and Sociology of Religion), Dr. Cha has also served as a member of the CORE (Committee of Race and Ethnicity) of ATS and participated in the Lexington Seminar's Academic Leadership Mentoring Project. His recent writings include chapters in *This Side of Heaven: Race, Ethnicity, and Christian Faith* (Oxford University Press, 2006), *Growing Healthy Asian American Churches* (InterVarsity, 2006), and *Revitalizing Practice: Collaborative Models for Theological Faculties* (Peter Lang, 2008).

Elizabeth Conde-Frazier is Vice President of Education and Dean of Esperanza College of Eastern University. Previously, she was professor of religious education at the Claremont School of Theology and taught Hispanic/Latino/a theology at the Latin American Bible Institute, in California. She is author of *Hispanic Bible Institutes: A Community of Theological Construction* (Scranton University Press, 2004), *A Many Colored Kingdom: Multicultural Dynamics for Spiritual Formation* (co-authored) (Baker Academic, 2004), and *Listen to the Children: Conversations with Immigrant Families* (bilingual) (Judson, 2011). She has also written on the subjects of participatory action research, Latina feminist theology, the spirituality of the scholar, and issues of justice as they relate to education.

Eleazar S. Fernandez is Professor of Constructive Theology at United Theological Seminary of the Twin Cities, New Brighton, Minnesota. His published works include *Burning Center, Porous Borders: The Church in a Globalized World* (Wipf and Stock, 2011), *New Overtures: Asian North American Theology in the 21st Century* (edited, Sopher, 2012), *Reimagining* *the Human: Theological Anthropology in Response to Systemic Evils* (Chalice, 2004), *Realizing the America of our Hearts: Theological Voices of Asian Americans* (co-edited with Fumitaka Matsuoka, Chalice, 2003), *A Dream Unfinished: Voices from the Margins* (co-edited with Fernando Segovia, Orbis, 2000), and *Toward a Theology of Struggle* (Orbis, 1994). He has taught in countries outside the U.S., including Myanmar, Cameroon, and the Philippines (Union Theological Seminary). As of June 2013, he is President of Union Theological Seminary, Philippines.

Mary Hinton is the Vice President for Planning and Assessment at Mount Saint Mary College, in Newburgh, New York. She serves on the Board of Directors of the Religious Education Association and the Association of General and Liberal Studies, and is the former president of the Mid-Atlantic Region of the American Academy of Religion. She actively publishes her research on the historic black church and frequently provides national presentations about assessment, strategic planning, and diversity. Dr. Hinton has a BA in psychology from Williams College, an MA in psychology from the University of Kansas, and a PhD in religion and religious education from Fordham University.

Willie James Jennings is Associate Professor of Theology and Black Church Studies at Duke Divinity School, Durham, North Carolina. Dr. Jennings earned his PhD from Duke University. He teaches in the areas of systematic theology and black church and cultural studies. The author of numerous articles, his research interests include these areas as well as liberation theologies, cultural identities, and anthropology. An ordained Baptist minister, Dr. Jennings has served as interim pastor of several North Carolina churches and continues to be an active teaching and preaching minister in the local church. He is the author of *The Christian Imagination: Theology and the Origins of Race* (Yale University Press, 2010).

Boyung Lee, a native of Korea, is Associate Professor of Educational Ministries at Pacific School of Religion, Berkeley, California. The breadth of her educational preparation extends from Korea to the United States. Among her published works are "From A Margin within the Margin: Rethinking the Dynamics of Christianity and Culture From A Postcolonial Feminist Perspective" (in *Journal of Theologies and Cultures of Asia*); "Realities, Visions, and Promises of a Multicultural Future" (co-authored with Mary Elizabeth Moore, et al., in *Religious Education);* "Caring-self and Women's Self-esteem: A Feminist's Reflection on Pastoral Care and Religious Education of Korean-American Women" (in *Pastoral Psychology),* and "Teaching

Justice and Living Peace: Body, Sexuality and Religious Education in Asian American Communities" (in *Religious Education*). She is the author of *Restoring Community in the Mainline: A Pedagogical Guide to Communal Faith and Ministry* (Westminster John Knox, forthcoming).

David Maldonado Jr. is President *Emeritus* of Iliff School of Theology and Director of the Center for Latino/a Christianity and Religions at SMU's Perkins School of Theology. His books include *Crossing Guadalupe Street* (co-authored, University of New Mexico Press, 2001), *Hispanic Christianity within Mainline Protestant Traditions: A Bibliography* (Asociación para la Educación Teológica Hispana,1998), and *Protestantes/Protestants: Hispanic Christianity within Mainline Traditions* (Abingdon, 1999). He also has held numerous denominational, national, and statewide service positions, and received many awards and recognitions, including 1977 Educator of the Year by the Dallas Mexican Chamber of Commerce and a W. K. Kellogg Foundation Fellowship, 1980–83.

Loida I. Martell-Otero is Professor of Constructive Theology at Palmer Theological Seminary/Eastern University, in King of Prussia, Pennsylvania. She is a licensed doctor in veterinary medicine as well as an ordained minister in the American Baptist Churches/ USA. She is a bi-coastal Puerto Rican who taught in various institutions of higher learning and pastored in urban centers for fifteen years. She co-edited *Teología en Conjunto: A Collaborative Hispanic Protestant Theology* (Westminister John Knox, 1997), and co-authored *Latina Evangélicas: A Theological Survey from the Margins* (Cascade, 2013). She has published various articles on *evangélica* soteriology, Christology, and vocation. Her recent research on Taíno religious beliefs has focused on its links with theological anthropology/embodiment, spirituality, and eschatology.

Fumitaka Matsuoka is Robert Gordon Sproul Professor of Theology *Emeritus* at Pacific School of Religion and was Vice President for Academic Affairs/Dean and Professor of Theology at PSR and at Bethany Theological Seminary. He also served as the director of the Institute for Leadership Development and the Study of Pacific and Asian North American Religion at PSR. His books include *Learning to Speak a New Tongue* (Pickwick, 2011), *Out of Silence: Emerging Theological Themes of Asian American Churches* (United Church Press, 1995), and *The Color of Faith: Building Community in a Multiracial Society* (United Church Press, 1998). He is currently working (co-edited with Jane Iwamura) on the *Encyclopedia of Asian American Cultures & Religions* (ABC/CLIO).

Paul O. Myhre, PhD, is Associate Director of the Wabash Center for Teaching and Learning in Theology and Religion, in Crawfordsville, Indiana. In addition to his forthcoming edited book *Religious and Ethical Perspectives for the Twenty-First Century*, he is the editor for *Introduction to Religious Studies* (Anselm Academic, 2009). He is also the Book Review Editor for *Teaching Theology and Religion*, a member of the Teaching Committee of the American Academy of Religion, and a board member of the Society for the Arts in Religious and Theological Studies. In addition to authoring a host of published essays on various topics, he is a practicing visual and recording artist. His current research interests are focused on intersections between visual and musical arts through the use of religious and theological imagination and reflection.

Nancy Ramsay is Executive Vice President and Dean and Professor of Pastoral Theology and Pastoral Care at Brite Divinity School, Fort Worth, Texas. Before coming to Brite in 2005, she served as the Harrison Ray Anderson Professor of Pastoral Theology at Louisville Presbyterian Theological Seminary in Louisville, Kentucky. She is active in the Society for Pastoral Theology, and served as co-editor of *The Journal of Pastoral Theology*. She holds clinical memberships in the American Association of Pastoral Counselors and the American Association of Marriage and Family Therapists, where she also has supervisor status. Her publications include *Pastoral Care and Counseling: Redefining the Paradigms* (Abingdon, 2004), *Pastoral Diagnosis: A Resource for Ministries of Care and Counseling* (Fortress, 1998), and *Telling the Truth: Preaching about Sexual and Domestic Violence*, co-edited with John S. McClure (United Church Press, 1998).

Archie Smith Jr. Archie Smith Jr. is former James and Clarice Foster Professor of Pastoral Psychology and Counseling, Pacific School of Religion/Graduate Theological Union; Pulpit Associate at the McGee Avenue Baptist Church; and adjunct research faculty at Sofia University (former Institute of Transpersonal Psychology), Schomburg Center for Research in Black Culture, New York.

Julia M. Speller is Associate Professor of American Religious History and Culture and Director of the Doctor of Ministry Program, Chicago Theological Seminary. She received her PhD degree from the University of Chicago Divinity School. Dr. Speller's research interests include American religious history and culture, in addition to the broader area of church history. She is particularly interested in twentieth century congregational histories with a focus on African American communities. She is the author of *Walkin' the Talk: Keepin the Faith in Africentric Congregations* (Pilgrim, 2005).

Mai-Anh Le Tran is Associate Professor of Christian Education at Eden Theological Seminary in St. Louis, Missouri. She is current Vice-President of the Religious Education Association (REA:APPRRE), with research and teaching focus on local/global intersections of race, gender, and class in religious identity formation and practices. She has contributions in the *Religious Education Journal*; *Christians in Education*; *The NIB's Pastor's Bible Study* series; *Ways of Being, Ways of Reading: Asian American Biblical Interpretation*; and *Poscolonial Interventions: Essays in Honor of R. S. Sugirtharajah*.

Acknowledgments

THIS PROJECT HAS A long history. It evolved out of the many seminars, consultations, and workshops I attended and a few public presentations I delivered. This means that I have many people and institutions to thank or to be grateful for. I may not be able to mention all of them here, but I would like to mention a few.

My graduate education did not intentionally prepare me to teach. It was simply assumed that, because I knew the core content of my field of discipline, I knew how to teach. While there is some truth to this assumption, it is not exactly true that knowledge of content automatically leads to acquisition of teaching skills on the subject matter one has learned; much less so if we speak of good teaching. I am glad that the Wabash Center for Teaching and Learning in Theology and Religion was there when I needed to reflect on my teaching practice and develop pedagogical skills. Even more, the Wabash Center offered workshops/seminars that dealt with the intersection of teaching and racial/ethnic identity. As some may recognize, the immediate context that informed the framing of this project was the Seminar on Teaching Effectively in Racially and Culturally Diverse Classrooms through the Wabash Center. I am grateful, in particular, to the leaders of that seminar: Nancy Ramsay, Shawn Copeland, Fernando Segovia, Fumitaka Matsuoka, and Matthew Ouellette. Also, earlier in my teaching career I received a grant from the Wabash Center that helped me to formulate benchmarks for a racially just institution, which have been used at United Theological Seminary of the Twin Cities to guide and assess its institutional efforts toward cultural diversity and racial justice. This concern for the educational institution as a whole is based on the understanding that teaching happens beyond the classroom and must spread throughout the whole institutional life. This understanding underscores the importance of implicit and null curriculum. I am thankful for Lucinda Huffaker, then Director of the Wabash Center, for her leadership and support.

I also would like to acknowledge the contribution of the Association of Theological Schools in the U.S. and Canada in the birthing of this project. The consultation for Effective Theological Education for Asian/Asian North American Seminarians, the consultation on leadership and governance, and my presentation on leading the faculty from within (A Roundtable Seminar for Mid-Career Faculty) have played roles in shaping this project. The ATS seminar on leadership and governance helped me see the crucial role of the institution in the whole educational enterprise, particularly its relationship to the implicit and null curriculum. This recognition led to my decision to include institutional life and governance as one of the parts of the project. I am thankful in particular to Daniel Aleshire, Janice Edwards-Armstrong, Stephen Graham, Frances Pacienza, and Lester Ruiz. Lester has been a conversation partner on matters related to theological education.

Other institutions and individuals have also contributed in the making of this book project. I am thankful to Fumitaka Matsuoka, whose advice I often seek, and to Mai-Anh Le Tran for helping me identify essay contributors from the field of religious education. This project would not have come into being without the institution that has given me the privilege to participate in the work of theological education—United Theological Seminary of the Twin Cities. For this I thank our former Dean, Richard Weis, for leading United Theological Seminary in the formulation of its new curriculum, advancing new programs, and instilling teaching excellence; and to our current Dean, Sharon Tan, for her generosity and openness to new possibilities. Also, I am thankful for our new president, Barbara Holmes, for the fresh vision, new initiatives, and empowering and hopeful presence that she brings. My gratitude belongs, as well, to my faculty colleagues for the countless conversations and meetings on the various aspects of theological education and for the support of staff, including Dale Dobias, Penny Truax, Deb Olsen, and Adam Pfuhl. I also would take this opportunity to express my gratitude to Catherine Pino for her skillful and meticulous editorial work, and to Karen R. Larson for her proofreading skills. I am also thankful to Christian Amondson of Wipf and Stock Publishers for overseeing this project, and to the essay contributors.

Most of all, my gratitude goes to my wife, Jo, for her generosity and support so I can pursue this project. In countless and multiple ways she has given so much of herself so I can pursue projects that I am passionate about.

Eleazar S. Fernandez
Fridley, Minnesota
Springtime, 2013, when lilacs were blooming

Birthing Culturally Diverse and Racially Just Educational Institutions

Teaching to Transgress and Transform

ELEAZAR S. FERNANDEZ

WHEN I FIRST STARTED my teaching career after completing my PhD studies, I simply assumed that I knew how to teach because I knew the content of my field, which is philosophical and systematic theology. This assumption was not completely baseless, because in the teaching of content one learns not only the content but how the content is taught. I realized before long, however, that knowledge of content does not automatically mean that one knows how to teach, much less how to be a good teacher. I, of course, learned how to teach, but my acquired skills were based mostly in what I learned as a student from my teachers and mentors throughout the years. I adopted the teaching methods and styles of my teachers into my classroom. While there was much that I could adopt from my former teachers and be thankful for, I needed to reflect on my own teaching experience and develop my pedagogical skills. To put it differently, I needed to be a reflective practitioner of my profession as a teacher. How could I ignore it if that was what I was doing in most of my waking hours and even what kept me awake in so many nights?

1

As I continued on my journey as a teacher, I realized that there is something about my identity and circumstances that was affecting, impacting, and informing my experience as a teacher. I realized or "was made to realize" by the wider society, particularly in the U.S., that I am a person with a "marked" body, that is, a "person of color" or a racial-ethnic minority, and this plays out in the classroom and beyond.

By the way, I have not always thought of myself as a person with a "marked" body. I have shared this story in various settings. Though I often tell this story in a humorous way, it is not funny. When I was in the Philippines I was simply a Filipino, even though, because of my physical features, I often have been mistaken to be Chinese, Korean, or Japanese. But when I came to the U.S. to study and reside, to my great dismay something strange happened: I became a person of color, a racial ethnic minority. I had been given a new identity, an identity that I did not and do not like, and an identity that hurts or kills. What kind of sin did my ancestors and I commit to bring all this trouble?

This story does not end here. I went to Yaoundé, Cameroon to teach in 2007, and an even stranger thing happened. I was shocked and could not believe that, for the first time in my life, I was called a "white man"—an "American." After my public lecture someone in the audience asked me if I was speaking as a Filipino or speaking as an "American." O my gosh, when did I become an "American"? How did this happen when, in the "land of the free and home of the brave," I was a foreigner—a non-American? My gut-level feeling was to deny my privilege (professor in the U.S.) and play the victim (racial minority, even if professor) role, but I believed it was not right to do so. This overall experience—from the Philippines to the U.S. and to Africa—deepened and expanded my understanding of identity, especially of its constructed, multiple, fluid, and shifting characteristic. Moreover, I became more aware how this constructed and shifting identity has been insinuated by racism in the U.S., and the very educational institutions in which I have given my time and skills are the very same institutions that continue to frustrate my longing for a culturally diverse and racially just world.

As a professor/person of color in a white society and in a predominantly white theological institution with two decades of experience in teaching, I surely have witnessed how race/ethnicity (and other forms of "marked" identities) has played out in the classroom, in research and publication, administration, and policy making. At first I tended to ignore or not mention it, but with other teachers and scholars openly sharing their experience, I have gained the courage to name racial/ethnic dynamics in the teaching and learning environment. The "marked" teacher encounters racism in multiple forms from various groups, including racism from students in her or his classroom. Though often subtle, it comes in the stereotyped expectations of students and faculty colleagues. If a racial/ethnic teacher, particularly one new to the U.S., introduces a little bit more of his or her country of origin's culture in the classroom, she or he may get the comment that she is into her ethnic stuff and not really teaching the core substance of the course. If the racially/ethnically "marked" person does not include her or his ethnic identity/culture, she or he may get the comment that her or his teaching or writing is generic, just like what one can expect from a white teacher and scholar. To add to the complexity, if the racial/ethnic person is identified as a liberationist theologian, she or he might be under observation to monitor whether she or he is teaching the "real stuff."

Teachers of "marked" bodies pursue their day to day work in and through the complexity of racial/ethnic dynamics. They have faced tremendous challenges and they have made significant progress, which can no longer be ignored by the predominantly white society. Yet, in every step forward, the racist system is cunning enough to do countermoves. As Gloria Yamato puts it, "Like a virus, it is hard to beat racism, because by the time you come up with a cure, it's mutated to a new cure-resistant form. One shot just won't get it."[1] Hence, teachers of "marked" bodies must be not only persistent, but strategic enough to prevent the racist system from putting them in a box—the "racial/ethnic teacher/scholar" box.

This vigilance should be true in choosing areas of teaching, research, and publication. One's teaching must feed into one's writing and publication, for if one's teaching does not lead to publication, where else would one find a time just to write for publication? There is no time left after teaching, student advising, committee meetings, and institutional citizenship. Moreover, one needs to strategize in one's publication so as not to make it easy for the system to pigeonhole the "marked" professor as only a "racial/ethnic scholar." In short, in addition to writing on issues of identity, the "marked" teacher may have to write and publish on topics that are considered core to the discipline.

Educational institutions, and theological institutions in particular, are at different places in their journey in relation to the issue of race and ethnicity, but there is a common thread of experience across the board. The good news is that there is a growing number of institutional supports to help teachers become more aware of the impact of the racial/ethnic dynamics and to develop teaching competence for cultural diversity and racial justice. Seminars and workshops have been offered to help teachers develop syllabi

---

1. Yamato, "Something about the Subject," 207.

and learn pedagogies that honor racial/ethnic diversity and promote justice. Two of the most helpful institutions are the Wabash Center for Teaching and Learning in Theology and Religion and the Association of Theological Schools in the U.S. and Canada (ATS). On the other hand, progress has been slow even as the ethnic/racial demographic of the U.S. has changed dramatically and will come to a point in which there will be no single ethnic majority.

Teaching, however, cannot be separated from the rest of the educational enterprise, which includes the context of theological institutions, the criteria for academic excellence, curriculum, faculty review and promotion, the whole matter of institutional life and governance, etc. My awareness of the significance of institutional matters and their bearings on our journey toward a more culturally diverse and racially just society has led me to initiate or to become involved in projects that attend to matters of curriculum as well as institutional life and governance. As my own journey progressed in those early years, I found out as an educator/teacher that the implicit and null curricula are as important as the explicit curriculum. It is easy to overlook the null: What is or what is not being taught? Who or what is excluded? Who is voiceless? Who or what is invisible? Who or what is intentionally or unintentionally critiqued? Who or what is demonized? Yet, the null, or that which is not spoken, speaks a lot; it is formative of theological formation. Knowing that the curriculum is more than the explicit, and that the implicit and the null curricula are as critical in the formation of persons, I have ventured into research and projects that address the larger institutional habitat in which the work of theological education is being done. We need to create and nurture the right institutional habitat if theological education is to move forward in the direction of cultural diversity and racial justice.

Part of the work of creating and nurturing the right institutional habitat is formulating benchmarks to help educational institutions, particularly seminaries, assess where they are in their institutional journey toward becoming a culturally diverse and racially just institution. Perhaps, contrary to the expectations of many stakeholders, the corporate culture, ethos, and institutional patterns of their beloved institution still remain largely under the "passive" and "symbolic" affirmation of cultural diversity, and therefore the institution is still very far from becoming a more fully inclusive and racially just institution in its identity and structure. Benchmarks are useful in making the assessment. Benchmarks may include the following criteria: courses will reflect the cultural, ethnic, and religious diversity of the nation; classes will prepare students from diverse cultural communities equally well to perform responsibilities of ministry appropriate for their communities or placement of call; programs will be designed to support

students in under-represented constituencies; the wider community will be aware of their institutions' various efforts to achieve diversity, such as courses, resources, and training; persons from diverse ethnic communities will see themselves and their ethnic communities represented throughout the building, including in the classrooms, hallways, library, café, chapel, and bookstore; the library will have resources needed to support the school's diversity; a culture of continuing education for staff and faculty will be evident in the opportunities offered for diversity training and in faculty and staff participation; proactive outreach and recruitment strategies will expand diversity throughout the seminary community; the retention rate of students will be comparable in all ethnic groups; communications (literature) will accurately reflect the school's values, expectations, and accomplishments in achieving diversity; the Board of Trustees will reflect the racial diversity of the nation; administrative and board officers will consistently develop strategies to ensure that diversity is achieved; the Board of Trustees will ensure that communities of color are among the constituencies to which the seminary is accountable; and proactive outreach, recruitment, hiring and evaluation practices will result in increase of staff diversity.

There is also the larger context to which we need to be attentive and in which we need to get involved if we are to effect transformation. This larger context includes academic guilds, both national and international. Our investment of social capital in these settings may have an impact on the current research and scholarship and in the formation of a new generation of teachers and scholars in our theological institutions. The Asian Theological Summer Institute, based at the Lutheran School of Theology in Philadelphia, has been helpful in mentoring scholars who are not only Asian American, but also Asian. I am proud to say that some of its participants are already heads of institutions in Asia.

Creating and nurturing academic societies for minoritized groups is an aspect in which we can slowly make a difference. The Society for Race, Ethnicity, and Religion has just been formed to address the issues raised by minoritized scholars. As other ethnic groups (Blacks and Hispanics) are pursuing some theological initiatives, Asian North Americans and Asians have also formed an academic society (the Association of Asian/North American Theological Educators—AANATE), a group that links Asian North Americans and Asian concerns, and a journal (JAANATE—*Journal of Asian/Asian North American Theological Educators*). These are what I have referred in my other writings as "alternative publics" for marginalized

groups or subaltern communities so as to have space to breathe as well as strategize.[2]

Also, as part of the larger context in which theological education operates, we need to form and nourish institutions that provide avenues for cooperation, mutual learning, joint programs, and peer institutional audit and accountability. My greater awareness in relation to this aspect has been largely through the work of the ATS. Through some of its program initiatives, I have joined colleagues from other theological institutions in serving as a member of a committee to decide on major faculty grants which, for me, is my contribution to the wider world of theological education. The ATS's program on Faculty Vocation and Governance has been important, particularly in my understanding of the role of faculty members in the governance of our theological institutions. Though often perceived as necessary "chores," faculty participation in these necessary "chores" is critical for transforming the corporate culture, ethos, and institutional patterns of theological institutions. It also provides a training ground for racialized and minoritized scholars to assume greater roles in governance and leadership. This is an area in which racialized and minoritized scholars have to work hard and make headway because, as pointed out by some essay contributors to this volume, minoritized scholars are underrepresented.

The discourse among member schools in the ATS has been that of "shared governance," and "shared governance" must be encouraged because our theological institutions need it, much more so acutely in a climate in which institutions of theological education have become, in Joseph A. Bessler's words, "endangered habitats."[3] This is a call addressed to all participants in theological education. However, as noted by some, there are barriers that block our journey toward shared governance. The larger culture is characterized by what John Bennett calls "insistent individualism."[4] The academic community has abundant institutional forms of insistent individualism such as disciplinary fields that have become specialty silos. These specialty fields, says John Cobb Jr., "constitute self-contained communities of research whose selection of topics is little affected by any needs but their own."[5] The hands-off agreement between specialty fields breeds a kind of indifference to common concerns that everyone must address. These critiques are valid, but something is seriously wanting: they do not include the effects of racism and white privilege as barriers to shared governance.

2. Fernandez, "Global Hegemonic Power," 66–67.

3. Bessler, "Seminaries as Endangered Habitats," 1–31.

4. Bennett, *Academic Life*, 1–45.

5. J. B. Cobb, Jr., cited in ibid., 15.

We also cannot forget or neglect our ties with churches and denominational bodies. They continue to exercise influence on our theological institutions, some more directly and others indirectly. Churches continue to exercise influence because they are still the main destination of our seminary graduates. Even though we have a growing number of students who are not directly affiliated with the churches, most of them are members of faith communities. And, as indicated by one of the essay contributors, students come from and are formed by homogenous or segregated churches and they bring this experience to the teaching-learning environment. How are we preparing our students who come from homogenous and segregated congregations who must have to deal with the changing ethnic and religious demographics of their ministry context? And how are we preparing students from new immigrant and racialized faith communities who must deal with their pressing issues?

This project is an outcome of my desire to think reflectively on my experience as a theological educator and a teacher in a world that is increasingly more diverse on one hand and increasingly contentious and divisive on the other. More particularly, this project grew out of my own experience as a teacher whose identity has been identified by the dominant society as a racially and ethnically "marked body." It is from this particular angle of experience that this project explores the various ramifications of doing theological education.

EXPERIENCES, PREMISES, AND PROPOSALS FROM RACIAL-ETHNIC MINORITY SCHOLARS AND TEACHERS

Creative theological constructions and biblical hermeneutics among racial-ethnic scholars in the North American context have grown tremendously in the past years. There is, however, a dearth from racial-ethnic scholars of religion and theology that reflects on their vocation, role, struggle, and hopes as religious/theological educators in the wider context of theological education in general and as teachers in particular. This book addresses that dearth of writings from racial-ethnic minority scholar-teachers in theology and religion on theological education as a whole and, in the specific, on the various aspects that include curriculum, pedagogy, institution, leadership, the teacher, the students, etc. An edited volume of such reflections, experiences, critiques, and proposals would have the advantage of gathering and presenting the rich and varied experience and perspective of racial ethnic minority scholar-teachers.

This book addresses the issue of theological education and teaching from seven major angles: (1) The general landscape of theological education in relation to cultural diversity and racial justice; (2) Knowing the teacher: The identity of the teacher; (3) Knowing the students: Who are our students? (4) Curriculum: What shall we teach? (5) Pedagogy: How shall we teach? (6) Institutional life and governance; (7) Perspectives from companions/allies.

1. The General Landscape of Theological Education in Relation to Cultural Diversity and Racial Justice

This section provides a critique of the landscape of theological education in relation to the plight and concerns of racial-ethnic minorities in general and of racial-ethnic minority scholar-teachers in particular. What is the status of theological education in North America with regard to cultural-ethnic diversity and racial justice? Has it challenged the hegemonic and homogenizing power of the Enlightenment paradigm and the dominant white culture, and explored alternative ways of doing theological education? Has theological education progressed in ways that match with the increasing cultural-ethnic diversity of its wider social context? Has it been responsive to the needs of its culturally and ethnically diverse constituencies? Is it preparing men and women for a culturally, ethnically, and religiously plural world? Where is it in terms of developing racial-ethnic minority scholar-teachers of religion and theology? What kind of training are they getting from major theological institutions? How are they being treated or valued as faculty members and part of the institution? What are the major challenges, the concerns that need to be addressed, the direction that must be pursued, and the steps that need to be taken?

2. Knowing the Teacher: The Identity of the Teacher

The identity of the teacher is an important factor in the teaching-learning process. What transpires in the teaching-learning process is filtered through this identity. Awareness of the crucial place of this identity in teaching is heightened especially when one is identified as a racially-ethnically "marked" body. In order to explore in depth the relationship between teaching and identity, some questions are useful guides. What experience(s) led to the teacher's discovery of her or his race or ethnic identity? What impact does that discovery have on the body of the teacher in classroom interaction when that body is "marked" by racial-cultural difference? How might the teacher's body affect evaluations of intellectual competency? How might the teacher's "marked" body affect racial and racist knowledges in the classroom? How does race shape the teacher's interactions with students, colleagues, and institutions? What does this mean for one's teaching?

3. Knowing the Students: Who Are Our Students?

Knowing our students is crucial in the teaching-learning process. Effective teaching demands that we know about aspects of their social locations, such as their backgrounds, communities of origin and belonging, personal life experiences, and learning styles. With knowledge of our students, we are at least able to teach in ways that best respond to their learning styles and to their current levels of awareness, assumptions, expectations, and information. We will also be able to judge whether we are using appropriate and realistic learning goals as well as anticipating questions or areas of confusion. Moreover, we are at least able to anticipate student reactions to our specific social group as instructors.

What do we need to know about our students? What issues are of greatest concern to them and what is their motivation for being in our classes? What is their prior experience with the range of social justice issues and what are their expectations? What are the multiple social identities of our students? What is the social inequality mixture of our students?

With the increasing ethnic and cultural diversity of our society brought about by the forces of globalization, greater sensitivity and responsiveness to our diverse student body is a demand of effective, empowering, and transformative teaching and is an act of justice. How shall we teach in ways that honor and celebrate racial-ethnic and cultural diversity in predominantly white institutions? How shall we teach in ways that honor and celebrate racial-ethnic and cultural diversity in racially, ethnically, and culturally diverse classrooms? Do our racial-ethnic students recognize their racial-ethnic identities in our courses and classrooms? Does our curriculum and teaching prepare them for the ministry in their ethnic communities, or are we doing racial-ethnic and cultural beheading?

Finally, what do we want students to know about themselves and about each other? What theories and practices are useful for teachers to understand their students and for students to understand themselves, particularly their racial-ethnic identities in relation to other social identities?

4. Curriculum: What Shall We Teach?

What is the content of our curriculum and our courses? What are we teaching to our students? What are the fundamental assumptions (e.g., educational and theological) underlying the school's curriculum? Are these stated or unstated? What are the fundamental assumptions underlying our school's curricular commitment to cultural, ethnic, racial diversity? Are these stated or unstated? Do these various sets of assumptions about curriculum and about cultural, ethnic, racial diversity clash? Does the curricular content include preparation for ministry in culturally and ethnically diverse settings? Are the experience, history, and perspective of racial-ethnic and cultural minorities present and honored? Do courses and syllabi include materials from racial-ethnic minorities? How are the racial-ethnic minorities represented? Are the courses that deal with racial-ethnic concerns integrated in required courses?

Racial-ethnic minority scholar-teachers need to develop critical consciousness about what they teach so as to use the resources of various racial and cultural heritages in ways that are respectful and appropriate and to avoid reproducing the assumptions of the dominant culture. Reacting to the dominant paradigm is not enough. Racial-ethnic minority scholar-teachers need to offer alternative content to the curriculum.

5. Pedagogy: How Shall We Teach?

How does one's racial-ethnic identity affect/inform pedagogy? How shall we teach as racially-ethnically "marked bodies" in ways that honor our identities as well as take our students' life experiences and multiple identities seriously, and promote cultural-ethnic diversity and racial justice? How shall we teach as racial-ethnic minority scholars and teachers in ways that do not perpetuate our marginalization and that prepare our students to do ministry in a culturally and racially diverse context? How shall we teach a course in which our experience and identity are so wedded to the subject matter? How shall we model what we teach? Do we have a broad repertoire of teaching methods to address various learning styles? What teaching methods are culturally sensitive and respectful for ethnic differences? How do we assess effective teaching in a multicultural classroom? What approaches, exercises, evaluative, or assessment tools are we going to use? What kind of teaching-learning environment are we creating? What is the classroom environment? What is the classroom culture and what are the classroom norms? Are we creating not just a *safe* environment but a *learning community* in which all members are committed to mutual learning and transformation?

6. Institutional Life and Governance

This aspect deals with the overall institutional life as well as governance structure and dynamics. What is the overall institutional climate? Does it proactively promote racial-ethnic justice and diversity? What has been the general experience of racial-ethnic scholar-teachers with regard to the issues of institutional life and governance and faculty vocation? How is institutional citizenship assessed? What forms of leadership have they assumed or exercised? How has their participation in institutional governance been perceived? In which areas have they made a difference, if any? What are some of the institutional barriers or challenges?

7. Views from Companions/Allies

While this volume is primarily about the thoughts and voices of racial-ethnic scholars and teachers on theological education and teaching, it is crucial for advancing the cause of cultural diversity and racial justice to include the thoughts/works of scholar-teachers from the dominant ethnic group who have become allies. Allies are those who not only recognize their own unearned privileges, but also are working to eliminate or transform these privileges into rights for all groups to enjoy. Allies are those who are willing to take both risks to try new ways of thinking and living and actions against social injustice in their own sphere of influence. Racial-ethnic scholars and teachers are not alone in the journey toward a theological education that affirms cultural diversity and racial justice, and they are not alone in exploring alternative teaching-learning practices that are responsive to the needs of our varied cultural-ethnic groups. They have educator-teacher allies from the dominant racial group, and the voices of these allies are of crucial importance and need to be included in this book project.

BRIEFS FROM THE ESSAY CONTRIBUTIONS

To respond to the seven concerns expressed above, I gathered eleven scholars and teachers from racial-ethnic minorities and I invited two white ally scholars and teachers. The essays from these scholars and teachers are here presented in the order outlined above. With the exception of the first topic, there are two writers for each theme or topic.

Opening the discourse on theological education as it relates to the overall history and experience of racial-ethnic minorities is the seasoned scholar and teacher Fumitaka Matsuoka, with his essay, "Theological Education of Not Yet." Without preliminaries, Matsuoka drives home his main point: "A large swath of theological schools in North America has failed to address race as a critical challenge facing theological education." This failure, according to Matsuoka, is due primarily to these schools' refusal to accept the pain of racism borne by racialized people and the lack of commitment of theological institutions to address the challenge of racism. We should not be surprised at this failure, because the difference that people of color bring is not affirmed or is not considered relevant to theological education. This, for Matsuoka, is the main culprit for the continuing failure. This racism that has corrupted and persisted in theological education must be named before we can proceed further. The foundation is corrupt, thus reform is not the answer. What is needed, argues Matsuoka, is the establishment of a "fair and equal representation of all voices—racial, gender, sexual orientation—in defining what theological education is." More particularly, what is needed, pursues Matsuoka, is a theological Bill of Rights.

Mai-Ahn Le Tran's, "When *Subjects* Matter: The Bodies We Teach By," opens the second topic, *Knowing the teacher: The identity of the teacher.* Debunking essentialist premises, Tran contends that there is no universal identity and role of teachers. Advocating for "thick description," she names the teaching subject (teacher) as raced, sexualized, classed, nationalized, etc. There is no neutral teaching body. The teacher's body has bearings on the teaching and learning process. While all "teaching bodies" are not generic and neutral, the bodies of racial ethnic minorities and women are distinctively "marked" and this presents serious challenges to the educational enterprise. Their "marked" bodies are marginalized in the educational enterprise that favors certain bodies—white, male, and heterosexual. This "marked" body constantly struggles for recognition in the classroom and academic community or for the ability to be taken seriously. Tran identifies four aspects or questions to pursue in dealing with the identity of the teacher: (1) Who is the teacher? (2) What are the sources of a teacher's authority? (3) What practices must the teacher hone? (4) What is the *telos* of the teaching life? The teacher who is identified as a "marked" body must be fully aware of the constructed and political nature of his or her teaching presence, and must continue to find ways to de-center the educational normativity of certain bodies. He or she must point to his or her "marked" body as "implicit" curriculum and expose in the explicit curriculum its vestiges of assumptions about "marked bodies" as "racial texts."

Loida Martell-Otero's essay, "From Foreign Bodies in Teacher Space to Embodied Spirit in *Personas Educadas*: or, How to Prevent 'Tourists of Diversity' in Education," follows Tran and pursues the point that the hallowed halls of academia are not, contrary to what they have been presented to be, neutral spaces. These spaces are inherently racist, *kyriarchal*, and inhospitable to teachers of color, especially women, who are classified as "marked" bodies. Martell-Otero names a few examples, including her own, of how academia has treated those with marked bodies. They are considered intellectually inferior and defective, and it is assumed that they cannot possibly represent knowledge. Martell-Otero's essay does not end with prophetic exposition of the *kyriarchal* space of academia, but articulates ideas and directions in which transformation needs to happen. She calls for a spirituality of education that is geared toward the creation of sacred spaces in which all the participants in the educational life participate in the creation of perichoretic communities of *personas educadas*—people who are hospitable, compassionate, and just, and who actively promote the dignity of all. We need to create, she continues, an educational system that knows how to welcome diverse *presencia* and promotes holistic *vínculos* (ways of treating each other).

The next two essays address the topic: *Knowing the students: Who are our students?* In his essay, "Racial/Ethnic Diversity and Student Formation," Peter T. Cha takes account of the changing ethnic demographics of the U.S. population in general and of theological schools in particular. While student enrollment in theological schools roughly mirrors the overall demographic change of increasing diversity of the wider society, the distribution among racial/ethnic minorities is uneven, with Hispanics significantly underrepresented while Asian Americans are highly represented relative to their number in the U.S. population. Strangely, even as the ethnic demographic landscape has become more diverse, religious congregations from which most seminary students are coming have remained relatively homogenous. After presenting his critique of the changing demographic landscape and challenges, Cha poses the question as to how we may best respond to our context. How shall we do theological education or formation for the "2040 reality" or for a multi-racially diverse world? With the greater possibility that students may be serving pastoral settings that are different from their ethnic-racial background, how shall we do theological education for that ministry? With white students mostly shaped by their more homogenous congregations, how shall we prepare them for a different world? And, how shall we prepare racial-ethnic minority students whose identities have been contested and precarious? Not only does Cha raise excellent questions, he explores some possibilities and presents an example of what might help us respond faithfully and creatively to our multi-racially diverse world.

Archie Smith Jr. pursues the conversation in his essay, "You Cannot Teach What You Do Not Know: You Cannot Lead Where You Have Not Been," by asking the question: "*Who is our student and who ought to be?*" We cannot go far without asking this fundamental question. The first part of the question calls us to take a sociological look at our student population, while the second part, the question of *ought to be*, calls us to take account of our vision of theological education and our priorities. If our theological vision and priorities are not in accord with what Smith names as the "biblical call to ministry," which involves "serving others while working to transform the social order toward increased justice and human betterment," then we will never get our theological education right. In spite of our best efforts and hard work in doing theological education, we will never get it right if we have not made right our relationship with those whose rights have been sidelined. Theological education that is dictated by the white power-knowledge nexus and oriented toward white middle class interests and values will declare the interest and needs of racialized communities to be "irrelevant" to theological formation. It is not a surprise, following Smith's forceful account, that those whose needs and interests are considered "irrelevant" will also find theological education conducted by our seminaries as "irrelevant." Theological education must get its theological vision and priorities right and must critique its existing ways of thinking and doing (about basic assumptions, context, students [class, race, sexuality], degree programs, courses, pedagogies, resources, etc.) if it is to serve the common good.

From the topic, *Knowing the Students: Who are our students?*, we move to address the next topic on curriculum or the content of theological education: *Curriculum: What shall we teach?* The first essay under this topic, "What Shall We Teach? The Content of Theological Education," is by Willie James Jennings. Jennings plays with an architecture metaphor to speak of the content of theological education and the various participants in theological education, particularly teachers, as inhabitants. Modern theological architecture, for Jennings, was not built with different bodies in mind or different minds in diverse bodies, which is defined by white, male, and heterosexual normativity. While most of the contemporary inhabitants of modern theological architecture had little to do with the architectural design or the process of building itself, and most have to make adaptations of various sorts, this is extremely acute for people of color and women. Teachers who are people of color and who are women experience serious psychical negotiation: they are committed to teaching the content of their fields of discipline for the realization of dreams both personal and social, yet they live in the shadows of foundational figures who continue to define and influence various structural and human surrogate standards of excellence, etc. Beyond naming the deep contradictions that teachers of color and women have to contend with, Jennings takes us to some of the possible ways the new inhabitants can take not only for the sake of survival but also for birthing new possibilities—new wineskins for new wines. To welcome or help give birth to the new, the new occupants (teachers who are people of color and women) first have to demystify design in relation to desire: design is fundamentally an artifact of desire. The content of theological education (curriculum), according to Jennings, is a constellation of desires materialized in designs. They have to challenge or position themselves in ways in which the architectural design more or less meets their desires for a new theological dwelling place that nourishes all and opens a place for future inhabitants.

Elizabeth Conde-Frazier's essay, "Thoughts on Curriculum as Formational Praxis for Faculty, Students, and their Communities," addresses the topic similar to Jennings's. Conde-Frazier's essay is informed by her extensive teaching experience and work, especially with the Latino/a communities. She is committed to the development of a curriculum that addresses the whole person as a member of the community and is transformative or liberational in its thrust. Noting the multiple dimensions in which the curriculum is at work, she calls for an extensive critique of the curriculum at various levels (explicit, implicit, and null). She exposes white privilege, power dynamics, disciplinary fields, professionalism, etc., as some of the factors that disenfranchise or marginalize certain groups and perpetuate oppression. After exposing some of the dimensions that prevent that development of a liberating curriculum, she advances some ideas on how we may proceed for both traditional and non-traditional settings. A great curriculum, for Conde-Frazier, must take account of the students and their context, the teacher, and the framework that holds the curriculum together. This curriculum should be emancipatory, integrated (vertically, horizontally, and diagonally), empowering, and acculturative for students in the practice of justice, and must develop performance skills and intercultural competency.

Boyung Lee's "Strategies to Teach Cultural Diversity and Race" names diversity in culture and ethnicity as the context in which disruptive education in general and pedagogy in particular must happen. Teaching for a culturally diverse and racially just world is disruptive because it must disrupt white hegemony. After naming white hegemony, Lee proceeds to articulate pedagogical principles and strategies for disruptive teaching. She adopts Robert Kegan's three-way meaning-making process (confirmation, contradiction, and continuity) in the development of one's identity to articulate these principles and strategies. Lee identifies four disruptive pedagogical principles under continuity, namely: teaching race as an integral part of the teacher's class subject, expanding the boundaries of textbooks, paying attention to the implicit curriculum, and creating a physical environment that embodies antiracist and justice pedagogy. She identifies another four for confirmation, which include performing needs assessment, assessing needs and creating a safe learning community through a liturgical rhythm, using multiple intelligences as kith and kin to antiracist and social justice pedagogy, and helping students learn through praxis. The final three principles under contradiction are these: asking "why" questions regarding school's curricula, practicing problem-posing teaching methods, thinking about evaluation before teaching and using focus groups to qualitatively evaluate one's class. Though all the principles are important, Lee underscores knowing the students' needs as a critical starting point to disruptive pedagogy. Lee concludes that if the teacher is to be faithful to the original meaning of education, then teaching must always be disruptive regardless of what is taught.

Julia M. Speller's essay, "A Pedagogy of the Unmasked: 'Unheard but Not Unvoiced, Unseen but Not Invisible,'" takes us to the topic of *Pedagogy: How shall we teach?* There is no direct route, for Speller, to a transformative and effective pedagogy (how we teach), without dealing with the "who" question or the life of the teacher and, in this instance, the teacher of color. The starting point for transformative and effective pedagogy is the teacher's self-actualization. While "self-actualization" is important for all teachers, the experience of teachers of color whose "marked" bodies have often been read as "distorted text" demands, for Speller, that we be critical of any claim that they have attained "sustainability of any level of self-affirmation." The challenge, she contends, is to remove the distorted mask and return the gaze with the full embrace and expression of power that comes from self-authenticity. Informed by Womanist epistemology, Speller speaks of this self-realization as radical subjectivity that has gained the power to unmask oneself from the debilitating and oppressive white categories that dominate academia. While this is a crucial starting point, it also is important to articulate the connection between the *who* that is teaching and the *where* that teaching takes place. This means that hierarchical structures and hegemonic systems must be challenged as well. While it is not going to be easy, when educators of color have claimed their authentic selves, they are in a better position to make use of their experiences and pedagogical tools to create a culturally diverse and racially just learning environment. When they gain their "full voice and visibility," they can bring their experiences, interpretations, and analyses to bear on their pedagogy so it becomes a powerful transformative tool.

The next couple of essays are on the topic of *Institutional life and governance*. Mary Hinton's essay, "The Vocational Cycle to Support Institutional Justice: A Pathway for Scholars of Color to Transform Institutional Life and Governance," takes us to the work of institutional change through the experience of racial and ethnic minorities in general and through her multiple experiences as an African American woman who has assumed various roles, including senior administrative posts. Vocation, for Hinton, is the entry point in effecting institutional change. Faithfulness to one's vocational aspirations must drive the daily work that shapes the institution. Anything that is less than this would be a violation of the person and a failure to make a just institution. It is through what she calls "Vocational Cycle to Support Institutional Justice" that scholars of color can support and bring forth institutional justice. The elements of the Cycle include: personal context and understanding, vocation, occupational choices within an institution, institutional life and governance, and institutional climate. The institutional climate, in turn, brings us back to the beginning of the cycle: it changes the personal context and understanding of agents, and they re-engage the institution so it continues to be transformed and transformative. Hinton makes two recommendations: first, one must be authentic in his or her approach to work and, second, the institution must be engaged at multiple levels to facilitate transformation.

In his essay, "Institutional Life and Governance: Realities and Challenges for Racial-Ethnic Leadership within Historically White Theological Schools," David Maldonado gifts us with his reflection on his experience as an administrator. He identifies specific areas that are problematic and areas in which transformation needs to happen. Maldonado calls theological institutions, which are mainly white institutions, to take seriously ethnic and religious diversity as the new habitat or context on at least two counts: as a matter of institutional integrity and a matter of survival. The integrity of our theological institutions is in question if they do not reflect the diversity that is present in society. Moreover, they have to experience transformation for the sake of institutional survival and the viability of theological education. Maldonado identifies institutional leadership as key in the transformation of our theological institutions and he contends that people of color are ready to step up to the plate. He continues to identify some areas in which challenges are present and areas in which transformation, i.e., active participation of people of color, needs to happen. He speaks of the need to have people of color on the governing boards—which are still composed mostly of whites and are still run mostly on white agenda—and involved in other related matters including the presidential search committee in relation to the selection of a minority president, the board's relationship to a minority president, and the minority president's relationship to the faculty and staff, the church denominational bodies, the communities of color, and the white constituencies.

The last topic of this book is devoted to responses from white allies: *Views from companions/allies.* Paul O. Myhre presents his perspective on what it means to be a white ally in his essay, "Angle of Vision from a Companion/Ally in Teaching for a Culturally Diverse and Racially Just World." The first small but significant step for white allies, according to Myhre, is the recognition of the pervasiveness of racism. The first few pages of his essay take account of the pervasiveness of racism in the wider society, where churches and theological education are not exempt from scrutiny. Beyond recognition of racism, Myhre calls for the work of undoing racism. Moreover, he proceeds to present ideas, practices, and resources to advance the cause of racial justice in the wider society and theological education in its various aspects: institutional and administrative oversight, faculty and curriculum, student recruitment and retention, pedagogy and syllabus, etc. Speaking in particular of the work of white allies, Myhre calls them to be attentive to the contours of the teaching-learning space. They must raise the questions, such as "Who is present, what histories do they bring, what epistemic frameworks are evident, what is missing, whose voices are privileged and whose are silenced?" Moreover, knowing how things are interrelated or interlocked, Myhre speaks of pedagogical, curricular, and institutional change moving together and the need for collaborative/alliance work among faculty members across the curriculum, and between faculty, administration, and students to advance the goal of creating culturally diverse and racially just educational institutions.

The last essay, by Nancy Ramsay, is "Faculty Colleagues as Allies in Resisting Racism." Ramsay names up front the main work of those who count themselves white allies: confront the issue of power and white privilege that pervades throughout educational institutions including board rooms, classrooms, departmental governance, faculty review and promotion, administrative practices, policies and procedural matters, recruitment, etc. Through vignettes, Ramsay presents cases and scenarios in which white privilege remains operative, but the vignettes also provide possible entry points for transformative interventions. There is no neutrality: to be neutral is tantamount to complicity. Allies must be intentional, which should not be equated with good intentions. Good intentions are not enough. The goal of white allies, says Ramsay, must be the intentional use of themselves to enact commitments to deconstruct white privilege, for without these intentional enactments white allies are simply contributing to the reproduction and perpetuation of their privilege. The goal then is "institutional transformation" because what is "*at stake,*" she argues, "*is the integrity of institutional and communal life and practices.*" Pursuing further the intentional work of allies, Ramsay names and articulates some of the skills that allies need to develop that touch the various areas of the academic life. Allies must engage in deconstructing any singular way of understanding an intellectual tradition and welcoming marginalized traditions. They must identify the ways in which white privilege limits imagination, expose teaching practices that undermine the noble intention to undo white privilege, act boldly to come to the defense of vulnerable faculty colleagues of color, and build strategic networks to undermine privilege, to name a few practical strategies among many.

FACING THE CHALLENGE WITH COURAGE AND CREATIVITY

There is no doubt that the challenge is enormous, but the work is worth pursuing for, as some of the essay writers indicate, what is at stake is not only the integrity of our educational institutions, but the integrity of our faith. Forces of reaction are always there, but so are openings and new possibilities. We just have to pursue and continue to explore creative ways of responding, ways that do not re-inscribe, normalize, and perpetuate what we are struggling against. Indeed, there are approaches that, with the noble intention of creating space for marginalized voices, often end up normalizing the dominant tradition. We must explore new ways of thinking and new strategic practices. Indeed, we cannot solve the same problem by using the same mind that created it or is responsible for its creation. It is a form of insanity, as someone said, to expect a different result while continuing the same strategy and tactic over and over again. The change that we must pursue must embrace the systemic and multiple dimensions of the educational system and the larger habitat in which we all dwell. This is clear in the essays of the various contributors to the volume.

Finally, as the contributors state and allude throughout, the systemic character of what we are facing demands collaboration and networking of various actors including teachers/scholars of color, administrators, students from various ethnic groups, boards of trustees, and white allies. While the context of this project is focused on the U.S. setting, white power and privilege cannot be separated from the larger or global context. Agents of transformation need to get better not only in articulating their demands, but also in organizing at various levels both locally and internationally. Transforming our educational system is political work, even as it is always an expression of our spiritual and theological work. We work politically not only in making the possible become real, we also work in enlarging what is possible and in making those that have been considered impossible come in the range of the possible.[6] Small beginnings should not intimidate us. We must remember that we are not called to do everything, but we are called to do something: to sew our piece in the larger quilt of our agenda for greater well-being.

6. William Lee Miller, cited in Hessel, *Social Ministry*, 163.

1

Theological Education of Not Yet

FUMITAKA MATSUOKA

THESIS: A LARGE SWATH of theological schools in North America has failed to address race as a critical challenge facing theological education. This failure is due primarily to their refusal to acknowledge the deep pain of racism borne by people of color and the consequent lack of institutional commitment to make race one of the major challenges facing theological education and the preparation of leaders in churches.

INTRODUCTION: THE ESTABLISHMENT OF THE THEOLOGICAL BILL OF RIGHTS

The thesis of this article is clear enough to those of us, teachers and scholars of color, who have languished in North American theological education for the past century: A large swath of theological schools in North America has failed to address race as a critical challenge facing theological education. This failure is due primarily to the deep pain of racism borne by people of color and the consequent lack of institutional commitment to make race one of the major challenges facing theological education and the preparation of leaders in churches. The reason for the failure was stated in the ATS Seminar for Racial/Ethnic Faculty Members at Predominantly White ATS Institutions that was held in October, 2001: "The values that we embrace

are not perceived as valuable by tenure evaluators. Our difference is valued
as a presence but not affirmed as a professional contribution to theological
education."[1] In other words, the effective exclusion of teachers and scholars
of color in shaping theological education for the past century is the primary
culprit of the failure. This failure mirrors the failure to address the matter of
race in a wider North American society. The failure is so fundamental to the
nature and definition of theological education that any attempt to reform it
cannot accomplish its intended purpose of "the increase among men [sic] of
the love of God and neighbor," as H. Richard Niebuhr stated.[2] Furthermore,
the words of Benjamin E. Mays about race in the U.S. some time ago capture
the fundamental problem of race facing theological education as well:

> I would submit that a nation cannot restore what it has not es-
> tablished. The nation exempted blacks and, to a large degree,
> Native Americans from the dialectics of freedom. It has not suc-
> ceeded to this day in including them. Whether blacks and other
> minorities will wait for the "quiet processes" to "confirm the
> obsolescence of our present commitments" is not yet assured.
> The multiplied consequences of white racism have created a ma-
> lignancy that will not wait for such gradual and self-interested
> therapy.[3]

The real critical issue facing race in North American theological education
then is not a reform, because the foundation on which theological education is built is corrupt. Rather, the primary issue is a new establishment
of a fair and equal representation of all voices—racial, gender, sexual orientation—in defining what theological education is. To put this issue in a
question form, North American theological educators need to address the
questions: "What is 'academic' and who defines it?" "Whose knowledge is
valued? Can we value communal knowledge alongside the cognitive bodies
of knowledge that are in tension?" How do we as an institution of theological education begin to recognize that community and institutional loyalties
are in tension?"[4] Theological education should have been one of the most
fertile areas of North American life where the moral integrity of the society
is to be established by embodying freedom and dignity to the captives it
held. But North America chose a meaner path where the insistent rhetoric
about liberty, freedom, justice, and love rang hollow against the pitiful cries
of the men and women whose freedom never reached the agenda of seri-

1. The Association of Theological Schools, "Issue: Tenure and 'What is Academic?'"

2. Niebuhr, *Purpose of the Church*, 31.

3. Mays, "Response to Sydney E. Ahlstrom," 24–25.

4. The Association of Theological Schools, "Issue: Tenure and 'What is Academic?'"

ous deliberation. Just as the civil rights movement and its leaders, such as Martin Luther King, Jr., lent an aura of credibility, however fleeting, to our most cherished presumption that we are a nation under God, Christian faith in the era of religious diversity and theological education where Christian leaders are nurtured and educated is indeed given an opportunity to be a fountain of redemption and reconciliation for all people. As the society anticipates the time in the near future when the current racial ethnic minorities are about to become a numerical majority, Christian communities and their leaders are given an opportunity for a higher way, a way in consonance with our professions of love and kinship in a just and humane society. This is to say that the task facing North American theological education today and in the future is no less than an establishment of the theological Bill of Rights, first within our own institutions that can become a beacon of freedom and equality for the whole society. This theological Bill of Rights serves as the revelatory paradigm of the very faith we affirm as it is incarnated in our societal life. The price for not acknowledging this critical task is very high, running the risk of the irrelevance of theological education and the total erosion of its credibility in our society.

THE HISTORICAL LANDSCAPE OF RACE IN THEOLOGICAL EDUCATION

And yet, this task cannot be carried out on a blank slate. The pain and sufferings long endured by the theological educators of color, the lessons learned by us, and the question of inter-racial reconciliation that is the theological expression of truth and reconciliation, constitute the initial step in addressing the establishment of the theological Bill of Rights.

The establishment of the Constitutional Bill of Rights in the U.S. was deeply rooted in the Enlightenment values. No wonder its rhetoric—life, liberty, and the pursuit of happiness—and the racial reality of life in the U.S. history display such a painful gap. The Bill of Rights was crafted by those who were of a single racial group and was then applied to the whole nation. No matter how lofty and noble the Constitutional Bill of Rights sounds, its fundamental flow is the absence of equal representations of all diverse groups of people. North American theological education is no less dependent on this historically shaped set of values. The establishment of the theological Bill of Rights must be rooted in another set of values and a totally new paradigm, that is, the reality of multiplicity and not of singularity. In the place of *e pluribus unum*, the starting point of the theological Bill of Rights is that reality of life is multiple! Unless this basic life orientation is affirmed, no attempt to reform theological education can be successful. Theological institutions cannot restore what they have not established, to paraphrase Mays.

But the affirmation of this multiple reality has not marked the history of theological education in North America. Daniel Aleshire, the executive director of ATS, acknowledges, "For all practical purposes, ATS schools and the Association were white institutions in the 1960s."[5] ATS began gathering data about racial/ethnic representations among student in its member schools only in 1977.[6] The dearth of racial/ethnic representations in both faculty and students meant the dismissal and devaluation of what people of color consider significant literature and resources by the White institution. To add an insult to this pain of injury, people of color repeatedly observed those members of the majority race who were rewarded for research divorced from the crucial issues facing the community.

In the subsequent decades of the 1970s through the present, the paradigm of theological education in North America has been that of inclusion, with the exception of a few institutions that are racially and ethnically formed. The often unstated purpose of theological institutions regarding race has been "to redress the institutional patterns and prejudices that had excluded primarily African Americans from enrollment and employment in many ATS schools," according to Aleshire.[7] Granted, some progress has been made over the last three decades in "redressing" the racial exclusivity of theological education, but the paradigm shift in addressing racial justice and representation has not taken place. The old wineskin continues to remain the pattern and culture of North American theological institutions. ATS is keenly aware of this problem, as Aleshire has stated, "Over the past forty years, the ATS focus has changed from inclusion to institutional capacity."[8] This shift is behind the current ATS project called "Preparing for 2040: Enhancing Capacity to Educate and Minister in a Multiracial World." The implications of this shift are very significant because the focus of theological institutions on "institutional capacity" points to the paradigmatic shift to the establishment of the racial Bill of Rights, the equal representation of all people, and the affirmation of "life, liberty, and the pursuit of happiness" for all people of faith, and not just for Christians. The question is whether the institutions participating in ATS's 2040 project as well as other theological schools are indeed aware of this paradigm shift as they struggle

5. Aleshire, "Gifts Differing."

6. Ibid.

7. Ibid.

8. Ibid.

toward the future of theological education in North America. "The future of the North American church and theological schools is dependent, in part, on our getting race and ethnicity right," says Aleshire.[9]

RACE IN THEOLOGICAL EDUCATION: THE MICROCOSM OF THE SOCIETAL HEALTH OF NORTH AMERICA

The issues of race in theological education and the reasons for its historic failure to address race are intimately related to the history of race and the racial health in North America. The critical issue of race for Christians and, for that matter for all people of North America, is this: The history of Christianity in America has failed to recognize that the "new land" is indeed built by the pain of racism inflicted on people of color. First and foremost, this pain needs to be acknowledged and addressed honestly by all people in order to move forward toward the healthy future of our society and the legitimacy of Christian faith.

An honest acknowledgement of the pain of racism centers on two primary areas in the history of race in North America: (1) the persistence of color line and (2) the illusion of precision about race.

THE PERSISTENCE OF THE COLOR LINE

The famous dictum of W. E. B. Du Bois, "the problem of the Twentieth Century is the problem of the color line," continues to manifest itself today.[10] To acknowledge the persistence of the color line and its associated experience of pain by people of color is to embrace negation that is bound with life in our history. North Americans are not good at facing the presence of negation in life. Theologically put, to acknowledge the persistence that continues to exist in the color line is to acknowledge the reality of the cross that is present in life. The primary reason the model of inclusion did not and does not succeed in addressing race in theological education is precisely because of the failure of North American Christians to recognize the presence of the cross in our societal life. This failure is the classic attribute of North American Christianity—the resurrection without the cross, or as Douglas John Hall describes it, "an officially optimistic Christianity."[11]

9. Ibid.
10. Du Bois, *The Souls of Black Folk*, 19.
11. Hall, *Lighten Our Darkness*, 73f.

The truth of the matter is for the Christian an integral part of the problem, perhaps the most problematic part, is—Christianity itself. As it has displayed itself of this New World, Christianity is the greatest barrier to its becoming the redemptive force in such a society, a light for our darkness.[12]

Theological education exists in this particular cultural and religious milieu of the officially optimistic society. The color line spills beyond the twentieth century into this century and the pain experienced by people of color has no reception precisely because our expectations do not coincide with the reality of the experiences of people of color, the forces of "negation" that have accompanied us, to use Hall's expression.[13] North Americans turn our eyes away from that which is painful and unpleasant in our midst. The cross for North American Christians is an "inconvenient truth" that is to be politely hushed over on our way to the resurrection. The pain of racism is another inconvenient truth that, at best, is noted politely and grudgingly in our efforts to reach the future of a multiracial and multicultural society. The cross is levitated and not grounded in life.

No wonder the color line persists. As long as its root cause is not confronted with honesty and courage, no attempt to achieve a more just and equal multiracial society or, for that matter, a just theological institution, can be achieved. A racially just and redemptive institutional capacity-building is possible only when the forces of negation that have haunted theological education in North America are acknowledged, addressed, and owned. Confronted with the persistence of the color line even in our own century, the question facing people of Christian faith is this: Who will join the redemption of our society that has been divided by the excesses of extraordinary racial privilege on the one hand and the continuing challenge of racial conventions on the other?

THE ILLUSION OF PRECISION: NOT BEING HOME IN OUR OWN HOME OF RACE

There is another reality that characterizes race in North America. Today we live in a racially liminal and in-between time. Race has become "unbound," complex, and malleable.[14] North America is not only becoming racially more diverse but also more fluid in its make-up. There is no longer

12. Ibid., 74.
13. Ibid., 73f.
14. Patterson, "Race Unbound."

a "correct" way of describing race, whether it is "blackness" or "being Asian American." There is an illusion of precision about the current state of race. Race is "a completely liquid shape-shifter that can take any form."[15] Asian American professor of comparative literature Lisa Lowe defines "Asian Americans" in terms of "heterogeneity, hybridity, and multiplicity."[16] In such a liquid state of race, post-black or post-Asian American identity does not mean post-racial. Racism mutates into a new form, sometimes invisible and not readily unknowable.

Furthermore, what is so disconcerting about the illusion of racial precision is that it creates a state of the Holy Instability, the state where one is not home in one's own home, as Theodore Adorno characterizes it.[17] In such a state, a temptation is to search for the illusionary sense of a secure identity. But such is not attainable in the form of nostalgia for the past, or in the shared experience of living with lingering racism. Such a temptation to long for a terra firma applies to all race since "race" itself is shifting and increasingly liminal.

Theologically speaking, North Americans live in between the persistent pain of the cross and the resurrection that is not yet, a place that is uncharted and totally unfamiliar. The Old Testament prophets were called at the time of turmoil and uncertainties, in-between times. They responded to such times by focusing their resources and gifts. The act of focusing gifts is their understanding of "calling." Where could we find the source of courage and tenacity to face this in-between time of racial mutation? Would the monotheistic faith identity that Christians have embraced in our history provide us with the sufficient foundation to navigate the heterogeneous, hybrid, and multiple landscape of race? In the era of the illusion of precision, theological discourse regarding race is no longer confined within the conversation about race. It extends into the raison d'être of the very singular and exclusive faith tradition we have upheld among the multiple and fluid landscapes of the world's faith traditions. "Religions are racialized!" says Neil Gotanda, professor of law.[18] What clues in the Christian faith tradition give us theological educators the healthy referential anchorage to face the racial and religious world of the Holy Instability—not being home in one's own home? The paradigmatic shift to institutional capacity from the model of inclusion is not merely an organizational, strategic, or pedagogical shift.

15. Touré, quoted by Patterson, ibid.

16. Lowe, *Immigrant Acts*.

17. Adorno, quoted by Said, *Reflections on Exile and Other Essays*, 564–65.

18. Neil Gotanda, his remark made at 2007 annual meeting of the Association of Asian Americans Religious Research Initiative (APARRI), Berkeley, California.

What is at stake is the very nature of theological education, the education of those who are harbingers of the very faith that speaks to the depth and reality of life through our particular history. In this respect, race in its illusion of precision challenges what we believe, the redemptive message and work of God in Christ even in the era of the liquid state of life.

RACE IN THEOLOGICAL EDUCATION: TRUTH AND RECONCILIATION

The one-sided history of American theology continues to downplay the insights of those who are the main driving forces of theological enterprise in this highly racialized world, a world increasingly made of people of color. What is needed in North American theological education is the creation of an educational system that minimizes the domination of power by a particular privileged group, based on the racial divide that has haunted the whole history of our continent. The creation of such a system is one of the most critical theological tasks facing the people of Christian faith and its theological institutions. How do we think about race theologically? This is the question facing theological education as North America enters the time when the racially "minority" population is expected to become the majority.[19] In order to respond to this question collectively, a necessary step is to acknowledge the pain of racism suffered by people of color throughout the history of this continent. The redemptive power of Christ is released only upon the people of faith who own up to the negation of life that has haunted North American history both personally and collectively. The necessary first task facing theological institutions today is to reveal the truth of our race history told by those who have been the victims of racism. What is needed is the restoration of victims' dignity and formulation of ways to assist with rehabilitation. This step will lead to the next step, which is to participate in the reconciling work of Christ among those who are estranged one from another. This much is clear about the avoidance of truth-telling: Unless we collectively own up to the painful truth of racism in our midst, our appetite for the evil of racism, a tolerance for it, an indifference for it, and eventually a distaste for good will be engendered within and about us. Human beings have a way of rationalizing the wrong we do, that is, a way of

19. According the U.S. Census Bureau, "Minorities, now roughly one-third of the U.S. population, are expected to become the majority in 2042, with the nation projected to be 54 percent minority in 2050. By 2023, minorities will comprise more than half of all children." U.S. Census Bureau News, released on August 24, 2008. www.census.gov/Press-Release/www/releases/archives/population.

insulating the heart. Truth-telling is a process of stripping away the built-in insulation. It does not come easy. It is a long, hard process. Truth-telling is also a communal act. We come before God in a communal judgment. This is to say that truth and reconciliation are the primary theological tasks facing theological education collectively as it anticipates its future. Truth-telling comes first from those who have been victimized by invisibility and historical revisionism. The purpose here is to not just chronicle the depth of the power of the negation of life that comes from the abuse of basic human rights and dignity. Theologically speaking, truth-telling is a powerful means of collective soul-searching just as the Republic of South Africa and other nations discovered in their attempts for truth and reconciliation. When we see and hear the ugliness of the institutional racism inflicted upon our own colleagues and students of color, we see the depth of our own nihilistic soul. Only then, in this realization, do we become open to God's grace.

In order to engage in the theological task of truth and reconciliation, there are pit holes that need to be noted: (1) The theological contributions of people of color have been relegated to what is classified as an ideological "liberation theology" and "contextual theology" without a giving of due accord to their key and fundamental roles in articulating the deep meaning of life through the lens of Christian communities of life; and (2) theological education has failed to acknowledge the true meaning of Christian faith that is being built by the "multitude" of diverse Christians.

History has shown that the rich and powerful are far more willing to alleviate the results of poverty than to attack its causes, and that their primary preoccupation is always with order rather than justice. But history has also shown that the concern for disorder over injustice invariably produces more of both. It is not enough to envisage a future, not even the future of North American theological education. The world of theological education demands a just future that only becomes open to us in our penitent act of truth-telling.

THEOLOGICAL EDUCATION OF NOT YET

As theological education in North America faces the future, this much is clear: it risks irrelevance unless the truth-telling of racism is earnestly engaged and the nihilistic soul of theological institutions is laid bare. What Christians believe is this: The redemptive power of God in Christ is released only when we meet God unprotected against the uneven and unyielding stony ground of life, as Rowan Williams reminds us.[20] God's redemptive power is released to us as "costly grace."

The story of Jesus and the woman taken in adultery (John 8:1–11) is instructive. Jesus allows a languishing moment in which people are given time to see themselves differently precisely because he refuses to make the sense they want. The divine power of reconciliation and redemption manifests in these languishing moments.

The future of race in theological education is still unknown. Reconciliation amid the painful history of racial divide comes unexpectedly, not according to any blueprint drawn by theological educators. We are only guided by faith that points to life in which there is never to be an end to love.

Jesus' most unprotected and languishing moment was on his cross. It was at this most vulnerable moment he uttered the words, "Why have you forsaken me?" His words are those of a question, not a statement. As Jesus asked this gut-wrenching question to God, he was stripped bare of any humanly conceivable clue to God's response. Donald Shriver points out that, in this most critical moment of his life, Jesus affirmed the "unnegotiableness of human relationships" by turning to God.[21] Theological educators become open to the reconciling redemptive power of God over the history of racial divide only when we become naked personally and collectively in acknowledging the weight of the pain of racism and our own enmeshment in the power of negation. "Every epoch sighs for a better world. The more profound the despair caused by the chaotic present, the more intimate is the sigh."[22] Where do we hear our collective sighs in North American theological education today?

20. Williams, *Writing in the Dust*.

21. Shriver Jr., "The Pain and Promise of Pluralism," 345–50.

22. Ibid.

2

When *Subjects* Matter

The Bodies We Teach By[1]

MAI-ANH LE TRAN

A POLITICAL STORY OF FITTONIAS

ONE ST. LOUIS AFTERNOON, my sister and I wandered into a local Lowe's to pick up some gardening tools. On the spur of the moment, Hoang-Anh went to look for some silver-veined fittonias, a garden plant of the family *Acanthaceae*, which she had once acquired back in her days in Berkeley, California. Not seeing them anywhere, my sister approached a store employee who was working in the plant section—an older woman of quiet demeanor—and asked if the store carried fittonias.

"You're looking for what . . . ?"

"Fittonias—particularly the silver-veined variety. Do you know if this store has them?"

"You mean pe–tu–nias?" She enunciated with deliberateness.

My antennas perked up. We are not twelve, nor hard of hearing: Why the slow speech?

"Oh, no, not petunias. I mean 'fittonias.' You know, I think they're called 'mosaic plants,' cute and small, they'd be just perfect for my desk! But I haven't been able to find them anywhere . . ." The sister rambled on.

---

1. Chapter title inspired by Dan P. McAdams's *The Stories We Live By*.

31

"Oh? Oh . . . I don't know . . . I've not heard of fittonias before . . ."
The woman looked increasingly perplexed. Then, with hesitation, "Are they
from *your* country or *my* country?"

Hoang-Anh and I looked at each other, dumbstruck. A simple question about a garden plant suddenly *ejected* us two naturalized U.S. citizens
right out of *this* country, and neither of us knew how to respond.

Visceral memories shot through my stiffened body: the "ching chong"
noises made by local teens as they passed by our house when we first moved
into the neighborhood . . . my fifth grade teacher flapping her arms in front
of the class to ask if I had left Vietnam by boat or by plane . . . the secret
shame throughout my sullen early-teens of having to eat "free lunch" at
school thanks to public aid for newly settled immigrants of the "Orderly
Departure Program"[2] . . . an overzealous colleague who got very close to
my face, asking if I could provide examples of how the cultural rules for
body contact might be interpreted differently by "my people back home" . . .
my first return to Vietnam after twenty years, being teased by the locals for
having the body shape and accent of "a little American" . . . . In that instant,
an inquiry about fittonias' origin created a convergence of memories: from
autobiographical memories of multi-ethnic lineage (Sino-Vietnamese)
and multi-religious heritage (ancestor veneration, Buddhist, Christian); to
episodic memories of relatives who had dispersed by boat or into "reeduca-
tion camps" at the end of a war just about everyone loved to hate; to social
memories of threats, taunts, jeers, jokes, platitudes and praises directed at
racialized and sexualized subjects like me who became "naturalized"[3] U.S.
citizens after a period of "alien resident" status; to historical memories of
laws and legislations that regulate the rules of belonging and the flow of
bodies for labor and love; to psychosomatic memories of sounds, sights, and
smells that congeal incidents of identity contestation . . . . There you have it,
"the personal is political" in plural modalities.

I think back to that occasion frequently and wonder why it is that a
seemingly innocuous question of whether fittonias came from *my* country
of origin would induce such acid reflux. After all, as a White male American
Facebook "friend" of my sister retorted when she recounted the episode
to her virtual compatriots, the store employee was just asking an innocent
question, and was not intending to insult. Why overreact with insinuations
of racial ignorance or prejudice? The commentator's rebuke rendered us
silent . . . but it was a torrid silence of quiet rage that cuts right to our core.

2. Rumbaut, "Vietnamese, Laotian, and Cambodian Americans," 179.

3. The 1952 Naturalization Act prohibited racial and gender restrictions in determining naturalization eligibility. Takaki, *Iron Cages*, 299–300.

If this country is *hers*, then what does that make us as inhabitants of this living space? Unsuspecting and repeated ejections thrust a body into existential limbo, for any incident that questions the legitimacy of our being *somewhere* reifies our ineligibility for rightful permanence *anywhere*. It is a comprehension that engenders inconsolable angst when the implications are followed through: as a theological educator, it is with this *impermanent body* that I teach, and despite all the confidence, gumption, and even arrogance built over the years from painstaking personal and professional discipline, I still teach each day in full anticipation of that eject button—for it has never failed to set off in moments suspecting or unsuspecting within the academic setting. No one taught me that in graduate school.

THE TEACHING BODY

> There is a body in the room. We ignore it . . . . Usually, of course,
> we ignore the body by ignoring it—we don't speak about it, we
> don't look directly at it, we change the subject quickly if there's a
> risk of noticing it. Sometimes, however, we have to ignore it by
> speaking about it—by saying the right things and then carrying
> on with our assigned topic.[4]

Most academics never learned how to teach. We are credentialed and authorized for having demonstrated some level of mastery over a cornucopia of "subject matters," but few doctoral programs focus on preparing scholars for the discipline and a life of *teaching*. Not only that, the *subjects* that arguably matter most in academic teaching/learning—the identities and bodies of the teachers—remain irreducibly complicated and vexing for educational research, policies, and practices.

Every academic institution recruits faculty who are *some*body—not just *any*body, and certainly not *no*body. The complications lie in determining which "body" counts in which matters. In legalistic terms, theological schools as Affirmative Action/Equal Employment Opportunity (AA/EEO) employers must, with varying degrees of explicitness, tout a policy against discrimination on account of age, race/color, sex, creed, religion, disability, and national origin, among other complicated stipulations. In reality, theological schools suffer from the same staggering gaps found in institutions of higher learning at large: the gaps between institutional *concepts* of anti-discrimination, diversity, inclusion, and actual institutional *practices* as

---

4. Greenwood, "Education in a Culture of Violence," 351. Citing Elbaz-Luwisch, "How Is Education Possible When There's a Body in the Middle of the Room?," 9.

experienced by their respective members.[5] The picture looks bleak: educators report feeling that they are teaching in "socially oppressive structures."[6] In deference to the "holy trinity" of teaching, research, and service, the educator negotiates his/her rights to academic citizenship within a matrix of institutional bureaucracies, curricular mechanisms, and governance fixtures (perhaps not unlike Weber's capitalistic "iron cage"[7]), the values, policies, and practices of which bend and buoy according to historical, socio-cultural, political, and economic undercurrents. In the process of proving that s/he is *some*body, the teacher finds herself embroiled in professional, cultural, political and individual "identity work,"[8] in which an attitude of *becoming* may potentially effect more moments of self-actualization than certitude about being some*thing*.[9]

The trouble is, there does not exist an authoritative "faculty manual" for this process of *becoming* for the theological educator. The ignored "body in the room" in the opening quotation refers to an educator's lament over the body dilemmas of those teaching in lands ravaged by conflict and violence in Israel and Palestine, where "X" marks the spots on the ground where bodies lay lifeless due to brutal, unceasing transnational identity politics. Few U.S. (theological) educators could fathom their "democratic" teaching/learning environments to be so deadly (unless one is teaching on the "wrong" side of town in parts of the country such as East Saint Louis?). However, articulators of a "critical pedagogy of place" remind us that every space of teaching/learning is an "ever-changing confluence of culture, environment, politics, and power," and the identity work of the teacher inevitably responds to the tides of their social location.[10]

Following this conviction, the ponderings about the teacher's "identity" in this chapter are both decisive and meandering. First, there is determined adherence to the Freirean premise that "since education is by nature social, historical, and political, there is no way we can talk about some universal, unchanging role [or identity] for the teacher."[11] As scholars of critical pedagogy and critical race theory point out, identity is a constructive project of "self-in-formation," catalyzed by the frictions of personal agentive

5. Prater, et al., "Disclose and Demystify."

6. Ibid., 16.

7. Takaki, *Iron Cages*, ix. Citing Weber, *The Protestant Ethic*, 181–82.

8. Clarke, "The Ethico-Politics of Teacher Identity," 186.

9. See this play on "body" semantics in Westfield, "Called out My Name, or Had I Known You Were Somebody."

10. Greenwood, "Education in a Culture of Violence," 356.

11. Freire, "Letter to North-American Teachers," 211.

will and socio-cultural-political forces. Second, subsequent to the previous point, in order to concretize the shiftiness of a teacher's identity work, there is intentional mindfulness of how teaching bodies are particularly raced, classed, nationalized, and sexualized in the academy, with a preference for thick description over against essentializing identity claims.[12] And that is why things get murky: given the uneven waters of identity work, we are held accountable to what New Testament scholar and Asian American theological educator Tat-siong Benny Liew calls "reading with *yin yang* eyes"—eyes which see "both the living and the dead," which refuse to idealize, valorize, or patronize the "sights/sites" of identity negotiations, but rather hold in tension contradictions, dissonances and paradoxes.[13] In this way, *yin yang* eyes are "queer"—they see identity *not* as fixed positive essence, but as unstable, unsettling positionality "marked" (i.e., constituted) in fluid situations and porous contexts.[14] "Thick description" of racial-ethnic "markings" of teaching bodies requires meanderings through these sorts of murky waters.

To queer identity thusly is also to denormativize prevailing sources of identity authorization, including the one preferred by many marginalized subjects: personal experience. The generativity of personal testimonials is not measured by how bad one has it (suffering quotient, if you will), nor by one's proximal or distal position from so-called centers of power. Rather, "witness bearing" of identity work done within in-between crevices (or "interstitial space"[15]) is instructive and constructive when it enriches thick description, expands the repertoires of counter-narratives, resurrects alternative standpoints and viewpoints, broadens collective consciousness, and catalyzes momentum for systemic change.[16]

With said presumptive hermeneutic bearing, four foundational questions serve as guideposts for the ensuing reflections on the racial-ethnic teacher's identity work:[17] *(1) Who is the teacher? (2) What are the sources of a teacher's authority? (3) What practices must they hone? (4) What is the*

---

12. This hermeneutic strategy follows postcolonial feminist cues, as modeled by Mohanty, *Feminism without Borders*, 5.

13. Liew, *What Is Asian American Biblical Hermeneutics?*, 13–15, 19, 25–33.

14. Loughlin, "What Is Queer? Theology after Identity," 150.

15. Kwok, "Fishing the Asia Pacific," 18.

16. Mohanty, *Feminism without Borders*, 77–78; Foss-Snowden, "Standpoint Theory and Discontinuing Denial of Racism, Sexism, and Ageism," 88.

17. Building upon Michel Foucault's notion of "ethics as self-formation," Matthew Clarke of the University of Hong Kong proffers a social constructionist framework for understanding the "ethico-political identity work" of the teacher, comprised of four axes: substance, authority-sources, techniques and practices, and *telos*. The four central questions of this chapter follow these four axes. Clarke, "The Ethico-Politics of Teacher Identity," 186.

telos of their teaching life? "Who is the teacher?" grounds explorations of the teacher's identity upon vocational-professional discernment. It pushes such questions as, what kind of teacher-scholars are we? What do we aspire to be? What parts of ourselves are involved in the teaching/learning tasks, given our identity "markings"? "What authorizes the teacher?" elicits generative themes related to the political negotiations and contestations of a teacher's credibility and authenticity, particularized in how racialized, genderized, or sexualized identities are *shuttled* back and forth between centers and margins of power.[18] "What teaching techniques and practices must they hone?" invites ponderings about tactics or strategies of minoritized[19] teachers who must improvise, adapt, and innovate to gain institutional footing and remain ingenuous to their vocational aspirations. "What is the *telos* of teaching?" presses for utopian ideals, for the freedom to imagine why we theological educators do what we do apart from socio-political determinism. After all, within the theological world, teaching is considered a "charism" and "calling," and such ideals may very well be the grace it takes to resuscitate teaching bodies for their vocation, and the motivation for institutional regeneration amidst the torrents of change.

Without further ado . . .

WHO IS THE TEACHER? GLADIATOR OF AMBIGUITY

". . . [A]ll teachers worth their salt regularly ask themselves whether they have made the right career choice."[20] The declaration comes from a renowned education theorist, prodigious author, award-winning teacher, Distinguished Professor of a major university—a self-identified White male with pedigrees from the U.K. to boot. Describing the teaching practice as analogous to white-water rafting, Stephen Brookfield asserts that the "skillful teacher" is one who "muddles through" the calm waters and turbulence of teaching with "practical reasoning"—or the ability to scan situations, make judgments, and respond with the best use of technical know-how. As "gladiators of ambiguity," they are prepared to expect the unexpected, and their "intuitive confidence" only grows through disciplined, persistent practice of their craft.[21]

18. Trinh, "Cotton and Iron," 330. Inter-spatial shuttling was an attempted metaphor before rediscovery of Trinh's use of it in her exquisite essay.

19. "Minoritized" is preferred over "minority" to emphasize the ideological and political processes of identity negotiations rather than fixed statuses.

20. Brookfield, *The Skillful Teacher*, 8.

21. Ibid., 6–9, 12.

Ambiguous an art as teaching is, who do teachers think they are? This question pivots *vocational discernment* to the center of identity exploration. Why did we go into teaching? What kind of teachers are we? What kind of teachers are we striving to *become*? This is no retreat to universal philosophical abstraction about the teaching life, for that would undermine the premise put forth earlier about the political/politicized nature of a racial-ethnic teacher's identity work. We will get to that. Rather, this is a brash attempt to force to the forefront one foundational dimension of "professional competence": How often do theological educators think about their identity, competency, and integrity *qua* "teachers"? How seriously do theological educators take their role as "reflective practitioners," maintaining disciplined critical reflection upon the *why* and *what* and *how* of their daily teaching practices? Arguably, there is such a thing as "bad teaching," albeit aggravated by identity politics, for no teacher is free of pedagogical malpractice: poorly prepared lessons, inappropriate teaching techniques, inability to know how students learn best, ego-boosting modes of instruction, unfair or uneven preferential options toward students, emotional abuse, disciplinary or departmental competitiveness . . . the list could go on. How do teachers reflect upon their ethico-political responsibilities and presence in the classroom and in the academic institution?[22]

Needless to say, this question is more complicated than it appears. "Professional competence" is *never politically neutral*,[23] and the variances of course outcomes assessment are a prime example of the politicized nature of (e)valuation. The material reality of the teaching life is defined by *body* politics: a teacher sits/stands/walks alongside learners as a "marked" body—wrestling with tensions between performance and perception, competency and credibility. The proverbial injunction "Do as I say, not as I do" may have been reversed for an emphasis on embodied pedagogy: "Do as I *do*, not as I *say*."[24] And yet, such pedagogical wisdom would only be heeded if the teacher manages to persuade others that she/he is worth being seen and heard in the first place. All "teaching bodies" are raced, classed, nationalized, and sexualized in the academy, but racial-ethnic minoritized bodies recall from (counter-dominant) history lessons that as far back as the early beginnings of the American republic, the "perfect body" and the "perfect intellect" was only reserved for the "perfect gender" of the "perfect race."[25]

22. Freire, *Pedagogy of Freedom*, 90.

23. Freire, "Letter to North-American Teachers," 212.

24. hooks, "Engaged Pedagogy."

25. Takaki, *Iron Cages*, 262–63.

Teachers who find themselves continuously minoritized on account of *ex-centric*[26] identity markings have borne frequent witness to the ambiguity of their bodies being the "non-written text" in academic teaching.[27] Like it or not, their impermanent, ambiguous body becomes an "implicit curriculum" that either underscores or undermines the subject matters being taught. This body's "otherly" eyes may only see what is *perspectival* according to the "rational, all-knowing"[28] standards of (Western/ized) academic discourse: inextricably bound to context and time, authorized primarily by *emic* intuitions and emotions, subject to verification and certification by "objective" *etic* norms. As such, judgments about "good" or "bad" teaching become as much an evaluation of the teacher's *identity performance*[29] (and the institution's forbearance of it) as it is an assessment of their teaching competencies. There lies a quandary for minoritized teaching bodies: discerning which performance is the *real* subject of scrutiny—their competence as teachers/scholars, their (in)ability to "look the part" of a competent teacher/scholar, or a combination thereof. Working doubly hard to "pass" as knowledgeable and credible has become an all too common refrain.[30] "Passing" turns eerie when ex-centric teaching bodies realize that it takes nothing short of "death masks" to project to nostalgic audiences the recognizability of the good days of yore. Look, they plead: the old standard-bearers are still here . . . look how well we can be mediums for their immortality.

"Who are you as a teacher?" may be a question of vocational discernment, but "Who do you *think* you are, anyway?" is a spin-off which, when uttered with a certain intonation, signals an interrogation of the teacher's "credit report"—the breakdown of their credibility and the sources of its authentication.[31] Aspirations to become guru, expert, sage, coach, guide, counselor, advocate, mentor, motivator, sojourner, pilgrim, co-learner—or whatever other functional images one may conceive for a teaching philosophy[32]—are tempered by nervous apprehensions over how such teaching roles are already being "typecasted." Playing it "straight" or outwitting the script becomes the creative tension for a teacher seeking legitimation, realizing that the performing body is a *de facto* locus of struggle.

26. Althaus-Reid, *Indecent Theology*, 22.

27. Pinn, "Reading the Signs: The Body as Non-Written Text," 87.

28. Trinh, "Cotton and Iron," 332.

29. Zamudio, *Critical Race Theory Matters*, 51; Carbado and Gulati, "Working Identity," 1301.

30. Sealey-Ruiz, "Reading, Writing, and Racism," 46.

31. Brookfield discusses "credibility" and "authenticity" as two values which students often say they most desire in teachers. *The Skillful Teacher*, 56. See chapter 4.

32. See Lines, *Functional Images of the Religious Educator*.

WHAT AUTHORIZES THE TEACHER? TEACHING BODY AS SITE/SIGHT OF STRUGGLE

It has been said that two maladies vex the life of academics: hero complex and impostorship anxiety.[33] It is one of the quintessential paradoxes of the ambiguous teaching life: we persist in our work believing we can "make a difference," if not a revolution; and yet deep in the recesses of our minds we fear that we are phonies. That said, research has shown that while the impostor syndrome may be ubiquitous, the severity of its effects has alarming correlations with the political markings of teaching bodies.[34] Savvy educator Stephen Brookfield refers to a principle articulated by English political observer Simon Hoggart: TATBTS—The Ability To Be Taken Seriously. Apparently, it is defined as "an ability to impress your colleagues, a knack of convincing them that you are someone to whom it is worth paying attention . . . ."[35] The problem is, following Paulo Freire's admonishment, TATBTS is *not* a neutral quality.

Visibility, Vulnerability, Viability

In recent years, women faculty of color have broken tough ground in bearing witness to the struggle to be taken seriously within so-called majority institutions of higher learning. Anthologies such as *Still Searching for Our Mothers' Gardens*[36] invoke the rallying cry of earlier generations of feminist/womanist scholars to continue the tradition of narrating counter-stories of the multiple jeopardy of scholar-teachers whose positionality is minoritized by the intersections of race, gender, sexuality, and nationality. With anecdotal honesty, empirical details, painstaking research, and analytic sharpness, these educators testify to inscrutable academic dilemmas imbedded in familiar taxonomies of struggle: diversity, difference, and problem of "blindness"; voice, power, agency, and "otherness"; normative gazes and territorialization in identity politics; profiling, prejudice, structural discrimination; curricular tensions and classroom dynamics; and collegial negotia-

---

33. Brookfield, *The Skillful Teacher,* 76–83.

34. See, for instance, Harvey, "The Impostor Phenomenon and Achievement."

35. Brookfield, *The Skillful Teacher,* 245; Hoggart, *On the House,* 46.

36. Niles and Gordon, eds., *Still Searching for Our Mothers' Gardens.* Cf. Alice Walker's 1983 classic, *In Search of Our Mothers' Gardens.* Early respected anthologies of Asian feminist voices include *Making Waves,* edited by Asian Women United of California, and *Dragon Ladies,* edited by Sonia Shah. A more recent contribution edited by Gabriella Gutiérrez y Muhs, *Presumed Incompetent: The Intersections of Race and Class for Women in Academia,* is garnering much attention.

tions and institutional politics. Three generative themes illustrate this web of complexity: "visibility, vulnerability, and viability."[37]

Visibility

Visibility—being seen—already means to be judged by what one looks like. This enfleshment of teaching bodies is not freeing, but rather fear-ridden due to the knowledge that one is constantly under the shadows of scrutinizing gaze. It is a form of psycho-political exposure that turns teachers into what educator Ana Maria Freire calls "interdicted bodies"—"forbidden to be," inhibited through self-monitoring.[38] At the intra-psychic level, the demands of physical, mental, and emotional health beckon prudent attention to care of self, but such concern is often difficult to negotiate within the *habitus* of institutional and academic life. Physiologically, sexualized female teaching bodies struggle with exposed bodily curvatures as much as menstrual flows, but who cares when the teacher is only supposed to be the disembodied "talking head"—mentally objective, emotionally persuasive, physically virulent? With biology being culturally and politically charged, we recall Audre Lorde's description of the "mythical norm" that haunts minoritized female consciousness: "white, thin, male, young, heterosexual, christian, and financially secure."[39] "Somatophobia" ensues as academics contend over which "ism" is more malignant (sexism or racism), forgetting that "flesh-loathing" attitudes arise out of "interlocking"—not additive—misogynistic, racist, heteronormative, classist, ageist, imperialistic, colonialist, jingoistic, capitalistic, and even militant typecasting of "difference."[40]

We keep that in mind when pressing for concrete examples for various typecasting of racialized and sexualized teaching subjects: How are they stereotypically deemed "dangerous" (angry, vixen, feminazi, terrorizing)?[41] How must they be stereotypically "nice" (compliant, "mule," exotic/tropic)? What would qualify them as "smart," "competent," or "authoritative" on a particular subject matter? A praise for a caricatured representation ("cute," "diminutive," "sexy," "curvaceous," "amazon"); cringing terms of endearment ("aren't you a dear!"); objectifying compliments ("work it, girl!");

---

37. Foss-Snowden, "Standpoint Theory and Discontinuing Denial of Racism, Sexism, and Ageism," 83. Citing Mitchell, "Visible, Vulnerable, and Viable."

38. Freire, *Teachers as Cultural Workers*, 9.

39. Lorde, *Sister Outsider*, 2nd ed., 116.

40. Spelman, *Inessential Woman*, 26, 126.

41. bell hooks does not mince words: "angry mean black bitch"! In *Teaching Critical Thinking*, 99.

inappropriate body contact (head-patting, chin-touching, face-cuddling, arm-brushing); sexualized advances from students and colleagues; overt inquiries or rumor mills about marital status or dating "preferences"; being passed over ("is there a teacher in this room?"), mistaken for someone else ("I didn't know there were two Asians/Blacks/Latino/as here"), put on the spot to defend one's teaching status ("sorry, only faculty are allowed here"); being spoken for by other well-meaning sympathizers, or tasked to enlighten so-called "ignorant" interlocutors . . . These are but minor anecdotal punctuations to the endless testimonials provided by teacher-scholars whose visible bodies render their credibility as teacher perpetually ambiguous.

Taking seriously the standpoint feminist concepts of *positionality* (identity work is place-based, situational and contextual) and *intersectionality* (identity is constructed and performed within a matrix of dynamic, intersecting identity statuses which are never fixed markers),[42] it is important to take account of the very particular ways in which oppressive body (stereo)types serve as identity straitjackets. This precludes the tropes of "true identity" or "essential victim," as third-wave feminist scholars have long argued. Rather, the blight of visibility—being seen—for the institutionally minoritized teacher seems to be inscribed by the "historical, geographical, cultural, psychic, and imagination boundaries that provide the ground for political definition and self-definition . . . ."[43] Thus, depending upon contextual configurations, a caricatured "woman of color" or "racial/ethnic minority" faculty may be desired in one institutional setting and not in another. Sadly, visibility often functions as a source of *de*-authorization. One must look the part, and it is a white-water rafting adventure to figure out which part is desired at which moment. Desperate attempts could result in "cultural impersonation," or the mimicry of projected identity (stereo)types in order to fit in or blend in at all cost—as in the schizophrenic vacillation between a hyper-performance of superwoman, villain, or femme fatale.[44]

Vulnerability

Here lies a catch-22: is it better to be *in*visible? That is a converse dilemma for the teaching body. For in both visibility and invisibility, the marked

---

42. See Harding, "Gendered Ways of Knowing and the 'Epistemological Crisis' of the West."

43. Mohanty, *Feminism Without Borders,* 106.

44. Mohanty, *Feminism Without Borders,* 102. Floyd-Thomas and Floyd-Thomas, "Emancipatory Historiography as Pedagogical Praxis," 127. The "superwoman-villain dichotomy" is attributed to womanist scholar Katie G. Cannon.

teaching body is *vulnerable* when it comes to various levels of performance evaluations. The cooperative of women faculty of color in the above mentioned anthology reports higher external and self-imposed expectations when it comes to identity and performance evaluations. Entrenched within academic institutions are invisible, implicit standards by which teachers are assessed, and according to which vulnerable teachers may be found wanting. As the assessment bar constantly shifts, ratings of teaching performance wax and wane based on what is deemed institutionally and politically "valuable" at various points in an academic's career and tenure. A teacher may have to perform by one particular set of standards for institutional approval (e.g., publishing or teaching), and yet is actually deemed valuable by a different set of standards (e.g., advising or administering programs). After all, there are different levels of needs and services expected of the teacher by the institution and the student body—particularly the bodies of minoritized students. A twisted form of academic *ventriloquism* is displayed when the institution needs some faculty for their appearance (how they make the institution look), some other faculty for their voice (what they have to say), and some for what they are able to do (how they are able to work behind the scenes to maintain day-to-day operations). "But you are so good at it!" is the accolade of which one learns to be leery, for it usually exacts a costly return.

Moreover, faculty of minoritized status regularly report the stress of having to bear the extra weight of representation: they must proudly demonstrate the institution's interest in diversity; they must be available as mentors to minority students who lack structural support; they must exercise teaching authority over minority students without subjecting the latter to public shame (sometimes, their ventriloquism and "death masks" are not even sufficient authority sources for minoritized students due to internalized sexism/sexblindness, racism/colorblindness, or colonialism); they must ensure the development of critical competencies to address social location in their own teaching and scholarship (because it is not an "innate" capacity or knowledge base); they must fight to make context-specific perspectives and concerns central to the "mainstream" curriculum, and they must not offend. After all, is it not enough that they get to teach "special interest" topics supplemental to the curriculum?

The fear of being the "token hire" or the fear of "not living up to standard" often results in self-censoring. Minority bodies suspected of having an "agenda" are subjects to be monitored and regulated.[45] "It sure is rotten to be a straight White male these days!" a student declares. The racial-ethnic

---

45. Foss-Snowden, "Standpoint Theory and Discontinuing Denial of Racism, Sexism, and Ageism."

minority female teacher (whose sexual identity might be suppressed if no one asks and she does not tell) suddenly realizes the vulnerability of her teaching task: on the one hand, she desires to expose a variety of "invisible" privileges at work in the student's statement and worldview; on the other hand, she is aware of the potential risks of being dismissed wholesale for alleged political bias. Recalling subaltern wisdom, she scans for possible "White allies"—male or female, gay or straight[46]—to assist her with a more cogent (and credible) critique of pervasive heteropatriarchy and white privilege. All the while, she wonders when her word alone would be enough.

Viability

One could charge that majority academic institutions operate by the principle of *unnatural* selection. It is not so much "survival of the fittest," for Darwinian natural selection assumes that species that can adapt to their immediate environment will survive. No matter how hard they try to "fit in," some teaching bodies remain vulnerable to (r)ejections from their host environments. The *viability* of the teacher as "outsider within"[47] is thus dependent upon their ability to cultivate coping mechanisms for both *pluricultural* and *fringe* existence.

As the "holy trinity" of academic life is teaching, scholarship, and service, the teacher unavoidably navigates a landscape of multiple institutional cultures and multiple lines of accountability. Within this web of connections, typical dilemmas of survival—*survivre*, to out-live—include the sense of self-shame, social isolation, lack of mentoring, lack of collegial support system, and lack of institutional security.[48] Academic coding of meritocracy and colorblind racism breed self-doubting questions: by what merit was I hired, and by what merit will I continue to be valued? Alliances for solidarity are easily subject to territorialized identity politics: Why are *they* hanging together? Is s/he a "sell-out"? "Token hire" carries more layered meaning in these crushing economic times, in which deliberations over faculty shape

46. Admittedly, this parenthetical dualistic rhetoric misses the mark when we account for the ambiguities of sexual bodies, in which "male or female" and "gay or straight" express a continuum rather than opposite polarities. Transgendered and intersexed identities further problematize the bifurcation. However, it is merely used as a rhetorical quip here to unsettle the wisdom that has become "convention" in conversations on dismantling racism: that "persons of color" need "White allies" to help them address institutional or structural racism. Problematically, gender or sexuality are often not factored into such equation.

47. Gordon, "Watching My B/lack," 47.

48. Prater, et al., "Disclose and Demystify."

and size, for meager-sized institutions, are driven as much by the economy as by institutional, curricular, or disciplinary politics. Therefore, "tokens" may very well enjoy some degree of political power (especially when it comes to accreditation), knowing well that such leverage is to be constantly bartered according to the rules of a market-driven, consumer-oriented academic space. That notwithstanding, racial-ethnic minoritized teachers are equally capable of colluding with and re-inscribing the very hegemonic values and structures used against them. This on top of institutional "divide-and-conquer" tactics makes *competition* more instinctive and eventually habitual than the work of solidarity and coalition-building.

To remain viable in a constant state of insecurity, isolation, or alien-ation, racial-ethnic minority teachers have called for a variety of fringe practices for institutional maneuvering, some of which will be highlighted below.[49] In all, when there is persistent discrepancy between institutional and personal expectations concerning diversity and anti-oppressive educa-tion, and incongruence between institutional *notions* of diversity and justice and its actual *practices*; when there is pervasive lack of basic command of cultural sensitivity, intercultural competency, and race literacy[50] within the teaching/learning environment, minoritized teaching bodies are no better than "strangers in the ivory tower," or "aliens" ineligible for permanent insti-tutional citizenship.[51] If academic institutions subscribe to a revolving-door doctrine to keep their faculty "fresh," then minoritized teachers may find themselves among the contingency of "day laborers" who are easily hired and just as easily dispensed according to need.

Aliens Ineligible for Citizenship

It seems worthwhile for an excursus at this point on how issues of "visibil-ity, vulnerability, and viability" play out for a racial/ethnic minority group (in)famous for their "model minority" status in higher education and the cultural mainstream, despite their marginality within (theological and reli-gious) educational research literature: Asian Americans and Pacific Island-ers (AAPI).[52] (Stereo)typically portrayed as minorities who have attained "universal and unparalleled academic and occupational success,"[53] AAPIs are often cited as exemplars of American meritocracy, in which upward

49. See Gatison, "Playing the Game."
50. Bolgatz, *Talking Race in the Classroom*, 2.
51. Wilson, "Strangers in the Ivory Tower"; Takaki, *Strangers from a Different Shore*.
52. "Oceanic" is recently the preferred term over "Pacific Islander."
53. Museus and Kiang, "Deconstructing the Model Minority Myth," 6.

mobility is attained through a perfected work ethic comprised of old world values and American (Protestant) individual self-help. Pitted against other racial/ethic minority groups (particularly African Americans and Latino/ as through malevolent "underclass ideologies"), AAPIs as an aggregated racial grouping serve as a foil for multiple sides of affirmative action debates. *The Rise of Asian Americans*, the 2012 Pew Research Center's "comprehensive" study of Asians in the U.S., is perhaps the most recent example of how obscured and over-simplified demographic data can serve to buttress dominant cultural anxieties about a minority population's alleged steady ascension to the top. Released in the thick of contentious national debates about immigration "reform," the report offers fodder for antagonistic delineations between "good" and "bad" immigrants/citizens.

Against this backdrop, educational researchers have begun to challenge how aggregate empirical data on educational performance and achievement have been used to obscure the actual struggles of Asian Pacific Americans in living up to the model minority trope.[54] Following the tenets of *critical race theory*, which will be further elaborated in the next section, researchers expose how the myth is sustained by misconceptions, misrepresentations, and lack of nuanced empirical data. For instance, the broad racial construct of "Asian American" or "Asian Pacific Islander" in educational research obfuscates vast ethnic differences, socioeconomic disparities, and the significant under-educated percentage within AAPI populations in the U.S. A multiple passport-holding executive from Hong Kong, a Korean grocery shop-owner, a Filipino doctor, a Laotian refugee in middle Tennessee, a migrant from the U.S. territory of American Samoa, and an Amerasian child of biracial heritage would all be homogenized under the "Asian or Pacific Islander" racial category.[55] Subsequently, based upon the ostensible "success" of a select few ethnic representatives within transnational market infrastructures or elite academic institutions (typically East Asians, and stereotypically thanks to American capitalistic benevolence), *all* AAPIs are typecasted in cultural discourse as the "new whites" or "almost white" by the model minority myth, in the midst of looming fears of immigrant infiltrations.[56] This misconception conveniently ignores AAPI collective and historical experiences of exclusion, prejudice, discrimination, harassment, pressure to conform, and survival struggles in mainstream America. When racism is casted

54. See, for instance, Nakanishi and Nishida, eds., *The Asian American Educational Experience*. More information may be obtained by following the research initiatives of the National Commission on Asian American and Pacific Islander Research in Education.

55. Palumbo-Liu, *Asian/American*. See esp. chapter 7.

56. Ibid., 110–13.

within a twisted framework of competitive suffering (to determine which racial groups suffer more), racialized infractions against AAPIs are easily dismissed as negligible individual biases or prejudices endemic to cultural diversity, rather than consequences of systemic racism. Aggregate research data suggest that AAPIs "in general" rank higher in educational achievement and rarely seek institutional resources and support. Such data fail to account for income disparities in hiring, the inability to gain employment, under-employment, and the lack of culturally appropriate social, governmental, or educational support. More ominously, the model minority trope and instrumental use of selective empirical data together force AAPIs into identity straitjackets.[57] As Asian American cultural theorists have shown, "the materiality of the [Asian] body as labor, commodity, and reproductive or sexual force" is *introjected* into the dominant American psyche for a "modeling" function within areas of containment. As inassimilable new immigrants, they must perform according to the model minority script, or risk being "re-foreignized" and ejected as "yellow perils," as has been proven throughout U.S. history.[58]

If cognizant of the dynamics of racialization described above, an Asian American teacher—or, more specifically, a one-point-five-generation Vietnamese refugee-turned-naturalized-U.S.-citizen—would step into the classroom wary of the various holographic identity constructs being projected upon her. Depending upon the boundaries of imagination, she is acutely aware of the cultural caricatures of the Asian female: beguiling geisha, diminutive mail-ordered bride, military sex worker, conniving brothel madam, innocent village girl, submissive Confucian wife, whip-lashing tiger mom, tradition-bound matriarch, plasma-breathing martial artist, nerdy Asiatic brainiac who "stole" an American job or admissions ticket to an elite academic institution, or (given post-September 11 xenophobia) an instrument for political or religious terrorism . . . Like the wives of East Asian migrant laborers once historically barred from citizenship by U.S. legislation,[59] this racialized and genderized teaching body wrestles with whether to perform or outwit the model minority morality play to attain legitimacy within the academic "iron cage." At the same time, she stands as an authoritative figure, granted a certain extent of institutional endorsement by virtue of the teaching office, her own charisma, and the body of knowledge over which she had proven acceptable mastery. This teacher

57. Museus and Kiang, "Deconstructing the Model Minority Myth," 6–11; Palumbo-Liu, 196; Espiritu, *Asian American Women and Men*, chapter 4.

58. Palumbo-Liu, *Asian/American*, 18, 146.

59. Takaki, *Strangers from a Different Shore*, 14.

does well to remember that just as identity is a performance rather than a fixed status marker, her authority as teacher is also a constant (and improvisational) performative contestation—and inevitably a compromise between the markers of her difference and the agentive choices she exercises over the constitution of her "otherness."

What techniques and practices might this teacher hone for such improvisational identity work? We turn to this question in the next section.

MAGICO-RELIGIOUS WAVERING BETWEEN WORLDS:[60]
TEACHING PRACTICES

In a letter penned for North American educators, the late Brazilian education reformer Paulo Freire wrote: "[A] teacher must be fully cognizant of the political nature of his/her practice and assume responsibility for this rather than denying it."[61] Freire was not alone in articulating the *political* nature of teaching. It is at base persuasive, if not directive; to varying degrees, it is an intentional effort to exert influence upon knowledge (what we know), affect (what we value), behavior (how we act). As such, scholars of critical pedagogy push the recognition that "knowledge is power" toward closer scrutiny of how power is configured by the boundaries of knowledge systems, and how the boundary coordinates of such systems can be "remapped, reterritorialized, and decentered" for multiplied reference points in our "reading of the world."[62] This epistemological disposition of "border pedagogy" assumes that learners are crossers of borders that are "historically constructed and socially organized within maps of rules and regulations that limit and enable particular identities, individual capacities, and social forms."[63] Teachers, therefore, are also border-crossers who might do well if they learn and apply what sociologist Aihwa Ong describes of the contemporary global "flexible citizen": "*trans*versal," "*trans*actional," "*trans*lational," and "*trans*gressive" practices that are "incited, enabled, and regulated by the logics" of the academic landscape.[64] These figurative abstractions can be broken down into a few components of "practical wisdom" for the teacher,

---

60. van Gennep, *The Rites of Passage*, 18.

61. Freire, "Letter to North-American Teachers," 211.

62. Giroux, *Pedagogy and the Politics of Hope*, 147. In his "Letter to North-American Teachers," Freire wrote that the skill to read the *word* generates the capacity to read the *world*. Also in Freire, *Teachers as Cultural Workers*, 18.

63. Giroux, *Pedagogy and the Politics of Hope*, 147.

64. Ong, *Flexible Citizenship*, 4.

following the cues of those who employ critical race theory (CRT) for educational analysis.

Subscribing to the concept that *race* is "an unstable and decentered complex of social meanings" transacted through social, economic, and political struggles, CRT treats race as an "organizing principle" of social relationships, practices, and structures.[65] For educational theory and praxis, CRT informs the examination of deep structural roots of institutional policies and everyday practices that contribute to racialization. Challenging notions of race as mere ideological constructs or essentialized, objective attributes, CRT scrutinizes the function of power/differentials in race relations, especially the power of White privilege ("whitestream"). In principle, CRT posits three central tenets. First, it highlights counter-narratives of marginal, subordinated voices as a strategy to decentralize and denormalize dominant grand narratives. Second, it takes advantage of "interest convergence" as leverage for championing equity, since the majority would be more prone to accommodate minority interest if there is overlapping benefit. Third, it targets systemic, structural change (social justice), informed by interdisciplinary and multi-issue analyses.[66]

Pedagogy of Dissent

Following CRT's first tenet, the teacher as "border-crosser" could learn to wield the *trans*gressive power of counter-stories that subtly offer "oppositional" definitions of reality.[67] Their own identity work as an ex-centric teaching body is the living enactment of *trans*versed norms: a "non-standard" subject asserting credibility and authenticity in ways that are slightly slanted, off-kilter, zigzagging, but enough to render problematic so-called normative coordinates of identity. Thus, the identity work of a Chinese-Peruvian ("Chinotino" for Chinese-Latino) teaching in the U.S. as a "global immigrant" unsettles various racialized binary oppositions.[68] A Black Caribbean narrative adds layers to the homogenized U.S. Black experience,

65. Omi and Winant, *Racial Formation in the United States*, 66, 68. Racial formation theory assumes that race is the *fundamental* organizing principle, but the Black/Asian/Latina feminist principles of positionality and intersectionality insist on multidimensionality.

66. Gillborn, "Critical Race Theory and Education," 26–27; Zamudio, *Critical Race Theory Matters*, 16, 22–23; Museus, *Conducting Research on Asian Americans*, 59; Brookfield and Holst, *Radicalizing Learning*, 193. See also Delgado, *Critical Race Theory*.

67. Zamudio, *Critical Race Theory Matters*, 16.

68. Kong, "Immigration, Racial Identity, and Adult Education."

calling to attention a longer history of colonial racialization and subordination of the non-White "other."[69] A queer faculty of color forces serious consideration of "intersectionality" to expose power inscribed by both race and heteronormativity.[70] The identity work of these teachers, in effect, serves as counter-normative "curriculum," juxtaposed against the written curriculum of academic disciplines that are in themselves "racial texts."[71]

Oppositional narratives need not be mild, as womanist scholars have long insisted. What Audre Lorde called *symphonic anger*, "loaded with information and energy," may very well be the emotive response in the face of "exclusion . . . of racial distortions, of silence, ill-use, stereotyping, defensiveness, misnaming, betrayal, and co-optation."[72] Similarly, bell hooks found her confidence through risky "back talk," or presumptive speaking as an equal to an authority figure. Preferred over silent protest, and more directive than informal women speech, "sharp-tongued" talking back is for hooks "a gesture of defiance."[73] For other racialized subjects, however, "counterdiscourse" may take the simple form of a slightly modified "American Dream" that subverts linear trajectories of integration.[74] The teacher as "border intellectual"[75] would recognize that these strategies contribute to potent pedagogies of dissent that challenge normative readings of the world.[76]

Constructing or resurrecting counter-narratives is *not* to be confused with the facile celebration of diversity or difference typically found in what is called "repressive tolerance."[77] Resting on the metanarratives of liberalism and democracy (the product of which includes meritocracy based on sex-blindness and color-blindness), repressive tolerance assumes an already equalized playing field in the sharing and valuation of various texts of identity. In reality, due to pervasive ideological conditioning, minority/minoritized identity stories are easily considered "alternative" and therefore supplemental to dominant ones—overshadowed, co-opted, or exoticized,

69. Alfred, "Challenging Racism through Postcolonial Discourse."

70. Misawa, "Musings on Controversial Intersections of Positionality." Cites Kumashiro, *Troubling Intersections of Race and Sexuality.*

71. Kong, "Immigration, Racial Identity, and Adult Education," 240. Cites Pinar, "Notes on Understanding Curriculum as Racial Text."

72. Lorde, *Sister Outsider,* 2nd ed., 124.

73. hooks, *Talking Back,* 337–40.

74. Palumbo-Liu, *Asian/American,* 246–47.

75. Alfred, "Challenging Racism through Postcolonial Discourse," 212.

76. Mohanty, *Feminism Without Borders,* chapter 8.

77. Brookfield and Holst, *Radicalizing Learning,* 190–97. The notion of "repressive tolerance" is attributed to the work of philosopher Herbert Marcuse.

but not "normalized." Therefore, following CRT's third tenet, the teacher as border intellectual passes over banal tolerance in favor of educational practices that examine power and privilege in the nooks and crannies of macro-structures and micro-realities. Brookfield and Holst suggest three concrete practices: 1) "ideological detoxification," or deconstruction of implicit ideological values undergirding definitions of institutional "normal"; 2) intentional disruption of privilege of all forms (viz., racial, sexual, class, citizenship status), especially those enjoyed in daily routines and institutional configurations; and 3) deep, sustained immersion in "alternative conceptions of normality," a pedagogy of contrast that seeks opportunities for serious confrontation with difference rather than dismissing it as inessential.[78]

CRT's tenet regarding "interest convergence" is perhaps most elusive for the minoritized teacher, for they must seek ways to *trans*late their talents and interests to institutional cultures "incited and regulated" by fluctuating bottom lines. In this act of negotiation, the teacher as "flexible citizen" knows that individual interests are more readily considered if and when they align with institutional interests. Put differently, majority-serving educational, pedagogical, and curricular norms are unlikely to change as long as they continue to serve majority students (and teachers) who happen to be predominant and by all standards excelling.[79] Thus, viability (survival) depends on vigilance with useful cues for continuous *trans*lational work. It also relies on forms of "horizontal comradeship"[80] forged out of affinities or strategic alliances. Perhaps most poignantly, the teacher as flexible, mobile, "nomadic subject" lives by the practical wisdom that (institutional) *home* is not a point of origin or destination, nor is it a "comfortable, inherited, and familiar space"; rather, it is a matrix of locations in which *belonging* is the product of imaginative collective struggle, and *affection and commitment* is enlivened by bodily "magico-religious wavering" between "boundaries not delineated in space."[81]

78. Brookfield and Holst, *Radicalizing Learning*, 201–9.

79. Zamudio, *Critical Race Theory Matters*, 47–48.

80. Mohanty, *Feminism Without Borders*, 46. Citing Anderson, *Imagined Communities*, 11–16.

81. Ong, *Flexible Citizenship*, 19; Mohanty, *Feminism Without Borders*, 128; Kingston, *Woman Warrior*, 8.

FOR THOSE WHO DARE TO TEACH: TELOS OF THE TEACHING LIFE

> What we need more than anything else is not *textbooks*, but *text-people*. It is the personality of the teacher which is the text that the pupils read: the text that they will never forget.[82]

A Freirean teacher is reminded that education is "a form of intervention in the world," and it begins with the very presence of the "textperson" standing in the room, asking herself/himself: "Do I stand for what I teach? Do I believe what I say?"[83] For teachers of theological/religious institutions, these reflections are done within macro-contexts in which "the future has arrived."[84] That future, according to Dan Aleshire of the Association of Theological Schools, is characterized by incremental shifts of long-term seismic effect in North American religion and North American theological education. With discipline, courage, and the earthiness that is the root of humility (*humilis*),[85] ambiguous, impermanent, ex-centric, border-crossing, space-invading, transgressive "flexible bodies" may very well be receivers and proclaimers of "apocalyptic" (revealing, unveiling)[86] visions to propel theological/religious education into the twenty-first century.

---

82. Heschel, *The Insecurity of Freedom*, 237.

83. Freire, *Pedagogy of Freedom*, 90; Heschel, *The Insecurity of Freedom,* 237.

84. Aleshire, "The Future Has Arrived."

85. Cahalan, *Introducing the Practice of Ministry*, 75.

86. Liew, *What Is Asian American Biblical Hermeneutics?,* 135–36.

3

From Foreign Bodies in Teacher Space to Embodied Spirit in *Personas Educadas*

or, How to Prevent "Tourists of Diversity" in Education[1]

LOIDA I. MARTELL-OTERO

THEY SAY THAT TEACHING is an honorable profession. It certainly is a rewarding one. It can also be a difficult one; at least, it has been for me. I always thought this was so because I stumbled into it. At least, I believed I stumbled into it. Thirty-three years ago, when I was a recent graduate from veterinary school, the government of Puerto Rico called in its chips for service in return for its scholarship support. It wanted to begin a veterinary technology program, and I was to be the "go to" person to get it done. I had no training in academic administration and certainly none in teaching. Veterinary medicine trained me to distinguish viruses, not curricula. I could discuss the latest histopathology techniques, but not the latest creative teaching methods. I learned to teach through trial and error. The program

---

1. My thanks to van den Blink for the phrase "tourists of diversity" in "Empathy Amid Diversity," 5.

was little understood and underfunded—I was its only full-time faculty. I attributed my difficulties in the classroom to these factors.

With time, I realized that I had not "stumbled" into teaching at all. I was called. Through the affirmation of this vocation and my gifts for teaching, and with the guidance and mentoring by those who would later become colleagues and were already friends, I began to hone this new profession. It was one that I never expected to practice but found myself enjoying immensely. I slowly and truly became a teacher. Yet, in spite of becoming better at my craft, of understanding such terms as *pedagogy, teaching, learning, education*, and yes, even *curriculum*; in spite of learning creative methods of teaching both from books and colleagues; in spite of learning about Bloom's taxonomy, and even teaching teachers to teach; in spite of all that, each semester of my early years of teaching in the U.S. presented difficulties, some more than others.

During my first semester at the institution where I am currently located, I was verbally harassed and physically intimidated by a student. The situation escalated to the point that the dean and president of the seminary had to intervene. It almost seemed that each term thereafter, someone was at the dean's office lodging a new complaint against me. The initial sympathy of the then dean turned to suspicion. I detected in the hesitancy of her demeanor the unspoken question: "What is *wrong* with this new professor?" It has taken much reflection, much prayer, many conversations with colleagues of color—Latina/o and non-Latina/o—to realize that what I was experiencing went beyond the personal. In this chapter I discuss what it means to be a "foreign body" in the teacher space. I locate this narrative within the primary argument: that teachers of color, particularly women of color, are marked as "foreign bodies" in teacher spaces because the so-called hallowed halls of academia are not neutral spaces, but rather, inherently racist, kyriarchal, and inhospitable spaces for difference. Until we begin to address the foundational institutional assumptions of the educational space, teachers of color, and particularly women, will continue to experience what Carol B. Duncan refers to as a "kind of casual violence to our psyches."[2] I conclude the chapter with a "spirituality of education." From the perspective of a Latina *evangélica*, I argue that theological education must intentionally create a hospitable place—a sacred place—that nurtures diverse *presencia*, and thereby prepares *personas educadas* who can establish relations of hospitality, particularly with those perceived as other.

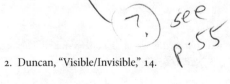

7.) see p. 55

2. Duncan, "Visible/Invisible," 14.

SPACE—NEUTRAL GROUND, WEB OF POWER, OR PLACE OF RELATIONS?

One of the earliest books about teaching I encountered was Parker Palmer's *To Know as We are Known*. In it, he expostulates on his now famous dictum, "To teach is to create a space in which the community of truth is practiced."[3] Yet years later, battered and wiser, I realize that while this seems to state a profound and altruistic truism, behind this statement are a number of questionable assumptions. The most fundamental assumption is that space is neutral. It is not. Space is not an inert vacuum. Space is occupied; it is a context. We do not simply exist in space. We "take place" in dimensions of time and space. We create a web of relationships. How we are organized in space is an expression of those relationships and therefore has sociopolitical, economic, and religious significance.[4] Those of us who have grown up in *barrios*, or have participated in schools with broken chalkboards, outdated books, and overcrowded classrooms, know that space is neither innocent nor neutral. Space can be sacred, but it can also represent structural "powers and principalities"—humanly constructed social institutions that seem to take on a life of their own and appear to be "natural" in the hegemonic influence they wield. No space we might think we create is neutral. We bring to such spaces the biases, worldviews, and yes, embodied beings—and therefore relations—that we are. We thus shape space. This means that the embodied community that is found in that space is not just any community, nor is the alleged "truth" that arises some spontaneous and profound insight.[5] It demands that we discern the spirits of truth that arise. One must always approach with intentionality the purpose of the space, the community, and whatever truth one seeks.

When I was growing up, racism was often defined in terms of how it victimized people of color. Today we have come to understand racism in broader terms. Racism is a systemic structure of power and privilege that empowers a dominant group through institutional means—legal, political, religious, economic, communication, cultural, and other foundational social structural means. Through a process of "racial formation," the United States has produced "structures of domination based on essentialist categories of race" as well as of class, gender, sexual orientation, and other "regions" of hegemony that appear to be "natural" or, at least, make some kind

3. Palmer, *To Know*, xii.

4. Soja, *Postmodern Geographies*, 6.

5. Carrette and King would argue that in the age of globalization and "neoliberal ideology" this is particularly true. See *Selling Spirituality*, 10–11.

of "common sense."[6] This process has led the white culture—particularly rich, heterosexual male Protestants—to believe that its worldview is the norm and standard for everyone, and that its privilege is its "just rewards."[7] Whoever does not conform to that norm or that standard is "other," and by definition "alien." In such a context, difference is a "weapon" that is wielded for exclusion and denigration.[8]

Elisabeth Schüssler Fiorenza defines kyriarchy as pyramidal multiplicative stratifications of dominance and subordination based on class, gender, and other essentialized categories of power and privilege. When coupled with racism—which includes not just privilege based on color, but that based on culture, and religion—kyriarchy creates a series of "interlocking oppressions." These oppressions form a matrix that impacts the communal living of most who reside in the United States.[9] These so-called "–isms" that plague our society and damage our communities are not simply passed on passively as if they were some giant DNA strand, invisible to the eye. The very system of racial formation and privilege that makes it invisible to the bearer of privilege also inscribes itself in ways to ensure that it is maintained and continued. It does so both overtly and covertly.[10]

Our educational system participates in this process of intentionality. It is a system that is constructed to (pre)serve this culture of power and privilege. If education is the "deliberate, systematic and sustained effort to transmit, evoke, or acquire knowledge, values, attitudes, skills, or sensibilities," as Lawrence Cremin suggests, then our educational system has served the dominant culture well.[11] Charles Foster observes that its purpose is to "empower the full participation of a privileged group" and limit the participation of others.[12] Gloria Ladson-Billings finds that

> schools, society, and the structures and products of knowledge
> are designed to create individuals who internalize the dominant

6. Omi and Winant, *Racial Formation*, 60, 68, 71. See also Barndt, *Dismantling Racism*.

7. Hobgood, *Dismantling Privilege*, 15.

8. Russell, *Just Hospitality*, 31.

9. Schüssler Fiorenza, *But She Said*, 115. Also, Kujawa-Holbrook, "Beyond Diversity," 144; and Turner, "Women of Color in Academe," 79. I would add that given the reality of colonization and globalization, recently defined as the new form of racism, such realities extend well beyond our borders. See Groody, *Globalization*, particularly chapter 1.

10. For more, see Coates, "Covert Racism," 208–31. Also, Barndt, *Dismantling Racism*, 88, 93, 156.

11. As cited by Foster, "Diversity in Theological Education," 24.

12. Ibid.

> worldview . . . The hegemony of the dominant paradigm makes
> it more than just another way to view the world—it claims to be
> the only legitimate way to view the world.[13]

Consequently, the educational space is not neutral. Edward Soja prefers the term "spatiality" to indicate that there is an intentionality of how it is organized and used to ensure the power and privilege of the dominant culture. Whoever enters that space must be well aware that its epistemological assumptions—the epistemological perspectives, ideologies, and the insistence on "educational excellence"—are already situated and serve the needs of a privileged group. In this space, knowledge is constructed. In so doing, it becomes an inhospitable space to anyone or anything it deems "other." This happens because a discourse is validated in this space, which "includes myths, symbols, [and] language patterns," that ensures that "we understand ourselves 'properly'—that is, hierarchically—classed, raced, and gendered persons."[14] It shapes and validates cultures and legitimizes *a* worldview. In that process, relations are constructed over time. Thus how we relate to and treat each other as a community is not a happenstance or a graced and fortuitous encounter. It too has been deliberately constructed. What is created is not a life-giving space, but one that declares some people as *personae non gratae*. In Spanish, we would say that such people are treated as *sobrajas* (leftovers)—as if they have nothing of worth to contribute to the life of the *communitas*.

Given this reality, it would seem that Palmer's invitation to create a space is not as easy or as innocent a task as it first seems. The space is already gerrymandered to be a particular space, the community to ensure the legitimacy of the truth of a dominant worldview, and the way of learning, the truths that are validated, and the very *presencia* (presence) and humanity recognized are those of a privileged group. It is into this space that teachers of color, particularly women of color, enter. It is in this space that we are called to create community, to teach, and to invite that community into a process of learning. It is in this inhospitable place that we seek to hear and find some modicum of truth, but not simply "truth" as an abstract notion. It is into this constructed space that we enter as embodied people to help form a community of *personas educadas*.

---

13. Ladson-Billings, "Racialized Discourses," 258.

14. Hobgood, *Dismantling Privilege*, 22.

FOREIGN BODY IN RESISTANT SPACES

"Body" is not a neutral term either. It can be defined in myriad ways. From a purely biological perspective, we can be attentive to the various anatomical and physiological systems that comprise "body." From a theological perspective one can plumb the depths of the Hebraic understanding of *bāśār* or the Pauline use of *sōma*.[15] Leaving Hellenized Greek, Platonic, Aristotelian, Gnostic, or other anthropological dualistic interpretations aside—what Eleazar S. Fernandez has rightly called "Manichean hermeneutics"—Christian anthropology has claimed that we human beings do not have bodies but rather *are* bodies.[16] The Hebrew *bāśār* points to the relationality of our embodied existence. The Mexican slang term *carnal*, literally "flesh" or "meat" that can be roughly translated as "sibling" or "intimate friend," actually comes very close to the notion of *bāśār*. To be an enfleshed, that is, an embodied people, is to acknowledge that we are created as social beings—the fact of our enfleshed reality is our perichoretic *ousia*. Insofar as Christian anthropology is concerned, the U.S. myth of the rugged individual has no biblical or theological basis. Recent trinitarian perspectives, particularly in the understanding of hypostases as persons-in-relations and perichoresis as diversified and intimate community, would also argue against an individualist anthropology as God's intention for creation.[17]

Thus embodiment not only points to the fact of our physical existence, it underscores the *who*-ness of our identity as persons and as social beings. It is the site of learning, relating, growing, apprehending, and knowing. This is not knowledge in a modernist reductionist understanding; i.e., an intellectual apprehension of facts, but rather the knowing of intimacy, as captured in the biblical concept, *yādā*. It is not reduced to "knowing about," but means truly to know the other. We can only know as an embodied people. We can only know through relationality, and relations take place in a given space.

Embodiment, like spatiality, therefore is not a neutral term. In particular, when the space is racist and kyriarchical such that the constructs of knowing are distorted, bodies are "misinformed"/distorted by what I have coined as "normatizing myths," reaffirmed and believed to be true by the dominant culture.[18] People of color are often familiar with these myths. For

15. Cf. Wolff, *Anthropology*, 26–31. Ridderbos, *Paul*, 115–17.

16. Fernandez, *Reimagining the Human*, 11. See chapter 1 for a deconstruction of this kind of "disembodied knowledge."

17. For more, see Zizioulas, "Community and Otherness." Also Boff, *Trinity*. LaCugna, *God for Us*.

18. Martell-Otero, "From *Satas* to *Santas*." Machado calls it "historical

African American women, there is the caricature of Aunt Jemima or the sacrificial "help" that lives to serve her white employers. Latinas are welfare "octomoms" or "illegal aliens" who are here to hustle the system. Asian North Americans are perennial foreigners who all look the same, or are good at kung fu and math. I could go on. In this sense, bodies are socially constructed. M. Shawn Copeland asserts,

> The social body's assignment of meaning and significance to race and/or gender, sex and/or sexuality of physical bodies influences, perhaps even determines, the trajectories of concrete human lives.[19]

This is why Elaine Graham asserts that bodies occupy "the intersection of nature and culture, construction and agency."[20] Embodiment points to this reality of the body as a site of constructed knowledge.

TEACHER SPACE: BRILLAMOS POR NUESTRA AUSENCIA

Because we live in a racist and kyriarchal society, the overall result of these mythologies is that "difference" is often equated with "inferior," "bad," "impure," "tainted," and even "mindless." It is not only the dominant culture that imbibes and believes such distortions and lies. People of color internalize this bombardment of misinformation/malformation as well. This is why bell hooks prefers to use the term "white supremacy" rather than racism: to underscore that racial and kyriarchal oppressions are not only about a dominant culture that seeks to ensure its power and privilege, but also about the internalized behaviors and beliefs of the oppressed.[21] What is now "common sense" is the value and recognition given to certain bodies. Beauty, intelligence, good, authority, and even respect become elements of privilege. The dominant culture determines a "norm," which is invariably based on "whiteness."

The halls of academia become a space in which the "norm" is the white, primarily heterosexual, male. In such places in particular, and in society in general, the "other" is marked by invisibility and absence, since presence

---

imagination"—or, "how those in the dominant group of a nation who have power to tell its history perceive the other," in "Voices from *Nepantla*," 93.

19. Copeland, *Enfleshing Freedom*, 8.

20. Graham, "Practical Theology of Embodiment," 80.

21. hooks, *Teaching Community*, "Talking Race and Racism," especially 28. See also Glascock and Ruggiero, "Relationship of Ethnicity," 204–5, where they note that students of color have internalized this oppression and often treat faculty of color in the same way that white students do.

is generally a mark of privilege. In Spanish we say, "*brillamos por nuestra ausencia* (we shine with our absence)!" To be present in a place where the "other" has *no right to be* means that one is marginalized. One occupies, then, a peripheral space that is often a site of conflict and despair. People, and especially women, of color are often relegated to such spaces. To occupy such a space marks one as "other"—more often than not perceived to be minoritized, racialized, ethnic, or "foreigner"—guilty of "transgressing borders." She is an "illegal alien," a "space invader," a "foreign body" occupying spaces that resist her, deny her humanity, and seek to isolate, quarantine, and if possible, expel her like the virus she is perceived to be.[22]

This space is thus fraught with obstacles that are not visible to the eye. In this space, one must play by the rules of a game that one is never taught, and rules change more often than the rooms in a Harry Potter novel. Palmer considers the act of learning an attempt to control one's reality. However, for people of color, particularly for those of us who are in the teaching profession, it is a survival skill.[23] We must learn the "campus culture"/ rules of the game to maneuver the political minefield. We learn quickly that the structures that determine scholarly recognition—tenure, promotion, recognition of the worth of one's work, even student evaluation forms—are "controlled by the dominant ideology" of white supremacy.[24] As hooks points out, we also learn that "the irony is that we are not actually allowed to play at the game of race, we are merely pawns in the hands of those who invent the games and determine the rules."[25] It is an exhausting enterprise to be sure. This is why I often find unrealistic my current dean's requests that faculty members find time to write at least fifteen minutes each day. I want to explain to him that my creative energy is often sapped by my constant service to others or because I am focused on surviving the gauntlet that is the academic space.

To be in this space is not only to be marked as other, it also means to be isolated and alone. As of this writing, the Association of Theological Schools reports in 2011/2012 that of its 250 member schools in the United States and Canada, only thirty-three faculty members are Latina/o, seventy-seven are African American, fifty-three are Asian/Asian North American, and two are multiracial, compared to 2,187 white men and 657 white women.[26]

22. Mills and Berg, "Gender, Disembodiment, and Vocation," 338. Pederson, "Nature of Embodiment," 366. Copeland, *Enfleshing Freedom,* 15.

23. Cf. Palmer, *To Know,* 24.

24. Ladson-Billings, *Racialized Discourses,* 267.

25. hooks, *Teaching Community,* 35.

26. These are not percentages, but absolute numbers. See Association of Theological Schools, "2011–2012 Annual Data Tables," Table 3.1A.

There are no reports of American Indian women faculty, and the report does not include any of the myriad other groups that now represent our diverse populations since it is limited to the Census Bureau's myopic categories. This isolation of teachers of color in academia translates into very real consequences.

To begin with, we are often exposed to rejection, disrespectful behavior, ostracism, sexual harassment (because our bodies are often eroticized in stereotypical fashion), and other unacceptable behavior. Furthermore, our scholarship is ignored or devalued. Too often, rather than seeing a scholar—a biblical scholar, an ethicist, a theologian, and so forth—students and colleagues see a Puerto Rican, an African American, or a Korean first. Additionally, stereotypes associated with ethnicity and race are superimposed upon our bodies. Difference is equated with ignorance or the inability to bring quality scholarly work or teaching to the classroom. Lastly, Caroline Sotello Viernes Turner and others have found that too often teachers of color have been isolated and overworked—forced to split their allegiances among academia, family, and community concerns, while asked to "represent" their constituencies since they are the "only one." She also finds that often their authority is undermined, and the legitimacy of their roles questioned. This leaves them feeling shattered, and exhausted, or in Nancy Lynne Westfield's words, wondering if they should apply for combat pay.[27]

I can resonate with many of these findings throughout my professional career, not solely in my teaching institution. In spite of the fact that I teach at a school whose student enrollment is 50 percent African American students, each time I walk into a classroom, I am at risk of there being at least one student whose body language indicates his or her displeasure that a Latina, a Puerto Rican woman, has transgressed the teacher space. Though the ethnicity/race and gender of the displeased student can vary, the intention of their overt or covert behavior is the same: to communicate their displeasure that a foreign body has invaded what they believe to be a sacred space that should be occupied by a different body. Each semester, a silent and intense negotiation of establishing my right to inhabit the teacher space, be respected as a human being, and be regarded as an intelligent person with knowledge takes place. There is a silent and continuous battle against a myriad of stereotypes and expectations. In this battle, whether I believe it right or not, fair or not, I gain legitimacy only if I bring into the classroom space the disembodied voices of the (predominantly white) bodies that students expected to find. Thus the oft repeated question to anything

27. Turner, "Women of Color in Academe," 75, 80–84. Westfield, "Called Out," 63, also 65.

new I teach, "Where did you read that?" with the expectation that I must legitimize my knowledge by citing "experts" (since clearly I am not one) and those experts must certainly include Euro-centric/white authors. Only then is there an unconscious exhalation, a sense of relief and legitimacy, an "it must be true-ness." Thus a disembodied white voice carries more weight than my embodied presence—which at times becomes an obstruction for learning—in the classroom. My greatest sin is that I am not white, not male, not tall, not anything that students were expecting.

Each semester, I must "earn my keep" and "pay my dues" to prove once again that I have the right to occupy the teaching space in which I stand. At times, well-meaning students share with me the hurtful things that have been said about me by students past. They then insist, "But you are not any of those things. I don't know why they say that, and I am glad that I did not listen." My embodied presence is not only an insult to disapproving students, someone they feel they have the right to assault in overt and covert ways in the classroom; it is also a presence that they freely disembody outside the classroom with innuendo and gossip. They add to the stereotypical fires. They build the walls of non-learning. It is no wonder that I resist Stephen Brookfield and Palmer's call to become vulnerable in order to allegedly remove the "psychological, cultural, interpersonal, or pedagogic barriers" that get in the way of learning since often the perceived barrier is my embodied self![28] Vulnerability for "foreign bodies" means being vulnerable to psychological, spiritual, emotional, and even, albeit rarely, physical assault.

In one particularly egregious incident, an African American student spent most of the semester communicating her displeasure, both with her body posture and gestures (eye rolling, arms crossed, facial gestures of displeasure, tonality that bordered on the disrespectful when countering anything I said) when she saw I was the teacher for the Systematic Theology course. After all, if it is true that African American women are oppressed, what right did I as a *trigueña* (Latina of color) have to occupy a space of authority and power over her?[29] Latinas are not supposed to occupy spaces of intellect, much less ones of authority, and certainly not one that she perceived to be as "authority over her." Insofar as she was concerned, at some deeply unconscious (and maybe conscious) level, I was being "uppity." I unwittingly provided her with the perfect excuse to report me to the dean on an occasion in which I had to cut short a discussion for the sake of time.

The then dean, a white woman, sat me *next* to the student in *front* of the dean's desk, while she and the student's advisor, a white male, sat *behind*

---

28. Brookfield, *The Skillful Teacher*, 12.
29. Cf. Quiñones Rivera, "From Trigueñita to Afro-Puerto Rican."

the desk. The spatial and embodied messages were clear: as a woman of color, I had no authority or power in the school's academic hierarchy. This is why I often question books on pedagogy written from perspectives of privilege that unrelentingly assert that teachers have power and authority. That day, sitting in that office, I was made very much aware that I was a foreign body, there at the largesse of white privilege. The dean reinforced the message, addressing me not by my title, as is customary, but by my first name. She assured the student that she would be treated with respect, but in so doing, disrespected me, quickly obliterating my position as a professor. The student left with a smirk on her face because I had been "put in my place." It was a reminder of the "ambiguous authority" and the ever-shifting rules of the game that women of color face in academia.[30]

While I mention incidents with students, they also occur among scholars, particularly when I am in other venues outside of the "safe" spaces of my institution. The difficulty and emotional toll of these incidents are exacerbated by the fact that there are so few of us in theological education. Isolation has three consequences: first, there is often no one with whom we can debrief and safely deconstruct these incidents. I am quite fortunate to be in an institution with a diverse faculty that has African American, Latina/o, and Asian North American faculty members, as well as white faculty who serve as able allies and friends. Yet for most faculty of color, it is often the case that there is no one "like them" with whom they can share their experiences. Second, isolation brings with it the risk of personalizing these incidents. It is easy to blame the teacher: the conflicts must be arising because of something the teacher is doing wrong and not because the system itself is deficient. Being isolated does not allow professors of color to effectively demonstrate how these spaces are racist and kyriarchical, damaging to all. Third, if there is no community of significant presence or numbers, there is little political power. These incidents continue to occur because faculty of color, particularly women of color, do not have sufficient political power or voice in their respective institutions to force significant changes. On the contrary, often subject to the racist and kyriarchical power structures already in place, to counter them is to risk being ostracized, being further marginalized, or losing one's position altogether. *Brillamos por nuestra ausencia.*

---

30. Turner, "Women of Color in Academe," 75.

A SPIRITUALITY OF EDUCATION: FORMANDO PERSONAS EDUCADAS

Thus far I have shared my experiences as a woman of color in academia and as being a "foreign body" facing resistance in the teacher space. Those are painful experiences to be sure, but they are not the whole story. I am not, after all, a passive victim. None of my colleagues of color with whom I have met and shared are, either. I have gained great wisdom and strength from them. I can attest that I have remained in teaching these thirty years and have in the midst of experiences of pain, fatigue, and frustration also experienced great joy, wonderment, and growth. Teaching is not a one-way street, nor is it a one-lane road! It is a multi-dimensional journey, a rich landscape filled with a multiplicity of experiences, events, encounters, and above all, people who enrich our lives along the way. What then is the saving grace for teachers, especially women of color?

This last section of the chapter I dedicate to writing about teaching not from a generic "women of color" or even "Latina" perspective, but from much more concrete context. I am, after all, not "Latina" but a bicoastal, bilingual, multicultural Puerto Rican. I am an *evangélica*, a designation that points to a particular form of popular Protestantism that includes foundational roots of indigenous, African, and Iberian Catholic popular piety and spirituality, and therefore never to be translated as "evangelical"—with its own particular theological, and political connotations. From this perspective, I want to discuss a spirituality of education that includes three important concepts: place, relationality as perichoretic *presencia*, and *persona educada*. It is an embodied spirituality that forms a kind of community that is hospitable to difference because diversity is part of its life-giving essence. It is my contention that as long as our educational system continues to privilege a dominant worldview of racism and kyriarchy, it will produce people with degrees, yes, but not *personas educadas*.

It would seem almost counterintuitive to write about spirituality in a chapter on embodiment and racism, but from a Latina *evangélica* perspective, these two things are not oxymoronic in the least. Here I define spirituality as all that entails a profound encounter or experience with the divine.[31] From the perspective of *evangélica* theology, it denotes the development of intimate relations with the Triune God, who is Community and therefore Diversity-in-Godself. This God who is Diversity-precisely-because-God-is-community is One because of the perichoretic intimacy of the Persons.

---

31. Regarding the use of spirituality as a consumer item, or a capitalist venture, see Carrette and King, *Selling Spirituality*.

Perichoresis is a term that literally signifies "to dance around" and in the tradition became synonymous with "interpenetration" and "interdependence." I believe that the Spanish word *vínculo* (literally, intimate ties that bind) captures this well. The Three are so intimately involved in a dance of love that they are one, yet not so involved that they cannot invite others to dance as well. We, and all of creation, are invited to dance with God through the Person of the Spirit precisely because we are *not God*. There are no foreign bodies in this dance.

Zaida Maldonado Pérez has described the Spirit as "the wild Child" who invites us to dance a *bachata*.[32] To speak of spirituality in terms of dance is not to envision an abstract immaterial or idealized utopia. On the contrary, spirituality is profoundly incarnational, and therefore "embodied," because this God is incarnationally present in human history, not only through Jesus Christ but also through Spirit who is Person intimately present in the lives of people, particularly the marginalized, forgotten, voiceless, oppressed, and poor of the world. This is the Spirit of truth who "springs forth" with life and hope, who is found in dusky wells outside the gates of polite society, and who inevitably moves to change the world.[33] The powerful fear this Spirit, this "wild Child" who they cannot control or dominate, but the powerless sing, "Come, oh Holy Spirit" and open their arms in worship.

Perhaps it is the Puerto Rican *evangélica* theologian in me who resonated so well with Rendón's proposal for a spirituality of education. Under the rubric of "sentipensante" (literally, "feelingthinking"), such a pedagogy envisions education as a process that takes into account the "whole human being," considering not only the intellectual life of the learner, but also the social, emotional, and spiritual life as well.[34] Rendón considers the relationship between the learner and teacher equally important. Indeed, one of the principal precepts of her book is valuing the quality of life of both in order to develop a healthy and balanced relationship of respect and dignity in the classroom. Elizabeth Conde-Frazier and others echo similar perspectives when they argue for the need to create an ambience of "hospitality" and "empathy." For Conde-Frazier, this begins with the creation of a "borderland" or a "space" that allows for mutuality and discovery amid difference throughout the educational journey. For her the heart of education is to create a "place" that is hospitable, defined as a "space that is safe, personal, and comfortable" in which people can connect to one another. According to Conde-Frazier, hospitality is related to "human dignity and respect for

---

32. Maldonado Pérez, et al., "Dancing with the Wild Child."

33. Costas, *Christ Outside the Gate*, "Epilogue."

34. Rendón, *Sentipensante*, 135. See also Russell, *Just Hospitality*, 15.

persons," particularly when persons are different, so that people can respect "the image of God" in each other.[35] That is to say, a spirituality of education is attentive to *presencia* (presence) and place.

Other educators beside Rendón have also emphasized the importance of the teacher-learner relationship. Yet in a society that glorifies competition rather than cooperation, individuality rather than communality, hierarchy rather than egalitarianism, segregation as "purity" rather than diversity as the Triune God's call for all creation, it is difficult to establish holistic, balanced, or healthy relations. We do not know how to be *presente* (present) to each other. In the Latina/o culture, where *vínculos* (relations) and people take precedence over time and productivity, the issue of *presencia* is foundational. Harking back to our indigenous and African roots, when the gods were *presente* in the spaces of the everyday / *en lo cotidiano*, people learned to be attentive to the presence of the sacred in and through the daily spaces. The sacred is to be encountered in and through our daily *vínculos*. The sacred is thus embodied in concrete ways through people, our *vínculos* and our ways of treating each other. This view of the sacredness of creation is expressed in the works of some non-Latina/o scholars. For example, reflecting on the concept of theosis, Robert Kress asserts that "God's holy will" is that "creation be holy" and that nothing has happened to creation to have it "lose its original holiness and communion with God."[36] Russell affirms this sense of the sacrality of creation further insisting that as part of God's creation, human beings are also holy and must be treated as such.[37]

This concept of *presencia* means that we are attuned to the value of people in the *communitas* because they are holy, and are conduits of divine blessings for us all, even as we are conduits of blessings for the community. That God is foundational for our understanding of *presencia* points to a Trinitarian nuance to the concept: as the Three Persons are perichoretically *presente* to each other, intimately related as diverse and yet one, in an eternal and intimately loving dance, so humankind is called in its *imago Dei* to be *presente* before God, and *presente* in its *vínculos* to each other and all of creation. This understanding of *presencia*, embodiment, and diversity as *imago Dei* does not allow for anyone to be treated like a foreign body in any space. Rather, it helps us to attune our ears to hear the invitation of the "wild Child" to invite us to a new dance, to hear music to a different beat, that welcomes a diversity of people to learn new things in new ways.

35. Conde-Frazier, "Prejudice and Conversion," 105–6. Conde-Frazier, "From Hospitality to Shalom," 171–72. See also Anderson, "Seeing the Other Whole," 11–12, and van den Blink, "Empathy Amid Diversity," 6–7.

36. Kress, "Unity in Diversity," 66.

37. Russell, *Just Hospitality*, 87.

Presencia, vínculo, and embodied holiness shift the notion of space from an inert and neutral vacuum to what I call "place." Place is more than space. There is an intentionality to "place." We inhabit place. Relations take place. Place is the cross section of time and space, but not simply any time or space. Place is the cross section of *kairos* and sacred space. Kairos has often been defined in terms of a divinely appointed time, but it also has a locative meeting: being at the right place at the right time. Sacred places are often geographical spaces imbued with memory and power.[38] They have a historical narrative that ties people and communities together. The divine has left an imprint in such spaces. In Puerto Rico, the national rain forest, *El Yunque,* is such a place. Regardless of the colonized narratives imposed on it, and its takeover by the U.S. federal government, the natives of Puerto Rico know it to be the home of the Taíno gods. *Evangélicas* recognize it as the place where we can hear the voice of the "wild Child" speak to us in the wind and amid the *coquís* (tree frogs).

Unlike the dominant culture, many indigenous cultures do not give priority to time as *chronos,* measured finite time. Unlike the Western anxiety over time—e.g., the obsession about "wasting time," "killing time," or of "time running out"—indigenous people emphasize *place* because place is where we develop relations. This is especially evoked in the common indigenous prayer: "to all my relations." For many indigenous people in the Americas and the Caribbean, their "relations" include the land and all of creation. This is what makes the land upon which they reside "sacred space." It is where God and all holy things are *presente.*

Our educational system does not allow for the formation of place. It is ironic that we pay so little attention to the classroom space as place. It is symptomatic of a disembodied system that is not attentive to relations and does not nurture diversity-in-community. We are too busy cramming full our schedules to take time to be *presente* to one another or to create a sacred place where we can experience the holy, and learn from the "wild Child." We live so much under the pressure of schedules and deadlines that I think they at times become the gods before whom we too often sacrifice its adherents, whether students, faculty, administrators, or staff. How are we to teach about a Life-giving Spirit, this wild Child, who liberates us to go forth with joy, if we live under the continuous cloud of something that begins with the word *dead*? Rendón reminds us that "learning takes time; it cannot be rushed. In an educational culture obsessed with sorting and grading, it is obvious to me that we have lost track of trusting the notion that learning is

38. See Friedland and Hecht, "Powers of Place," 17–36.

not bound by a specific timetable."[39] In such a system, I am not only foreign body, I am also one who has been robbed of "breath," of the Spirit of life that allows me to dance to a different beat.

I realize that I am proposing a different way of visualizing education. Yet unless we dismantle the current system of race and privilege, teachers of color will continue to experience being "foreign bodies" in teacher spaces. The current structures seem to ensure the success and well being of a select and privileged group at the expense of many others who are undeservedly marginalized and dehumanized. Such a system may produce experts in particular fields, but it does not produce *personas educadas*. How ironic! Though the phrase *persona educada* is literally translated "educated person" it does not necessarily correspond to a person with degrees. In fact, I would posit that racist and kyriarchical people who are socialized and conditioned to demean others, to be blind to their sinful acts of power and privilege, and to treat teachers and peers like foreign bodies are far from being *personas educadas*.

Rendón translates *persona educada* as synonymous with wise person, and citing Antonio Pulido notes that it can refer to someone with insight and common sense.[40] I believe that the term denotes something more profound. A *persona educada* is a person who is welcoming—especially to the stranger—compassionate, respectful, and accords human dignity to all who enter their home. That is to say, it is someone who embodies hospitality. It is someone who is unfailingly polite and attentive to the needs of others. A *persona educada* is someone who creates a sacred place and is attentive to the embodied *presencia* of the other. In a sense, this is part of what is interpreted as "wisdom." Irrespective of their educational, economic, or social status, to be *educada* is related to how one treats others. The community acknowledges their status. Our current educational system, in failing to create sacred spaces where we respect each other's embodied *presencia*, develop holistic *vínculos*, and learn to celebrate diversity as reflecting the *imago Dei*, has failed to produce compassionate *personas educadas*. We need to do better.   Won't pass Orals!

In recent years, my pedagogical approach has been not so much to teach a given subject as much as to try to create perichoretic communities of *personas educadas* that respect diversity. Each semester we learn that we do not know how to be a diverse people together even as we learn that we know something about being a diverse people together. Along the way, we create a place of communal *vínculos* and learning, and I cease to be a "foreign

39. Rendón, *Sentipensante Pedagogy*, 120.
40. Ibid., 87.

body" in these sacred spaces. I remember anew why I remain *presente* in the classroom. There is such joy in seeing the dance.

CONCLUSION

All of us involved in education need to create places where we all, not just students, can hear the music of God's call to hospitality, relations, compassion, care, and true perichoretic relations with one another. In short, where true loving justice is practiced in holistic ways. We need to create a place where we can be *personas educadas* who stop *talking* about diversity, stop being what van den Blink calls "tourists of diversity," and have the courage to live out what being a diverse community means—with all its messiness, conflict, and loss of power and privilege.[41] We need to stop silencing people and treating teachers of color as foreign objects, and justifying such mistreatment and "casual violence" with the false excuses we make up. The minute anyone is robbed of her human dignity, we have violated the sacredness of God's creation. For that, there is no excuse. It is sinful. It is wrong. We need to let Spirit be the Life-breathing wild Child in our classrooms and show us what it means to bring life into an educational system that thus far has been *matándonos a paso lento*.[42] I pray and hope we can hear the invitation to dance *en otro son* (to a different tempo).

41. van den Blink, "Empathy Amid Diversity," 5.

42. *Matándonos a paso lento* is a riff on a popular saying: literally, killing us slowly. It is equivalent to the English, "killing me softly."

4

Racial/Ethnic Diversity
and Student Formation

PETER T. CHA

There is another element that must be present in our struggle that then makes our resistance and nonviolence truly meaningful. That element is reconciliation. Our ultimate end must be the creation of the beloved community.

~MARTIN LUTHER KING JR.

WHEN COMPARED TO PREVIOUS student generations, racial and ethnic diversity is perhaps the most striking new characteristic of today's seminary student body. This shift in student profile, in turn, compels today's seminaries to reexamine their approach to theological education as traditional teaching and learning practices become increasingly less effective. Who, then, are today's seminarians? What different life and church experiences have shaped them? What might be ways in which today's seminaries can be attentive to their students' changing and varying needs? How can seminaries creatively facilitate their students' learning and formation in light of this increase in student diversity? This chapter explores these and other related questions, focusing particularly on students' formational experiences as they go through their theological education. The chapter concludes by look-ing at my seminary's pilot project in which students from different racial/ethnic backgrounds go through a two-year formation group experience that aims to increase students' intercultural competency and their capacity to promote justice and seek reconciliation.

DIVERSE BACKGROUNDS OF TODAY'S STUDENTS: WHERE DO THEY COME FROM?

Diversity in Racial/Ethnic Backgrounds

According to the data provided by the Association of Theological Schools (ATS), racial/ethnic diversity among its member schools' student bodies has increased dramatically during the past four decades. In 1977, when ATS first collected data about the racial background of students attending its member schools in the U. S. and Canada, about 6 percent of the total enrollment were non-white students. Forty years later, in 2007, the figure has increased to 35 percent,[1] a six-fold increase.

While the overall increase in diversity among ATS school students roughly mirrors that of the broader population in the U. S., a further analy-sis of the demographic data reflects more complex realities of ethnic/racial representation among today's seminaries.[2] According to the 2007 ATS data, the percentage of black students in seminaries (11 percent) is similar to that of the percentage of blacks in the U. S. and Canada combined (11.9 percent). However, Hispanics are significantly under-represented in today's seminar-ies; only 4 percent of today's seminarians are Hispanics although 14 percent of the general population is from this racial/ethnic background. Asian/Asian Americans, on the other hand, represent 7 percent of the seminary student body while they make up 4.8 percent of the general population.

Furthermore, racial/ethnic students are unevenly distributed among ATS member schools. According to the 2007 ATS data, the largest racial/ethnic student group in mainline Protestant seminaries is African American while in evangelical Protestant seminaries and Roman Catholic seminar-ies, Asian North Americans and Hispanics are, respectively.[3] These demo-

---

1. This figure includes international students who make up 9 percent of the student population. See Aleshire, "Gifts Differing: The Educational Value of Race and Ethnic-ity," 2–4.

2. Ibid., 10–16.

3. In 2007, more than 58 percent of all racial/ethnic seminarians were attending evangelical seminaries. See ibid., 10

graphic pictures indicate that seminaries of different "theological camps" tend to draw particular racial/ethnic students, resulting in different primary and under-represented racial/ethnic groups on their campuses. Therefore, while overall racial/ethnic diversity among seminary students has increased significantly, the uneven representation and distribution of racial/ethnic students make it necessary for each school to give attention to its own racial/ethnic composition of the student body and develop responses that would best fit its own cultural diversity context. In short, when it comes to addressing students' racial/ethnic diversity in U.S. seminaries, one size does not fit all.

Racialized Ethnic/Racial Identities

Influenced by multiculturalism present in educational and the broader cultural settings, most students who come to today's seminaries acknowledge and celebrate their ethnicities. For whites of European descent, their constructed ethnic identities are largely subjective, individualistic and voluntary in nature.[4] For them, the construction of ethnic identity is largely a volitional process of self-identification, pursued to attain a sense of self-fulfillment. Since their identities are neither contested nor resisted by others, these identities are generally "optional" and are highly symbolic in nature.[5]

For people of color living in a racialized society, however, their racial/ethnic identity formation involves profoundly different processes. First, the process involves a continuing negotiation between outsiders' coercive designations—"who they think you are"—and individuals' self-ascription— "who you think you are." For many Asian Americans, for instance, the race-based panethnic "Asian American identity" is an artificial identity category created and imposed by the dominant group. It is a categorical identity that conveniently lumps all Asians as a homogeneous group and is defined by reference to their differences from or inferiority to the dominant group.[6] Yet, over the years this same identity has become more than a coerced ascription by outsiders, as Asian Americans have learned to appropriate it as a useful resource for social and political actions. As Cornell observed, "the language of subordinate-group categorization and control has become the language of subordinate-group self concept and resistance."[7]

4. Waters, *Ethnic Options*.

5. Gans, "Symbolic Ethnicity," 577–92.

6. Espiritu, *Asian American Panethnicity*, 6–7.

7. Cornell, *The Return of the Native*, 146.

For people of color, the construction and maintenance of such contested identities require ethnic/racial communities in which their identities are regularly affirmed, "plausibility structures" in which particular worldviews are shared and internalized. In the U.S., religious communities have historically played a significant role in this process, providing cultural socialization as well as theological resources that enrich and energize the ongoing process of identity construction. Particularly when their identities are negated and threatened by the dominant group, these faith communities provide means through which their members' individual and group identities can be grounded in a transcendent reality. For them, therefore, their ethnic/racial identities and their spiritual identities are deeply intertwined.

Furthermore, for many students of color, the process of negotiating ethnic/racial identities may involve the production of multiple identities and multiple "layering" of identities.[8] In a racialized society, minoritized individuals carry a "portfolio" of ethnic/racial identities, allowing them to put on different identities for different settings. For instance, I am a South Korean native (but whose parents were displaced North Korean refugees), a 1.5 generation Korean American, an East Asian American, an Asian American, and an American. The presence of multiple ethnic/racial identities, in part, enables individuals to respond to and negotiate with racial oppression or prejudice they encounter in different settings.

In sum, for students of color who come to our seminaries, the formational experiences of racial/ethnic identities are often contested and precarious. What social, cultural, and spiritual setting should seminaries offer to these students as they continue to work on their ethnic/racial identities? Particularly, what theological and spiritual resources should schools offer that would enable all students, including whites, to form individual identities in the context of the presence of "others"?[9] Finally, how might today's seminaries enable members of their learning communities—students, faculty, and administrators who come from diverse racial/ethnic backgrounds—to move towards the formation of a new "peoplehood" that respects shared values and differences,[10] the "beloved community" Martin Luther King, Jr. prophetically imagined?

---

8. Nagel, *American Indian Renewal*; Heggins III and Jackson, "The Collegiate Experience for Asian International Students," 379–91.

9. Volf, *Exclusion and Embrace*, 99–165.

10. Matsuoka, *The Color of Faith*, 5.

Diversity in Congregational Experiences

Another characteristic of today's seminarians is that they come from diverse church backgrounds. In the past, when denominational schools drew the majority of faculty and students from the same denominational and racial/ethnic background, schools assumed that their students were coming to seminaries with similar church experiences and theological orientations. Today, seminaries recognize that their students come from a far wider range of ecclesial backgrounds and therefore bring with them different formational experiences and perspectives.[11] The task of understanding today's students, therefore, needs to include a careful study of the churches that have shaped and continue to shape them.

A major characteristic of today's congregations in the U.S., a trait that might have played a critical role in forming seminary students' views on and experiences with racial/cultural "others," is that these religious communities are overwhelmingly mono-racial. According to a recent study,[12] about 90 percent of American congregations are made up of at least 90 percent of people of the same race; only 7 percent of U.S. congregations are considered multiracial churches.[13] Given that public schools are six times more likely to be racially diverse than religious congregations currently are,[14] our seminary students' multicultural awareness and experiences are far more likely to have been formed on their school playgrounds than in their church's youth group activities or other fellowship events.

Recent sociological studies further indicate that the racial and cultural homogeneity of congregations significantly impacts their members' perception of racial "others." In their study of how religion intersects with race relations in the white evangelical community, sociologists Emerson and Smith identified two primary ways through which a mono-racial congregation can increase its members' prejudicial race perceptions.[15] First, white Christians who attend such a church tend to be even more racially isolated than the general white population, a condition that then leads to a higher degree

11. Klimoski, "Evolving Dynamics of Formation," 29–48.

12. Emerson, *People of the Dream*, 35–36.

13 Sociologists who study congregations define the multiracial congregation as one in which no one racial group comprises 80 percent or more of the people. Twenty percent is used as the cutoff because a number of studies indicate that 20 percent constitutes the point of critical mass. The same study found that while 15 percent of Catholic congregations are considered racially heterogeneous, only 6 percent of evangelical Protestant and 3 percent of mainline churches are estimated in this category (Emerson, 39).

14. Emerson, *People of the Dream*, 37.

15. Emerson and Smith, *Divided by Faith*.

of racial prejudice and of inter-cultural unawareness. Secondly, the study also found that racially homogeneous churches contribute to the formation of a particular type of "cultural tool kit" that shapes how their members interpret and evaluate their world, including race relations in the broader society. In particular, Emerson and Smith identified the following as racially important cultural tools in the white evangelical tool kit: "accountable freewill individualism," which minimizes and individualizes racial inequality; "relationalism," which focuses on interpersonal relationships—such as family ties—as the main causal factor contributing to poverty and racial inequality; and "anti-structuralism" that causes individuals to overlook the structural aspect of racial inequality.[16] Given these and other related factors, Emerson and Smith conclude that racially segregated churches sustain and deepen the process of racialization not only in the Christian community but also in the wider society.

Emerson and Smith's study identifies a number of critical religio-cultural challenges for predominantly white evangelical seminaries if they are to become learning communities that aim to nurture ministers who are well-prepared to serve in a culturally and racially diverse world. More immediately, given that more than half of all ethnic/racial seminarians are currently attending evangelical schools, these institutions—including the one in which I serve—need to analyze carefully their own institutional cultures, including those religio-cultural tools that profoundly shape how we view "others" and their experiences.

At the same time, this sociological study also raises a number of key questions for all seminaries that are experiencing growing ethnic/racial diversity. What might be the intended and unintended consequences of attending racially homogeneous congregations for black, Hispanic, Asian American, and non-evangelical white seminarians? What "cultural tool kits," developed and maintained in these homogeneous faith communities, guide and shape their self-understanding and their view of "others"? What are some perspectives or assumptions in these areas that need to be challenged and affirmed during their seminary years? Given that the majority of seminary students have not had multicultural faith formation experiences in their own congregations, how might seminaries provide such experiences for them? These questions require seminaries' attention as they seek to better understand and serve their students who come from today's congregational experiences.

16. Ibid., 76–80.

HOW DO STUDENTS EXPERIENCE SEMINARY EDUCATION?

Given the rapid and significant changes taking place in today's student profile, it is becoming increasingly imperative that each school finds ways to understand who its students are, to identify the interests and needs of its students, and to discern how students are experiencing the school's theological education. An intentional practice of listening to students, an active form of listening that informs and reshapes how the faculty and the school view teaching and learning, is an essential pedagogical activity. In this section, I will briefly describe how two seminaries—one mainline and the other evangelical—learned to practice this type of attentive and constructive listening.

Claremont School of Theology: Developing a Culture of Listening[17]

As the school was beginning the curricular revision process of its MDiv program in 2000, the administrators and faculty at Claremont School of Theology (CST) wanted to explore how their students who come from very diverse backgrounds experience the current curriculum. During the school year 2000 to 2001, assisted by a grant from the Lexington Seminar, two CST faculty members facilitated a year-long process of listening to a group of first year MDiv students. After selecting seven students who reflected the diversity in the school's student body, they interviewed these students four times throughout the academic year, probing into how they are adjusting to their new learning environment and how students from different backgrounds experience the MDiv program differently.

Being mindful of the power dynamics that exists between the faculty and students, the two faculty members were very intentional in creating a particular culture of listening in these small group sessions. Each session began with the question, "Tell us about your experience so far at Claremont," inviting students to express their thoughts and feelings. Because their desire was to empower students to voice their concerns and expectations freely, the faculty team decided to interview these students in a group

---

17. For more details about the CST's experience, go to the archives section (year 2000) of the Lexington Seminar website (www.lexingtonseminar.org). In 2007, funded by the Lexington Seminar, I had an opportunity to visit CST to interview faculty members and administrators, to do a further follow-up study on the school's practice of listening. The study report from this visit is included in my article "Student Learning and Formation."

setting rather than individually, since the latter might have been too intimidating for some students. Also, faculty members intentionally minimized their own participation by asking questions of clarification only, since their intention was to encourage the students to identify key issues and concerns that demand the school's attention.

After each session, both faculty members reviewed the videotapes and the transcripts of the interviews, paying attention to nonverbal as well as verbal communication that took place during each session. Throughout the year, the faculty team aimed to identify themes and categories that emerged repeatedly during their listening sessions and possible connections among them. After the year-long process of listening and analyzing what they heard, the two faculty members then presented the findings at a faculty retreat. Their presentation deepened and enriched the faculty community's conversation about the increasing diversity among their students and its implication on how they should think about the task of curricular revision of the MDiv program.

Recognizing the rich contribution of this particular exercise, the faculty and administration decided to continue to develop different ways of listening to their students by hosting multiple town meetings with larger groups of students and by adopting a portfolio approach to assessment, thus creating opportunities for students to express how they are experiencing their education at Claremont. At Claremont School of Theology, two faculty members' ethnographic interview of seven students led to other institutional practices of listening to students, promoting some key educational and institutional changes to better understand and serve its diverse student body.

Trinity Evangelical Divinity School: A Strategic Listening Session

Each year, the dean's office of Trinity Evangelical Divinity School (TEDS) sponsors several faculty development meetings. Lasting three to four hours, these gatherings bring together faculty members to engage in a number of significant issues in teaching and learning. In May of 2008, with the help of a small grant from the Wabash Center, two faculty members collaborated with the dean's office in facilitating a faculty development meeting that focused on how racial/ethnic students experience the school's MDiv program. Given that black and Hispanic students have been historically under-represented on our campus, several recent alumni from these backgrounds were intentionally invited to converse with faculty members. Instead of current students, a group of recently graduated alumni were invited because they had had the opportunity to experience the entire MDiv curriculum; they also could reflect critically on their MDiv educational experiences in light of their current ministry experiences in their particular cultural contexts.

The listening session began by inviting alumni to reflect upon their MDiv experiences, including challenges they had faced as minoritized individuals in classroom settings as well as in the broader institutional life. The two facilitating faculty members then invited these pastors to assess how their educational experiences prepared them for their current ministries, and what areas of the program might need critical attention if the school's MDiv program were to better serve students who are from or are preparing to serve in diverse cultural contexts. As at Claremont's interviews, TEDS faculty members took the posture of active listening while several took notes. After the alumni had finished communicating their perspectives and reflections, faculty members entered into a dialogue with them to further clarify some issues and to express their gratitude for the shared insights. The alumni pastors were thoughtful and very honest in their reflections, affirming several positive aspects of their learning experiences at Trinity while also identifying a number of academic and social experiences on campus that caused them to feel invisible and marginalized.

The second half of that morning's faculty development meeting focused on faculty members' reflections on what they heard. The process began in small groups; each group aimed to identify some key issues and themes that emerged during the listening session and then spent some time exploring ways through which faculty members and the school could respond to the needs expressed by the black and Hispanic alumni. Finally, faculty members came together in one large group, to hear the reports from all small groups, looking for repeated themes that needed the school's attention and a way to prioritize the school's responses to the expressed needs of the students.

One of the critical issues that emerged during the listening session was that many black and Hispanic students—as members of the two underrepresented, minority groups on campus—frequently experienced a sense of isolation and alienation.[18] Their experience of curricular and social marginalization made their overall seminary education less than positive, if not painful, and a few alumni mentioned how helpful it would have been if they had belonged to a more intentionally diverse formation group.[19] As a result,

18. A number of recent studies also indicated isolation, alienation and vulnerability to self-esteem as significant challenges many racial/ethnic students face in predominantly white colleges and seminaries. See Marchesani and Adams, "Dynamics of Diversity," 9–17; Ramsey, "Teaching Effectively," 19–20.

19. At Trinity Evangelical Divinity School, all MDiv students are expected to participate in a formation group that meets weekly, each led by a faculty member. During

a multiracial formation group called Mosaic Fellowship was established in the fall of 2009, and I began to serve as the group's faculty advisor.

One of the important roles Mosaic Fellowship has played since its inception is that it provides a valuable context in which the practice of listening to ethnic/racial students can continue. Each week, twenty-four members of the Mosaic Fellowship and I come together to converse on a number of topics that intersect race, culture, and theological education. Furthermore, the group regularly invites a number of administrators and faculty members to join the conversation, providing opportunities for them to hear, among other things, how students from diverse racial/ethnic backgrounds experience theological education at Trinity.

If the first rule of good teaching is to know our students, each seminary needs to develop ways to listen to its students, particularly to those whose voices are often not heard. The above experiences of the two institutions offer weighty support for the value of such practices. However, in order for such a listening process to be constructive, certain conditions must exist and a certain ethos must be in place. Does the school embrace values such as dialogue and mutuality? To put it differently, do faculty members want to hear about the students' experience, particularly of those who are marginalized or under-represented on their campus? Would faculty members and administrators hear stories of their students without being dismissive and defensive, a kind of listening that can lead to concrete changes over the years? As the student population increasingly diversifies and as most seminaries continue to struggle with the challenge of low enrollment, it is becoming increasingly necessary for seminaries to cultivate an institutional culture of adaptive listening, for their educational effectiveness—if not the institution's very survival—depends on it.

PASTORAL FORMATION AND STUDENT DIVERSITY

The Role of Student Formation in Theological Education

In *Educating Clergy*, Foster and colleagues argue that formation should be at the center of educating clergy because, compared with the education of other professions such as medicine, the training of clergy is particularly concerned about "meaning, purpose, and identity."[20] To put it differently, the process of preparing future ministers should involve more than the ac-

---

these weekly meetings, students and the faculty member attend to the issue of spiritual formation in the setting of theological education.

20. Foster et al., *Educating Clergy*, 8.

quisition of knowledge or even cognitive tools, for its primary aim is to enable the student to become a person who thinks, feels, and acts in a way to foster "pastoral imagination."[21] The process of theological education in seminaries, therefore, must include at its center a set of formational experiences that are both multidimensional and integrative.

Currently, seminaries are seeking to offer a formation-oriented theological education through a number of different venues. In classroom teaching and learning, an increasing number of schools emphasize the importance of integrative learning, a pedagogical approach that aims to enable their students to learn how to integrate their intellectual, emotional, and spiritual development into a coherent whole.[22] Such an approach, it is assumed, would produce learners who can, among other things, respond to new and different challenges wisely and who can effectively serve in diverse ministry settings.

Another site for significant formational experiences is shared community worship. While the role chapel worship plays in theological education may vary from school to school, these regularly held worship services offer students and faculty members opportunities to express and experience their beliefs, emotions, and spirituality. Because it is often during chapel worship service that students experience their faculty members and administrators not only as lecturers and advisors but as preachers and co-worshippers, that students find role models in the rich context of sharing life's joys and tragedies, and of cultivating shared spiritual practices and theological reflections.

Finally, seminaries aim to provide formative learning experiences to their students through the provision of programs in the area of supervised ministry or field education. By offering opportunities for their students to learn how to apply theories and skills in particular ministry contexts, schools aim to help students to integrate their "being," "knowing," and "doing."

Pastoral Formation for the "2040 Reality"

The task of student formation in theological education becomes even more challenging when seminaries take seriously the changing racial/ethnic landscape of the U.S. In 2008, the Brookings Institution assessed the rapidly changing racial demographics in the following way:

> The Census Bureau's new projections through 2050 portend
> a more accelerated transformation of the nation's population

---

21. Dykstra, "The Pastoral Imagination," 2–3.
22. Klimoski et al., *Educating Leaders*, 49–51.

on race-ethnic dimensions than was previously supposed. These new projections show that the minority majority tipping point—the year when the white population dips to below half of the total—will occur in 2042, eight years sooner than in the Bureau's projections just four years ago.[23]

How should seminaries think about the task of student formation given that their students are to be prepared for ministry in tomorrow's fully multiracial world?[24] With the increasing possibility that a growing number of students might have opportunities to serve in cultural contexts different from their own, how might seminaries seek to equip their students so that they might be able to competently serve in cross-cultural or multicultural ministry settings? Given these emerging issues and concerns, what should formation look like in today's seminaries?

Many formational approaches mentioned above—integrative teaching and learning, communal worship experiences, and various supervised ministry programs—might require some significant revision and modification if they are to prepare students for the "2040 reality." In recent years, many schools have designed and adopted creative, integrative learning approaches to encourage their students to see how different elements that they are learning in various classes fit together. However, an emerging assessment is that many integration-oriented approaches developed in predominantly white seminaries might have cultural blind spots (e.g., they might be framed too individualistically, and so reflect the cultural ethos of the dominant culture), thus making it more challenging for those who come from different cultural backgrounds to experience the intended integrative experience.[25] How might an integrative learning approach look if it took seriously the diverse backgrounds of students and their future ministry in intercultural and multiracial settings?

Currently, many seminary chapel programs also encounter challenges as students and faculty members from diverse backgrounds bring with them different understandings of and expectations for their shared worship experiences. On the one hand, many predominantly white seminaries continue worship practices that reflect their own liturgical and cultural preferences and biases, relating to those who come from different cultural and liturgical

23. Frey, "The Census Projects Minority Surge."

24. The Association of Theological Schools provided a four-year consultation program called "Preparing for 2040: Enhancing Capacity to Educate and Minister in a Multiracial World." In this program, thirty-six seminaries from the U.S. and Canada participated to find strategic ways to enhance their institutional capacity to educate diverse students for ministry in a multiracial world.

25. Cha, "Student Learning and Formation," 39–44.

backgrounds as if they were guests who are visiting their worship space. On the other hand, a growing number of schools fully embrace liturgical and cultural diversity in their chapel worship; however, unless done carefully, their practices can be less than helpful to their students' formation experience. They need to continue to wrestle with questions such as, "How much diversity is conducive to students' formation in their own cultural and ecclesial tradition?" and "At what point does diversity of worship forms limit the ways in which shared worship can be formative to any?"

Finally, the supervised ministry programs on many campuses are also facing limitations in this area of multicultural pastoral formation, largely because most churches in which their students serve are racially and culturally homogeneous. For most seminary students, the task of finding suitable mentors and field education ministry sites that would enable them to grow in multicultural awareness and intercultural competency is challenging and can be discouraging. Given these and other challenges found in today's approach to student formation, schools need to find creative ways to think about alternative approaches to formational experiences that might enable their students to be better prepared for the "2040 reality."

MOSAIC FELLOWSHIP: A MULTIRACIAL FORMATION GROUP FOR RECONCILIATION

Begun in the fall of 2009 at Trinity Evangelical Divinity School, Mosaic Fellowship is a multicultural student formation initiative that seeks to address a number of key issues and questions mentioned above. The project brings together a group of students from diverse racial/ethnic backgrounds to reflect upon their identities, to facilitate their growth in intercultural competency and leadership, and to deepen their theological understanding of those themes that promote justice and peace in today's multicultural world. In particular, the group has chosen reconciliation as its theological vision towards becoming a "beloved community" and as its over-arching theological theme that integrates other themes such as race, culture, diversity and social justice.[26]

26. The Mosaic Fellowship has been significantly influenced by the programs offered by the Center for Reconciliation of Duke Divinity School. During the past four years, a number of Mosaic leaders and I have participated in the Center's week-long Summer Institute on Reconciliation program.

Who Participates?

Currently, Mosaic Fellowship has five leaders and twenty student participants.[27] As its faculty advisor, I co-lead the group with four doctoral students and administrative staff members who come from different racial/ethnic backgrounds.[28] This leadership team, which meets monthly to plan and to evaluate various aspects of the program, collaboratively serves twenty MDiv or MA students who are in either their first or second year. One of the important roles of the leadership team is to select ten students each year by reviewing submitted application essays and interviewing—either through Skype or in person—those who have expressed an interest in joining the two-year program. Given the group's explicit intention to be a multiracial learning community, the leadership intentionally aims to maintain a certain racial/ethnic composition, in particular, to ensure that half of the participants come from the two under-represented groups on our campus, namely blacks and Hispanics.

What Kind of Formation?

While the Mosaic Fellowship does not have a formalized curriculum, its two-year program is broadly divided into four semester-long sections, each focusing on one of the following four formational themes—spiritual formation, community formation, leadership formation, and missional formation. During the semester in which spiritual formation is the main focus, the group aims to explore different approaches to and practices of spiritual formation that might be more suitable for its multicultural context, and to identify those spiritual disciplines that are particularly helpful to those who are engaged in the intercultural ministry of reconciliation. During the community formation semester, the group seeks to imagine what a reconciling, multicultural Christian community might look like in a predominantly white seminary setting, and to take concrete steps that would enable the community to journey towards that direction. During the semester in which leadership formation is the focus, the group explores how represented cultures view leadership differently, and aims to develop a set of leadership skills and habits that might be helpful to those who seek

27. In order to facilitate more relational and experiential formation experiences, we decided to cap the size of the group although more students showed interest in participating.

28. Currently, our leadership team consists of an Hispanic man and woman, an African American woman, one Anglo American man, and one Asian American man.

to serve in cross-cultural or multicultural settings. Finally, during the missional formation semester, Mosaic Fellowship aims to identify and analyze various forces that continually perpetuate racism and other forms of injustice in society, and to examine different ways that Christian communities can confront these forces. While each of these formations receive particular attention during a given semester, the group's aim is also to integrate them intentionally while students go through their two-year program, helping them to see these four dimensions of formation as an integrated whole.

How Are Formational Experiences Facilitated?

How does Mosaic Fellowship aim to facilitate the formational experiences of its student participants? Each semester, the process of formation begins with an overnight retreat away from campus. The retreat, organized around one of the four formational themes mentioned above, includes group worship time, three or four thirty-minute teaching presentations, and several small group discussion times. Through these activities, the students reflect on how the given formational theme intersects with their racialized identities, challenges/opportunities of cultural diversity, and the ministry of reconciliation. Particularly during their small group time, all participants are invited to share how their life/faith journey stories relate to those themes and issues mentioned above, learning how to lament as well as express hope with others in the group. Given that most Mosaic students come from racially homogeneous congregational experiences, retreats at the beginning of each semester provide for students a critical opportunity to forge significant multiracial relationships and to regularly immerse in multicultural communal experiences.

How might significant conversations and formational experiences that began at the weekend retreat be sustained and even deepened throughout the semester? The Mosaic program aims to achieve this goal primarily in two ways. The first is through the weekly formation group meetings that meet for ninety minutes during lunch on Thursdays. On certain weeks, led by the faculty advisor, the formation group time is used to explore a particular issue that relates to the semester's formation theme (e.g., students' past or current church experiences and their impact on students) or a specific challenge the group is currently experiencing (e.g., how to respond to different communication patterns in multicultural settings). On other weeks, the group invites guests from diverse cultural, racial, and vocational backgrounds. These guests are "veterans" who have already had a life of negotiating through or coping with racial/ethnic/gender related challenges, sharing their life stories and perspectives with the group. These formation group meetings also serve the important function of strengthening a sense of communal bond among all Mosaic participants, as they share a meal together—prepared by different small groups each week—and have opportunities to hear how everyone is doing.

The second venue through which Mosaic members continue their significant conversations throughout the semester is a biweekly small group gathering. Each small group, formed at the fall retreat, continues to meet throughout the academic year, providing more intimate support for one another as well as opportunities for Mosaic students to experience the joys and challenges of forming intercultural relationships. The small group time also provides a setting in which students can further process the formational theme of the given semester. To help facilitate this particular conversation, copies of a selected book that focuses on the semester's theme are distributed to all members at the beginning of each semester, so that questions and insights emerging from the reading can deepen formational conversations in small group.

In addition to the regular gatherings mentioned above, Mosaic Fellowship seeks to provide integrative formational experiences to all student participants by offering them supervised leadership experiences. To begin with, all second-year students are invited to serve as small group leaders and as peer mentors to first-year Mosaic students. As they participate in this year-long leadership experience, supervised by Mosaic leaders, these students fulfill one of the school's field education requirements while also being mentored by Mosaic leaders who are experienced in multicultural ministries.

Another important aspect of second-year students' field education experience is the leadership role they play at Mosaic winter retreats. While the fall retreat is designed and led by the Mosaic leaders, the winter retreat is led entirely by that year's second-year students. This particular leadership exercise offers them an opportunity to demonstrate and integrate various insights and skills they have gained from their participation in the Mosaic program, including their ability to work collaboratively with those who come from diverse cultural backgrounds. For Mosaic leaders, winter retreats provide important opportunities to observe second-year students' "performances" as well as to evaluate the overall impact of the program.

At the end of each academic year, as the group of second-year Mosaic students complete their participation in the two-year program, Mosaic Fellowship celebrates the occasion by holding a "commissioning service," reminding each person of God's calling upon one's life to be an agent of reconciliation and justice. Particularly, the Mosaic leaders charge these second-year students to think strategically about getting involved in some aspects of campus life to practice what they learned at Mosaic. During the past two years, a number of former Mosaic participants have served in strategic leadership positions, ranging from the chapel worship team member to the president of student government. During this phase of "internship," Mosaic leaders aim to provide ongoing support to these Mosaic alumni who are on campus, offering resources and encouragement. In short, while its formal program is two-years long, Mosaic Fellowship seeks to serve its ethnic/racial MDiv students during their entire theological education period at Trinity.[29]

More Than a Program: Constructing a New Culture

In their rich ethnographic study of seminaries in the U.S., Carroll and colleagues conclude that the factor that shapes and forms students most is the school's educational culture.[30] If so, a predominantly white seminary like Trinity Evangelical Divinity School needs to critically assess its institutional culture and begin to make sustained and significant institutional changes if it is to become a school that can effectively educate its students for the 2040 reality. Such a process, however, will require—among other things— a lengthy period of time. Mosaic Fellowship, given the situation, aims to construct a distinctly different cultural space on campus, an intentional subculture that forms its students while it also plays a role in facilitating some needed changes in the broader educational culture of the school.

In his work *Organizational Culture and Leadership*, Schein emphasizes the critical role a set of shared values and artifacts can play in the shaping of an organizational culture.[31] Mosaic Fellowship, since its beginning, established and practiced a set of values that contributes towards the formation of a certain communal culture: shared values such as Christ-centeredness, reconciliation, justice, intercultural boundary-crossing, and collaborative

Values

---

29. Recognizing that the Mosaic program requires a significant amount of time from participating students and to support and promote student body diversity, the school offers a 40 percent tuition reduction scholarship to all Mosaic students, for the entirety of their MDiv program.

30. Carroll et al., *Being There*, 203–68. Building upon the works of Clifford Geertz and Ann Swidler, the authors of the study described a seminary culture as an entity that "consists of those shared symbolic forms—worldviews, beliefs, ritual practices, ceremonies, art and architecture, language, and patterns of everyday interaction—that give meaning and direction to the life of the schools and the people who participate in them" (268).

31. Schein, *Organizational Culture and Leadership*, 23–34, 197–234.

partnership. These values, in turn, are reinforced and strengthened by the group's intentional use of certain artifacts, ranging from its own language to a set of rituals such as small groups taking turns in providing lunch for the weekly formation group meetings.

Furthermore, Mosaic Fellowship's structure and program are intentionally designed to promote and practice the values mentioned above. For instance, its value of collaborative partnership is expressed and experienced at multiple levels. The group is collaboratively led by a small, multiracial team of faculty, staff, and PhD students, each small group is co-led by a pair of second-year students who come from different cultural backgrounds, and each winter retreat is designed and led by a team of second-year students. These institutionalized activities and formats strongly shape the emerging culture of the group, even while countering strongly individualistic cultural practices that are pervasive on campus. Through these intentional culture building activities, Mosaic Fellowship seeks to provide a distinctly multicultural "plausibility structure" in which participating students can constructively engage in their identity, leadership, and vocational formations.

Finally, Mosaic Fellowship strives to find ways to get strategically involved in the process of reshaping the school's institutional culture. The group aims to accomplish this goal through the following four ways. First, it invites a number of key school administrative leaders to the weekly formation group meetings, offering them a chance to listen to the Mosaic students' experiences and to discuss the school's current and future goals, which include the goal of preparing all students for the 2040 reality. Secondly, the group also invites several faculty members to its meetings each year, asking each person to give a short presentation that connects one's scholarly interest with the theme of cultural diversity or race relations. These faculty presentations offer opportunities for Mosaic students to interact with materials that are often not covered in their MDiv courses. Perhaps even more importantly, these experiences encourage participating faculty members to see the value of including such themes in their teaching, thus contributing to the formation of these faculty members as well. Thirdly, as many Mosaic students and graduates serve as key leaders of other student groups on campus, they are influencing their peers with the insights they have gained, promoting collaborative partnership within and among several student groups on campus around the shared Mosaic values mentioned above. Finally, through a number of key initiatives begun by Mosaic leaders and members, Trinity has started a number of growing conversations with leaders of nearby black and Hispanic communities. Recognizing the significance of developing further conversation and partnership with these communities, the school recently created a new full-time position to coordinate these growing partnership ventures, and offered it to a Mosaic Fellowship leader.

In small but strategic ways, Mosaic Fellowship is serving as a catalyst, starting new and generative conversations in and around our campus that, in turn, promote change in the school's institutional culture. For this multiracial formation group, this in fact may be one of the most significant lessons it can offer to its students, to those who are called to be leaders in their faith communities: how to intentionally promote change in their own institutions as they journey towards becoming "beloved communities" that welcome and embrace all God's people.

CONCLUSION

As the student population becomes increasingly diverse, one of the foundational tasks today's seminaries face is to know who their students are and what their needs are as they engage in theological education. Trinity Evangelical Divinity School's Mosaic Fellowship aims to create a space in which administrative leaders and faculty members can attentively listen to a group of diverse students, and in which is found a cultural space where students can encounter meaningful formational experiences. This pilot project is a small but important beginning of the institutional journey for the school as it wrestles with the task of forming students for the 2040 reality. Each seminary in the U.S., given the uniqueness of the United States' theological and socio-cultural context, needs to find its own way of listening to its diverse students and of responding to their formational needs. In today's rapidly changing educational context, each school's ability to effectively fulfill its educational mission depends on it.

5

You Cannot Teach
What You Do Not Know

You Cannot Lead Where You Have Not Been

ARCHIE SMITH JR.

The one thing we seem to learn from history is that we never learn.

~SOURCE UNKNOWN

Hi Whitney
Brun!

PROLEGOMENON

There are five things students ought to know. They are: (1) *Context*—The learning context is all-important. Context weaves together and shapes the meaning and significance of things. (2) *Teachers*—Who are the teachers that impart knowledge and wisdom and serve as trusted guides to the student's learning experiences? Teachers are also students when they learn how better to reach their students. (3) *Fellow students and self-awareness*—Students need to know who they are learning with and how peer interaction can greatly influence what they think. Students must also become aware of their own uses of self and how issues of selfhood reflexively affect the relationship between self and others. (4) *The school and its mission*—Students need to

88

know the foundational values and mission of the school from which their formal learning, degrees, and certificates come. Upon graduation, students carry their learning with them and become ambassadors of the very institutions that informed their learning. In this way, they extend the school's mission to a wider world. (5) *History and classic texts that help interpret the struggles of their people*—Students need to know and remember the communities that birthed, invested, and sent them to learn. They need to know the struggle of their people, how they embody the lessons of the people and extend the values of that struggle in a world that continues to unfold. These five things are not identified under the rubrics above. Rather, they permeate the essay as a whole.

What does it mean "to learn" something? Do we ever learn? Do we ever graduate?

When I graduated from high school, I knew that I was saying goodbye to Ponnie, Gary, Tall, Claude, Ronald, Donald, Patricia, Stanly, Grace, Linda, Carl, Randolph, Roy, Deloris, and Jimmy. They were particular and cherished classmates and co-learners with whom I had shared the classroom since kindergarten. We were from native peoples and Chinese, Japanese, Jewish, Filipino, Mexican, African, Eskimo, Italian, and Irish backgrounds. Unknown to us at the time, we were part of a great migration of people and from different language groups. We were part of a multicultural experience. We knew that we would never be co-learners in the same schoolhouse and classroom ever again. We were saying goodbye for the first and last time.

There was another sense in which we were co-learners, students, and teachers. Our families, and especially our parents, were the ones who taught us the deepest lessons of living and dying. Their influence, embedded in various cultures, was implanted in us. They helped shape the many ways we learned from one another and from life's experiences both in and outside of the classroom.

If we are, as Martin Luther King Jr. reminded us, "wrapped in a single garment of destiny," then we are destined to be co-learners with and teachers of one another. If it is the case that life itself is an ongoing learning experiment, then there is a broad sense in which we are co-learners and teachers in a wider world and in a classroom without walls. We are challenged to build a safer world and share resources in the one world and planet we have in common.

I want to think about the aforementioned experiences and influences as cultural knowledge and background influences that help shape the general and evolving human condition where we play our part. Culture, in this interpretation, is both in us—i.e., a part of us—and around us in much the same way as water surrounds the fish of the sea. Students and teachers wittingly and unwittingly co-construct specific learning environments. We do so from different social locations, and within surrounding cultures. We realize certain educational values. Still, we emerge differently and as co-learners together. The roles of student *and* teacher are intertwined and intentionally held together in a relationship of mutuality and desired diversity. But we, finite and limited creatures, cannot control all of the variables that go into our learning experiences. It is from this broad perspective of desired and novel diversity that the rest of the essay is framed.

YOU CANNOT TEACH WHAT YOU DO NOT KNOW

It was the summer of 2007. I was on sabbatical leave in London and thinking about the Senior Seminar that I was to lead when I returned to Berkeley. The seminar was a required course for graduating seniors. It was intended to be an opportunity for students to integrate their theological, historical, and biblical learning with social and pastoral analysis. The seminar was to be organized around a single case that all would share. Research and discussion were to be integral parts of the integrative paper or project. Students were expected to develop their own perspectives on urban and suburban ministry. I thought about how this might happen. I found the case study that I had been thinking about in *The Guardian*, a leading London newspaper. It was the murder, in broad daylight, of Chauncey Wendell Bailey Jr., a news reporter in Oakland, California. He was assassinated on August 2, 2007. This story made the international news.

I recalled that when I first moved to Berkeley to teach, Patty Hearst and Wendy Yoshimura and the Symbionese Liberation Army captured the news of the day. Marcus Foster, a Black school superintendent, recently had been assassinated. I remembered that a high school classmate had been shot down in Oakland. The Black Panther Party frequently had shootouts with the Oakland police. Drive-by shootings were common in Oakland. And now there was another murder, this time of a news reporter, gunned down in broad daylight for investigating a local situation. What in the world was going on here?

There was a long line of urban violence. There were problems of police corruption, high unemployment, poverty, poor housing conditions, and urban blight. This was a community with lots of churches and liquor stores. Oakland was the home of a famous Chinatown, and of congressman Ron Dellums, congresswoman Barbara Lee, a symphony chorus and orchestra, a major newspaper, *The Oakland Tribune*, and celebrities such as movie star Danny Glover. It was the home of the Oakland Raiders and the Oakland

A's. It was the site of the Oakland fires and the burial site of the murdered victims of Jonestown, Guyana. A Street of Oakland was the place where a former Black Panther Party leader, Huey Newton, had been murdered in a drug deal gone bad. One might wonder, "Does God have a special theatrical interest in Oakland?"

Oakland borders on the famous University of California in Berkeley and a large complex of theological schools, the Graduate Theological Union. Oakland, Berkeley, and the San Francisco Bay Area, facing the Pacific Ocean, can be important places for theological reflection. This case study, situated in the Bay Area, would challenge us on many different levels. It would test certain limits of knowledge, and help us to see that we cannot teach what we do not know and we cannot lead where we have not been. What more could one ask for in a case study, I thought.

There was rich material here for theological reflection, biblical interpretation, historical and educational wisdom, and social and pastoral analysis. Research material was available in a host of surrounding university and college libraries. This case study was a goldmine for learning in our midst, I thought. I decided to investigate and write about this as a way to join with the students in a stimulating learning experience. I was excited about the possibilities. We could learn together and realize certain ideals of a learning community.

So, is it true that we never learn the lessons of the past? Upon return from my London sabbatical and with much excitement about learning from the events that surrounded the Chauncey Bailey murder, I was met by a strange situation. The dean of the school where I taught was approached by a group of white students. They carried the complaint that my focus on urban violence, specifically my choice of the *Chauncey Bailey vs. Your Black Muslim Bakery* news item was "irrelevant" to their ministry (ministries).[1] This complaint was made in the wider context of the school president's policy statement of "Zero Tolerance for Racism." My colleagues were confused. They did not know where to stand. The president distanced himself from the controversy and was not supportive. Only one student voiced the idea that this was a good case study. He was a Black male student and concerned about what was happening in Oakland.

The white students who approached the dean were probably right about this issue being "irrelevant" to *their* ministries. Ideally, the goal of an ongoing theological education, as H. Richard Niebuhr reminded us, is the

---

1. No one could have known then that gun violence, which has been an everyday occurrence in Black communities for years, would surface as a major issue in the presidential campaign of 2012 and in suburban communities such as Newtown, Connecticut, or in the murder of Trayvon Martin.

increase of love of God and neighbor: to grasp life's purposes, find meaning in existence, practice the will of God as far as this is possible for a human being, and to lead others to do the same. In this light, and ideally, seminary is a place where questions about moral purpose and ethical pathways to truth are valued. Faith, faithfulness, and reason are kept together in critical correlation. Commitments and significance can be pursued in the context of higher theological education. Questions that appear to be "irrelevant" are taken seriously along with context. Interpretations of the past can be accessed and can illuminate the present. In these ways, we might be able to go where we have not yet been. The student, then, may experience her- or himself on a voyage.

I was led to reflect on the above events because of a headline that recently appeared in the San Francisco Chronicle: "'Enough is enough': Black pastors emerge as strong voice pushing city to combat violent crime." The opening sentence of this article by Matthai Kuruvila read, *"Frustrated with the city leadership and a spiraling crime rate, a group of pastors from Oakland's historically black churches have been flexing their political muscle to bring change to the city."*[2] (Italics added.)

There are at least two different, contrasting, and stereotypical understandings of ministry implied in the responses of, on the one hand, certain white students who brought the complaint of "irrelevancy" to the dean and, on the other, certain Black pastors in Oakland, California. Is ministry primarily a professional role choice or is it mainly a biblical calling? There are tensions between these two different interpretations of ministry. Both need to be critically explored. The difference can lead to misunderstandings and racial polarization in the classroom and on seminary campuses. Context and the nuancing of information matter.

Generally speaking, the former understanding of ministry (ministry as professional choice) may be represented by certain white students' context and understanding of "my" ministry, as "profession" and possession. The core emphasis may be on "me" and "mine" and whatever else is relevant to self-interest.

Generally speaking, the latter (ministry as a biblical calling) may be understood by certain Black pastors and their context. There is, among some, a strong push to address an urban crisis, to care for the welfare of the city, to "fight violent crime," and to seek safety and justice for everyone. The core emphasis may be on the biblical call to ministry and serving others while working to transform the social order toward increased justice and human betterment. Ministry as such refers to serving God's purposes in the

2. Kuruvila, "Enough is enough."

world. "The household of faith" and "the one Body of Christ" may be central metaphors for understanding biblical calls to ministry.

The Christian seminary has not always been clear about its role in preparing students for either form of ministry. Is ministry to the whole people of God within the overarching contexts of biblical faith or not? If "Yes," then how might this play out in various contexts where tensions already exist? John W. de Gruchy made an important observation: "Ordained ministers often end up serving particular groups, indeed, becoming captive to them and their interests rather than being ministers of the church of Jesus Christ . . . [C]ulture, class, and ethnic uniformity and interests have been determinative for the shaping of many congregations in most parts of the world."[3] Endemic to the human condition are issues of relevancy and falling captive to local interest, as well as emerging problems of idolatry, such as greed, the glorification of money, self-promotion, and survival. The significance of these in relationship to transcending values, religious experience, critical inquiry, and the meaning of the gospel for all people might be among the issues explored in a seminary education. The latter are distinguishing focal points for higher theological education. This includes the academic preparation of religious leadership, faithful living, and confessing faith in God today. Who then *ought to be* our student?

WHO IS OUR STUDENT AND WHO OUGHT TO BE?

Gayraud Wilmore observed ". . . most predominantly white theological seminaries have little understanding of the world in which these [Black] pastors and their people live, or the coping mechanism by which they have been able to carry out a ministry of survival and liberation for masses of Blacks caught in the web of the deteriorating structures of urban life"[4] (brackets are my own). Wilmore reflected upon the future of theological education from the standpoint of the 1980s: "To what extent is the theological seminary, presently oriented to the white middle class, prepared to learn something about the experience of the black inner city church in order to serve this 'underrepresented constituency?' Can theological education be made more relevant to ministry and mission in the rapidly 'blackenizing' metropolitan environment?"[5]

Ideas about "ministry as profession" and "ministry as a divine calling" can be polarizing. They still hold challenges for seminaries and institutions

3. de Gruchy, *Theology and Ministry*, 37.

4. Wilmore, "Introduction," 87.

5. Ibid., 87–88.

of higher theological education. Looking back we can see that different understandings of ministry have intensified and contributed to vastly different interpretations. Vastly different interpretations of ministry may raise the questions, "What is desired diversity?" and "Who is our student and who *ought* to be?" Different interpretations reflect our different social locations and may underlay student and faculty inability to understand each other.

Wilmore's observations take on added meaning when theological education is seeking ways to be sustained financially. Can an education that encourages white students to be immersed in Black inner city situations be offered online? Can an education that encourages Black students and pastors to be immersed in white suburban situations be offered online? Context matters along with teachers, the interactions with fellow students, and one's own self-awareness and uses of self.

Theological institutions may have certificates of legitimation to hand out, but not necessarily the required cultural wisdom, resources, and accompanying skills. Culturally competent expertise, critical historical inquiry, good questions, research, and relevant knowledge are essential to sound higher theological education. Many white-controlled theological institutions are under the pressure to survive financially. They look to their donors and sources of financial support to sustain them. Ties to donors may limit or help determine the meaning of ministry and diversity, and who our students are. When financial survival becomes all-important and lifestyle becomes the dictator of academic values, then critical inquiry narrows. Certain moral/ethical concerns such as a sense of "call" to ministry and ministries in Black inner city churches can become secondary, if not irrelevant. Who then are our students and who *ought* to be? How is relevancy determined?

Certain questions may be more important than "answers." Answers tend to settle the issues or close the conversation. Questions open conversations and may point to other questions. Here are some important questions to ask: "Into what past patterns of history does this (any current decision or bright idea) fit?" "How does it help perpetuate or disrupt certain oppressive practices?" Others are, "In what sense is this (the new idea or direction) brand new or really novel?" and "Why are we encouraging it, now?" These may not be questions that administrators or educational leaders are interested in pursuing, but they can help determine the meaning of diversity and have value for the learning of student and teacher.

Looking back, seminary professors, including myself, never explored what on earth was the meaning of "my" ministry. We failed to explore its relationship to culture, the city, the gospel of Jesus and the cross. We might have asked, "What is being done today to help *all* students address and deal with the clash of culture and lifestyles, and the complex realities of urban ministry amidst growing poverty and violence with guns?" The big and unaddressed observation is one I heard when I was a student at Colgate-Rochester Divinity School. John Howard Griffin spoke at Mechanics Hall, Rochester, New York in November 1963. This was shortly *before* the assassination of President John Fitzgerald Kennedy. John Howard Griffin said that Black Americans and White Americans view their same community from vastly different perspectives. Later, his observation was confirmed in the 1968 Kerner Commission Report, which was also known as the "Report of the National Advisory Commission on Civil Disorders." Here was an often quoted piece of that report at the time: "What white Americans have never fully understood—but what the Negro can never forget—is that white society is deeply implicated in the ghetto. White institutions created it. White institutions maintain it, and white society condones it."[6] This statement serves as one measuring rod among many for where we are today. How can this view from the past inform the educational wisdom of theological students today? How can it become relevant?

True, the statement is "dated" because its focus is limited to Blacks and Whites. What about the larger picture that included my former classmates—those I knew from kindergarten through high school? What about Asians, Latino/Latina, Native peoples, poor whites, and mixed-race citizens who also know subjugation, refugee status and migration, long term discrimination, the effects of structural inequality, and class warfare? With structural inequality on the increase, the increase in gun violence, the new poor, race/class divisions, and the new Jim Crow being what they are, this Kerner Commission statement continues to hold relevance for everyone. The language of yesterday may have been industrial education, but today it is replaced by vocational technical education. Either way, patterns of class and racial divisions in society are perpetuated. Who then is our student and who *ought* to be? Who are the teachers? What is being taught and caught?

I know that our dean addressed some of these issues when she introduced the Emmett Till case in the senior seminar. She was brave! I believe she received little or no encouragement or support from the majority of her faculty colleagues. No support at all from the president. If it is the case that one cannot lead where one has not gone, then what lessons of relevancy do our students learn from this?

6. Kerner et al., *Kerner Commission Report*, 2.

WHERE IS THE CLASSROOM LOCATED?

Parts of Oakland appear to be mobilizing religious and theological resources to combat urban violence. Certain themes in the research of Walter Rauschenbusch's social gospel, William Hamilton's "death of God" theology, Harvey Cox's secular city, and James A. Sander's monotheizing process will surface again and again as timeless resources for the thinking and rethinking of higher theological education. Awareness of the interrelatedness of diversity and personal and social issues will intensify. The urban crisis, now surfacing around the most recent budget cuts in social services, will intensify. Changing beliefs and questions around what to believe will force inner city pastors to respond in ways unfamiliar to them. A sense of inadequacy will grow. Hence, an unsuspecting group of Black clergy caught in the vortex of urban violence will need to fashion or refashion their theological beliefs and understanding of ministry as they extend care to a variety of individuals, families, groups, and the new poor. Who then are our students and who *ought* to be? Where will they be taught? Who are the teachers? The urban crisis that pastors face will challenge them to intervene in the immediate crisis without losing sight of the universal claims of the gospel for all people. Narrow views of ministry will be challenged. Who then are the teachers and students in this classroom without walls?

Gun violence and safety, poverty and available health care coverage, social services, and issues of class long have been relevant to ministry and Black communities—from slavery to rural KKK activity in the South, to Detroit and Chicago's South Side, to Harlem, Philadelphia, Fort Lauderdale, Richmond, Oakland, etc. These are symptoms of increased diversity and stratification, social change, migration and urbanization, social and family organizations, and other deeper, entrenched social challenges that are not unique to America or American cities. Gun violence and issues of safety have spread to suburban communities, such as Newtown, Connecticut. These signify urban, mental health, and social policy issues. A Jeremiah or Isaiah or Micah would go further and address what on earth God is doing and calling us to be and do in all of these situations. Who is the student now and who *ought* to be? Where are the teachers? Where is the classroom located now?

THE THREAT OF BECOMING ONE DIMENSIONAL:
THE BIND

Is it true that we never learn from history? It becomes true when the questions above are ignored. It becomes true when we turn a deaf ear to the distilled wisdom of the past and the universal claims of the gospel, and allow ourselves to be defined by the immediate crisis. When we work with tunnel vision in the present and tune out alternative views that do not conform to our own desires, then we and our educational processes have become one dimensional. Then wisdom traditions become irrelevant and the lessons of the past are lost to us. This is unfortunate and lamentable. A certain direction is considered lamentable when it hinders the leadership from working with a broad constituency that can enable seeing from multiple directions and advocate relevant connections between the concerns of the Prophets, culture, the gospel, the city and the quality of our minds. A lamentable situation exists when leadership proves unwilling or incapable of seeing this bigger picture and wider challenge. When the leadership cannot hear the voices that cry out from different social locations and articulate things differently, then it is time to think about the lessons unwittingly imparted to students. It is time to rethink the priorities of a theological education in the light of culture, biblical values, and ethical norms of justice and compassion. Often different and seasoned voices are told "you do not understand!" They are dismissively referred to as "irrelevant," " a hindrance," "extremely angry," "alienated," "resistant to change," "a distraction," "opinionated," "old fashioned," "ivory tower idealists," etc. Other standpoints, critical perceptions, bigger pictures, and wider challenges may indeed appear to be irrelevant to a seminary's particular vision of higher theological education.

When a seminary community becomes polarized in tribal-like enclaves of staff, students, administration, and faculty, and is unable to communicate within and across borders, then it appears to be misguided and hopelessly divided. It will become increasingly one dimensional. This appearance is derived from an increase of derogatory remarks, silencing, and diminishing trust and cooperation within and between groups that once pulled together. More fragmentation and divisiveness can be seen, if one chooses to look. Then the seminary, in reality, becomes a place that is tragically self-focused, "my" ministry- and self-survival-oriented. The ideal aims of a higher theological education have been lost when money dictates priorities, limits thought, and controls vision.

Seminary, then, may not be the ideal place where critical questions of moral purpose and ethical pathways are valued, and the development of an inner spiritual life and tradition are intentionally encouraged. This is not new, but still it is a tragic and disturbing view when compared with certain ideals for higher theological education. This is tragic and disturbing when this particular view—the priority of monetary, market values, and a corporate model for education—has gained the lone high road with little resistance. One student, referring to an increase of online college courses put it this way, "What a boon to the administration, which now can collect tuition without providing services or hiring faculty. The people who lose are the students. It's just another quick step toward the day when only the children of the rich actually go to college, while the children of the poor and middle class go to the coffee shop to stare at screens."[7] This view of things is confirmed at the seminary level when a corporate model of industrial education is replaced by vocational technology rhetoric. We unwittingly repeat certain mistakes of the past without appearing to have learned anything. What happens to the student's learning when the seminary's focus becomes one dimensional? Who are the teachers and what are the teachers teaching?

YOU CANNOT LEAD WHERE YOU HAVE NOT BEEN

We believe it is important to enable students to work toward a sense of unity that includes a developing sense of desired diversity. This unity embodies certain ideals of similar and dissimilar perspectives, and a beloved community of practical, critical, and scholarly inquiry. We reflect upon selected past experience that may guide us in the present toward a desired diversity.

We can see from the Chauncey Bailey case above that there may be some problems associated with attempts to teach diversity. How does the teacher prepare for desired diversity in the classroom? This and many related questions have been central to my own understanding of what it means to be a teacher. For the majority of my teaching career, I have been the minority in the classroom. What has it meant for me to think and plan from the perspective of the majority culture, and to downplay my own, perhaps unshared, lived experiences and point of view? What does it mean to select case study material from my own Black cultural background and from within American society? Is self-denial necessarily a virtue? Cries of "irrelevancy" may be heard.

In order to achieve a diverse and systemic point of view, a Japanese colleague and I decided to offer a course together to see what we could learn and where to expand, adjust, or curtail certain teaching practices. We told students during the course interview period that we were experimenting

7. Grossman, "Online College."

with a new course called "Ministry in a Multicultural/Multiracial Society." We had not worked out all the issues. We had never taught together. We would learn together from our mistakes and successes. If students were willing to journey with us in this face-to-face classroom experience, then well and good.

We began with storytelling. We talked about our own early childhood experiences of growing up in American society. My colleague talked about his experiences in an internment camp, the memorable stories he heard from elders and other interned people, and the role of white missionaries. I talked about my school experiences and about hearing stories of discrimination from my parents, who were born in the Deep South: stories of the fear and distrust of certain white people, reprisals such as lynching and discrimination, and the values of self-reliance. They tried to instill values of integrity and communal care in my siblings and me as we grew up in the Pacific Northwest. We learned about Chief Sealth (Seattle) and his understanding of the unity of nature and the Web of Life. We learned about the care and spiritual power of the Black church community.

Each student began with a personal narrative about how he or she got his or her start in American society and a major metaphor, statement, theme, or value. Through storytelling we employed a nonthreatening therapeutic strategy that kept resistance at a minimum. Each student was interested in what others had to say. Each was eager to share his or her story. In this way, we were able to identify common ground as well as differences in our experiences. We were then able to talk about what were the challenges of the gospel's call to follow Jesus all the way. Though we were many, we still could cooperate and find unity in the Body of Christ. We visited several churches in the community that had multiracial and multicultural ministries. What were the challenges, the promises, and pitfalls of such a ministry?

We interviewed pastors and laypersons in their church settings. The last part of the class experience required each student to present a paper in class. The paper would meld themes in personal narratives and assigned readings, and address the perceived challenges in carrying out ministry in a changing multiracial and multicultural society. The pastors and laypersons we visited earlier were invited to participate in these presentations.

Given the affirming comments about process and content throughout and at the end, we came to believe that this was a successful course. Unfortunately, we were unable to continue offering this course. It was considered not cost-effective to tie up the resources of the only two ethnic minority professors in one classroom.

A Selected Past Experience

Another way to prepare for diversity in the classroom was to take sabbaticals outside of the United States. In my case, I went to London and trained medical doctors, psychiatrists, social workers, and educators from so-called third and fourth world countries and regions, such as Bangladesh, Pakistan, India, Hong Kong, Singapore, North Africa, Sierra Leone and Ghana, to become family therapists and psychotherapists. I was able to offer workshops, work with families, consult, and develop video teaching clips and other resources that I believe would bring difference and rich diversity into the classroom where I regularly teach.

I was exposed to new experiences. For example, I was able to work with a Muslim couple from Iraq. The father was a political prisoner of Saddam Hussein. My co-therapist was a Jewish psychiatrist from Argentina. We were all foreigners. London, England was our common denominator. This experience was not possible within the United States. I was fortunate to have permission to use one of our taped sessions in my regular teaching of theological students. We were able to learn what it might mean to develop new questions of diversity and face the "strange situation" not as obstacle, but as opportunity to forge beneficial change. Sometimes, my co-therapist was a Muslim woman. We were able to work with a traditional Muslim couple. Experiences such as these informed my teaching and helped me to become more curious about questions such as, "What is culture and where is it located?" and "Who is my student? Who *ought* to be?" The latter is especially important when working across cultural differences. I could also recognize when I was the student and needed help.

Sometimes, when you are able to work outside of your typical work environment and in a different country and culture, you may be able to notice things back home that you might not otherwise see. I was able to return to the United States with new insights, for a different and more informed way of working. I could offer choice and challenge to my students. But this did not always work out in the ideal ways that I had hoped, as indicated in the Chauncey Bailey situation above.

Another Selected Past Experience

"Who are our students?" and "Who *ought* to be?" are very good questions. They should be raised rather than ignored. Still, they are difficult questions to answer. Few want to struggle with them. When our students come from the majority culture, and have had minimal contact with Black people or other people of color, difficulties can arise.[8] Who then, is our student and who *ought* to be? My mother (a Black woman), for example, came from rural Mississippi. She worked as a domestic for white people. They only knew her in a servant role or as "the help." Neither she nor my father (a Black man with a sixth-grade education) were ever seen as valued persons in their own right. They were socially trapped in their lowly status. My father once shared the humiliating story that, when he would go to work, a white neighbor would come and urinate on his front porch. This happened again and again. So, it may be difficult for some from the dominant culture to take their ethnic minority and degree-bearing teacher seriously. Some may come to believe that their teacher is there only because of affirmative action, but not as someone who has anything relevant or real to offer. Ethnic minority students may also share this same perception of their ethnic minority teacher.

An ethnic minority woman from Pakistan, whom I had helped train as a therapist, was assigned a client who sought mental health assistance from the clinic where we worked. When the client arrived for his appointment, he was shocked to find that his therapist was an ethnic woman. He protested, walked out of the room, and demanded that the receptionist assign him a "real" therapist. To my surprise and to the dismay of the therapist, the white receptionist complied with his wishes, thereby maintaining a dominant pattern of discrimination and humiliation. A similar pattern holds true when our students are able to avoid taking classes from ethnic faculty, and also to gain support from the white administration to do so. True, this is hard to prove. But it happens. In 2008, Manning Marable observed, "Once black PhDs are hired at predominantly white colleges, they appear to encounter the same old racism that generations of earlier African-American scholars faced within white institutions . . . . [T]he patterns of racial inequality and unfairness . . . continue to exist."[9]

One ethnic minority student, after graduating, told me that he did not take any of my classes because he wanted to take classes with someone who had real life experiences. Really?! How can you possibly be a successful role model, if you are not an athlete, entertainer, or President of the United States? How can you be a real educator when the majority of the people who look like you are deemed intellectually inferior, unsuccessful, living on the street, poor, in jail, and/or in prison?

---

8. The meaning of the term "Black people" is arbitrary and context-dependent. In some cultures of the world, "Black" means anyone who is not identified as "white" or European. Still, in certain places, the Irish, for example, have been referred to as "Black." Typically, it is associated with racial, ethnic power minorities, and inferior status.

9. Marable, "Losing Ground?"

Still, many other students gravitate to us because they know us to be serious, hard working, competitive achievers, and wise. They believe we will take them seriously and give timely feedback. They know the idiom, "You cannot teach what you do not know! You cannot lead where you do not go!" If they know that you have learned from your experiences, grown strong from your trials, and kept compassion alive, then they want to journey with you. Below are examples of feedback offered to my students after the second class assignment was made. The assignment was designed to stimulate a diversity of standpoints and conversation among the participants. This particular class was on family narratives, pastoral theology, and care. The teaching style was reflexive and dialogic.

1. Where Am I and What Do I Think about Work with Family Narratives?

The following is a composite view of class members' answers, narrated in the first person: "I am familiar with dream work; Jungian, Gestalt and Adlerian techniques; and some aspects of a dialogue between psychology and theology. I am formed by and reminded of certain experiences in my family of origin (some are pleasant, others are very painful, still others continue to be confusing). I have worked as a pastor, hospital chaplain, family therapy supervisor, family therapist, clinical psychologist, and teacher with children in my care and with families who come from cultures different from my own. I have worked with kids who have been identified as 'troublemakers' or makers of trouble and have helped them to change. I have listened to stories of family members."

2. What Literature Have You Already Consulted or Read— Literature that Already Guides Your Thinking and Approach to Family Life?

The collective responses ranged widely from those who have not read or consulted family life or family therapy literature to the following: texts on childhood development, developmental psychology, and moral development; works of Russian novelists and playwrights, certain existentialists, and others such as Borges and Kafka; Bowenian family systems theory; John Gottman, *Why Marriages Succeed and Fail*; Harville Hendrix's Imago Therapy; certain literature in clinical psychology; works by Sekbong Han, and Gildong Hong; Watzlawick, Weakland, Fisch, Gregory Bateson, Kuhn;

Edwin H. Friedman, *Generation to Generation: Family Process in Church and Synagogue*; Charles Gerkin, *Introduction to Pastoral Care*; Maxine Glaz and Jeanne Stevenson Moessner, *Women in Travail and Transition: A New Pastoral Care*; Wayne E. Oates, *Grief, Transition, and Loss: A Pastor's Practical Guide*; Edward P. Wimberly, *Counseling African American Marriages and Families*; Charles F. Kemp, *The Caring Pastor: An Introduction to Pastoral Counseling in the Local Church*; Howard W. Stone, *Strategies for Brief Pastoral Counseling*; Robert Kegan, *In Over Our Heads: The Mental Demands of Modern Life*; Monica McGoldrick, *You Can Go Home Again: Reconnecting With Your Family*; Wanda M. L. Lee, *An Introduction to Multicultural Counseling for Helping Professionals*; James B. McGinnis and Kathleen McGinnis, *Parenting for Peace and Justice*; Michael True, *Homemade Social Justice: Teaching Peace and Justice in the Home*.

Professor: "What do we *notice* from the above listing? A few observations are in order.

"First, only a few references actually point to the literature on family therapy written by practitioners themselves.

"Second, it is important to recognize that the literature on pastoral care and counseling is not the same as the family therapy literature. The training, theoretical orientation and conceptual frameworks, paradigms, and credentialing process differ between the two disciplines (pastoral counseling, on one hand; and marriage, family and child therapy, on the other).

"Third, the bulk of the literature on marriage, family, and child that informs our thinking is primarily from white, mainstream America, with little exception. Unfortunately, this fact is also largely unquestioned in seminary and in training programs. Do social class, ethnicity, sexual orientation, gender, age, religion, and culture make a difference in the way we define, think about, and approach family realities, and train folk to work with culture and class differences? Furthermore, what is the difference between family and household?

"Fourth, the social sciences such as anthropology, sociology, economics, and cultural and social policy studies may not play a very strong role in the literature cited above and in family therapy literature. The contributions of systematic and practical theology are largely ignored.

"Fifth, are there any theoretical references to *narrative theology* or *narrative approaches* to families? Hence, we are led to ask, what is *narrative* and what would a narrative approach to family life look like? How can we distinguish a *narrative* from a *non-narrative approach*?

"We can identify more issues, but we have done enough to *notice*, from this collective picture, some things that we were not aware of before the assignment. Perhaps we can gain some clarity on these issues before the class is over. I will leave it to you to raise the issues."

3. What Assumptions in the Literature or Popular Press Are or Are Not Being Made about Families?

Professor: "Caring aims at improving humanness in both those who are cared for and those who are caring. There is an assumption that families are safe, happy places, havens from the storm(s) of life. There is another assumption in the idea that there is some order in what appears to be disorder. Certain assumptions held by family members are not always beneficial; and sometimes people get cast into roles that are hard to break out of. Some of these hard-to-break roles are reinforced in the media. Hence, certain myths become socially and culturally entrenched (institutionalized). The mass media greatly influences ideals of family life. Committed heterosexual family life is the ideal. BGLT, polygeny, polyandry, celibacy, and other non-heterosexual styles are viewed as deviant, incomplete, and/or immature."

4. What is Covered/Neglected?

The following are additional comments and exchanges between student and professor:

Student: "How can I apply the Western style of family pastoral care to Korean contexts of care?"

Professor: "Note that there may not be 'the' Western style of care. Rather, there may be a variety of Western styles of care that emerge from a diversity of cultures. Neglected are good and detailed descriptions of poor children and children from wealth—who both may experience the family as a broken and hurtful place. Such neglected descriptions may be relevant to the Korean context when a Korean therapist or pastoral care provider attends to these. How can families help one another? How can mother-daughter, mother-son, father-daughter, father-son, and sibling relations in non-mainstream or culturally different families contribute to our understanding of families? Non-mainstream culturally relevant descriptions are often neglected in the literature, in training programs, and in seminary education. A critical appraisal of the shaping influence of the mass media and of popular (televised) religious programs on family life is often neglected in training programs, seminary education, and church school."

5. *What Are Some of Your Concerns about Working with Family Narratives?*

Student: "I do not have a lot of happy stories to tell."

Professor: "If Crossan is correct—i.e., that 'everything is narrative, that there is no "reality" on which to stand'—then how do we do therapy? Where does the therapist stand or gain leverage to enable the family or family members to change? Where does the pastoral family therapist position her- or himself and why? Is there any standard model of family?"

Student: "How do I accept the thoughts of others who differ from my own about the role of parents?"

Professor: "How do family therapists deal with belief systems and values that differ from their own? Is it possible (or *how* is it possible) that the writer or storyteller affects the narratives they tell, and how are they affected by the narrative once it is told?"

The following are additional dialogical questions between student and professor:

Student: "Many of [the people with whom I worked] were depressed and some of them revealed manic-depressive symptoms. . . . I spent time with them listening to their stories . . . I realized that just listening to their stories attentively could be a good medicine to their depression. At the same time, I wish I had been equipped more with pastoral care and counseling skills."

Professor: "Listening is an indispensable part of competent pastoral care. But when is listening alone not enough? How can we tell?"

Student: "My main concern working with family members is that I will become too entangled with the problem and take sides, rather than remain neutral."

Professor: "Please note the term, 'neutral.' Is neutrality humanly possible? Let us ask: 'How do we remain *curious* about family belief systems and transactions?' 'How do we use *curiosity* to trigger the evolution of new ways of seeing and being in family life?' 'How do I think about and work with family structure?' 'Why is this important?' 'How do we avoid the dangerous belief or resist the temptation that "one theory fits all"?' This temptation is appealing when you are busy and overstretched, and feel pushed by pressure to 'hurry up,' fix it, be successful, now!"

Student: "Is a narrative approach a one-theory approach? Where do immediate context, cultural context, historical experiences, interpretation, and meaning come in?"

Professor: "Here is what I am thinking. If we did nothing more than to explore, in depth, the above issues for the remainder of the semester, we will have gotten more than our money's worth. There are issues and assumptions and questions to be addressed that would take us a long time to explore in depth. Perhaps, already, with this first assignment, there are seeds for a final project.

"It is important to ponder what we have already done, and attend to the questions already raised. A temptation in any educational experience, especially this one, is to rush through (surf the net of) our experiences, to remain on the surface, and to fail to achieve depth of meaning because we are moving too fast. We are too busy. Someone put it this way: 'Get in, get what you want/need, get out.' (This was wisdom passed from one seminarian to another.)

"What is the purpose of an education (or learning experience) if we already know, ahead of time, what we need? Where does discovery or the unknown come in? How do we help family members, who come with a similar mindset, to distinguish *need* from *want* if we fail to make such distinction for ourselves? How do we become curious about things we do not know? Where is there room for the kind of learning that can come from patient contemplation, critical discernment, and reflection? How/when/where do we learn to do creative waiting (vs. just wasting time)? How can we tell the difference? How do we savor experiences long enough to learn the lessons? How do we achieve depth of meaning and gain wisdom? Most important, when do we pray?

"I believe these are questions at the very heart of narrative work with families. It is at the heart of training pastors to be wise carriers of stories and to do narrative theology. Narrative pastoral family care, if it is to be therapeutic, is an opportunity for the whole family to stop, look, and listen. This entails patient, discerning work over time, and the tapping of the family's resources and wisdom that have evolved over time. This is not work for those who are stuck on speed mode and do not have time for it. What do you think?"[10]

---

10. Subsections under "Another Selected Past Experience" represent the kind of summary feedback and exchanges between students and professor near the beginning, middle, and end in many of my classes. The purpose of these exchanges was to raise questions, provide information, and stimulate discussion. In addition, students received individual feedback on their assignments. The feedback included things they should know. My teaching assistant, Susan Pohl, was a major help with the classroom process and discussion. Her participation allowed me to be in the observer/learner role. In this way we could learn from teaching and teach from a position of ongoing learning.

CONCLUSION

In closing, I return full circle to the five things our students should know and the questions at the beginning of this essay. The *context* matters where *student and teacher* meet and interact in formal ways. *Fellow students and self-awareness* are in constant interplay and together help shape the quality of the learning experience. *The school and its mission* help frame the foundational values of the student's learning. These foundational values meld with the *history and classic texts* that students have experienced. Students learn to interpret them and extend them to a wider world. Hence, the questions "Who are our students and who *ought* they be?" and "What does it mean 'to learn' something?" take on great meaning. These are important questions that our students should know if we are interested in transmitting wisdom from one generation to the next.

We have also asked, "Do we ever learn? Do we ever graduate?" It has been suggested that we are both student *and* teacher! Whether acknowledged or not, we are endowed with the inheritance of the past and we carry our experiences and voice where ever we go. We are never *just* in the moment. We are always at an intersection, negotiating things and always integrating past experiences in the living present while acting toward the future. We exist in time and space and are forever on the move. Learning, unlearning, and new learning are ongoing processes of spontaneity and adjustment, critical reflection, and decision-making. Where we start is important, but not as important as what we do with what we start out with. I was fortunate to start out with classmates who came from different cultures and language backgrounds. But there were always bigger pictures and wider influences that we could not have seen or known at the time. We are always a part of something that is infinite, novel and emerging. We "see through a glass dimly."[11]

Knowledge is always partial. Students need to know that, too. It may be hard to communicate the idea of partial knowledge and the values of a critical, reflexive inquiry when students come with an "it's all about me" attitude and a monolithic understanding of the world. As a teacher, I could come to know certain things if I pursued them like a student with an inquiring mind. I learned that my classmates were as different as they were similar. If I can build on what I learned from them, and on what I have been given by my students, teachers, and colleagues, then perhaps I will be fortunate enough to never graduate from the process of learning, unlearning, and new learning. Maybe I will be able to continue in a vocation as a student who

11. 1 Cor 13:12.

is willing to learn and as a teacher because I have been willing to go on a continuing journey.

6

What Shall We Teach?

The Content of Theological Education

WILLIE JAMES JENNINGS

WHAT DOES ARCHITECTURE DO to us? Alain de Botton, in an opening story in his book *The Architecture of Happiness,* reflects on a house that had been for its residents among other things, a ". . . physical but also psychological sanctuary . . . [and] . . . a guardian of identity."[1] Architecture, Botton goes on to suggest, can exert powerful influence over us, especially if we attend carefully to its details. We might learn important life lessons from its characteristics.[2] Teaching the content of theological education is about entering architecture, and entering that architecture continues to be an extremely complex negotiation for people of color and for women. The reason for this complexity is commonly known but not fully appreciated: theological education in the modern Western academy was not built with different bodies in mind or with due consideration of different minds in diverse bodies.[3]

The architecture of modern theological education has been likened to the white master's house built exclusively for his sons. Of course, we should remember the many qualifications often pressed against this observation

1. de Botton, *The Architecture of Happiness,* 11.

2. Ibid., 175ff.

3. Chopp, *Saving Work.* Chopp's reading of the problem is yet one of the most powerful and concise.

of architectural particularity. First, theological formation is ancient and reaches back behind its modern degenerative performances bound to white, male, heterosexual normativity, which means that we need not assign all of what is essential to theological education to Euro-male centrism. Second, numerous peoples of color have engaged in theological educational endeavors geared toward their own peoples, which suggests the viability of theological education for those formerly imagined at its margins. Third, the actual content of theological education, whether ancient or modern—that is, a curriculum and its courses as well as the "stuff" of individual courses—is either identity-neutral or so laden with multiple identities, peoples, perspectives, and ideas as to automatically attend to diversity when carefully taught. While these qualifications present some truthful elements, they don't capture the thorny problem of theological education's architecture. At heart, we are still confronted with living in a house we did not build.[4]

This is not unusual, especially if we stick with our architecture metaphor, because the vast majority of people who live in houses of any kind probably had little to do with the architectural design or the process of building itself. The numbers of people who actually design and build their own houses are relatively few, so most people are faced with the task of adopting and/or more often adapting to the given architectures of their domiciles. It is precisely this process of adaptation that I want to focus on in this essay in order to do two things. First, I want to analyze the complexity of *teaching the content* of theological education for people of color and women.[5] Second, I want to imagine a different way of thinking about "content." And in this regard, I also want to suggest some pedagogical and political strategies for that work of teaching the content of theological education. There is urgent need for more analysis of this complexity because the battle lines regarding what constitutes faithful theological education have moved directly into the content question. It is exactly in the content question where we encounter multiple arguments, much misunderstanding, and a great number of unacknowledged fears and hopes.[6]

4 Lorde's classic statement about the master's house informs this analogy at this point. Lorde, *Sister Outsider*, 110–13.

5. I recognize that the term "teaching the content" is quite unwieldy, but by this term I am attempting to capture the customary topics, actual subject matter, usual forms of presentation, and instructional paradigms for teaching the traditional fourfold division of theological education—Bible, theology, history, and ministry studies—and all the sub-divisions that have emerged out of these areas.

6. Warford, ed., *Practical Wisdom*. See especially articles by Samuel Escobar and Diamond Cephus.

THE SPACE OF SUBJECTIVITY IN THEOLOGICAL CONTENT

We who teach in theological studies (or more generally religious studies) spend a great deal of our life energy living and working in the space of content, whether we think of content as the contents of a curriculum or the content of our specific courses. It is a demanding space for all who teach, but it can be and very often is an extraordinarily contradictory space for those for whom it was not originally envisaged. The contradictions for women and people of color move in at least two directions. First, we have made a career-long (maybe even lifelong) commitment to a field of inquiry, a discipline that at some level brings us satisfaction and even pleasure, yet we live in the modern shadows of foundational figures of those disciplines who by and large would not have imagined us their conversation partners in the discipline. Even newer fields of inquiry yet stand on a stage constituted by these older modern fields of study soaked in white male hegemony. Second, we are committed to institutions of higher learning and academic institutionalizing processes (offering and conferring of degrees, certifications, and formal introduction into traditions of intellectual inquiry, etc.) as vehicles for the realization of dreams both personal and social, while we live in the shadows of foundational institutional figures who have defined, and continue to define through various structural and human surrogates, standards of excellence, evaluative habits of mind, pedagogical preferences, and ways of interacting with students and faculty colleagues that reflect cultural and aesthetic tastes born of the modern colonial moment and the desires of the ruling classes.

These contradictions create for so many women and people of color a love/hate psychical condition within the space of teaching the content of their disciplines and their participation in the ecology of their respective curriculums. What does it mean to love one's discipline yet be at war with many of its modern foundational figures? How is it possible to challenge the concepts, paradigms, shared assumptions, etc. of one's field of inquiry, yet demand that students learn and appreciate the "classical" texts and arguments of that same field? Why would someone participate in a curricular schema and its ecology of assessment within an institution while opposing the hegemonic operations activated by that very curriculum and its processes of assessment? For many in the academy, I am simply describing the nature of life within a scholastic universe where one becomes a proper participant in a tradition. Quite a few of our colleagues would not see these matters as real contradictions. Yet there is a density of life struggle that eludes a facile reading of these matters as simply the normal challenges of academic life. Many teachers experience a very serious psychical negotiation in inhabiting their disciplines, especially as they confront them *in the content* of teaching them.

What is at play in these contradictions is the struggle to establish a form of subjectivity that must reconcile the subject position of a teacher of a given content with the contingent and historical self of marked bodies.[7] That subject position represents a history of intellectual inquiry not only tied to its particular content, but also tied to the image of the educated one who would normally inhabit that position. What circulate around the subject position of teacher/scholar in the theological academy are the content of a discipline *and* the imagistic echoes of those normally associated with the discursive presentations of that content in teaching and research. That circulation continues to be strongly affected by the historical inertia of white male hegemony, which presses that subject position toward subjectivities that are, for many scholars, terribly troubled.

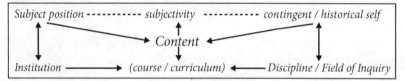

Subjectivity in this regard is a way of perceiving oneself in the world in which a perception of the world *together with* a perception of the self is presented as a way to narrate life. That narration includes both aesthetic and theological judgments that govern our behaviors and self-interpretation. Simply put, troubling subjectivities arise out of the confrontation of women and/or people of color with the subject position of teacher of a given content yet bound up in the historical inertia of white male hegemony. They are troubling because they create what should not be—a historical self constantly questioned and under continuous examination—never fully at home in the subject position of teacher of a given content. Troubling subjectivities in relation to the historical inertia of white male hegemony might be expressed in three ways.

First, it might be seen through a sense of captivity to a limited world of interpreters of the content of a given field. The modern theological academy is profoundly haunted by the ghosts of deceased European interlocutors. This is not new news. Moreover, in many sectors of the academy the prevailing sense of "serious"—that is, substantive—intellectual work in a field is directly tied to continued engagement with those interlocutors *and* their

7. Oliver, *Colonization*.

contemporary interpreters. The interpreters may on rare occasion represent a broad range of diversity, yet the trajectory draws new scholars toward an abiding limitation. The implicit agreement within this limitation is that properly introducing students to a given field of inquiry as well as broaching the frontiers of knowledge within that field require the constant conjuring of foundational European thinkers.

Where is the trouble here? Is it not the case that every discipline is constituted by a limited number of pivotal thinkers and commitment to a given field commits one to thinking alongside those intellectuals? Is it not also the case that disciplines are conversations that one enters into as a participant? Commitment and participation are givens; the trouble is not the trajectory, but its speed and its range. Choosing to enter a theological field of inquiry and teach its content is indeed entering conversations sometimes ancient and honorable, and yet that entrance also demands the expansion of those conversations through the joining of a scholar's own questions and concerns to wider sets of contemporary concerns, some which bear directly on that field's trajectory. The trouble here is the amount of time and energy required to expand those conversations as well as the viability and sustainability of that expansion. Here many scholars of color and/or women are confronted with resistance in the form of life-draining questions regarding the *how* and *why* of their discipline's expansion, which greets them not only in their scholarly research but in the content of their courses. They are often pressed into exaggerated intellectual justification for every attempt to expand and/or reformulate aspects of their discipline.

The demand for intellectual justification is an inherent aspect of scholarly participation in a field, yet the kind of intellectual justification bequeathed by the legacy of white male supremacy layers on to that demand the implicit requirement to show that difference (of opinion, position, or argument) is not rooted in a difference (of race, gender, sexual orientation) that is perceived as a deficiency (of knowledge, understanding, or appreciation) of the founding arguments, concepts, or figures of the discipline. Thus this kind of intellectual justification becomes a mental vise, squeezing us between the past founders and the present interpreters in an exhausting crush of accountability. This is why for so many women and people of color there is a need to escape the kind of intellectual justification demanded, and to demand instead a radical rethinking of the precise nature of their intellectual work.[8] Even if one imagines the decisive interlocutors of a field to be truly ancient originators—for example, Hebrew Bible writers, or New Testament figures, or writers of Christian antiquity, or medieval writers or

8. Westfield, ed., *Being Black, Teaching Black*.

figures—the layers of modern European interpreters and commentators are yet presented as inescapable sites of accountability.

This heavy cloud of accountability is connected to another tangled problem. *A second way that troubling subjectivities can be seen is in the struggle against disembodiment.* The presence of women and people of color in the space of content makes visible the operations of whiteness that have historically made white male bodies invisible, but powerfully present. Whiteness is both an object of sight and a way of seeing. Like the hidden narrator of a story, whiteness authorizes what should receive focus and what may remain in the background. Instructional authorization as such is in fact the cumulative effect of years of teaching practice through which the assumptions of what needs to be stated and what no longer needs qualification have been naturalized into the overarching pedagogical architecture of any educational program or presentation of course content. The problem here is the tying together of two forms of authorization, one arising from sheer pedagogical expediency and another drawing life from the normalizing gaze of whiteness.

These two forms of authorization, now tied together, play off of each other, mutually enforcing yet eliding each other's operations. The most profound effect of these dual operations is their control of the economies of display—that is, which ideas, concepts, or paradigms are quickly connected to bodies, especially bodies marked by race and gender, and which ones are allowed to linger in the space of the white universal as freely applicable to all places and times, and as such may reign as analytical arbiters. One example of this dual authorization is the schematic and all its variations that one yet finds in some syllabi or outlines of books that introduce Christian theology.

Syllabus for Introducing Christian Theology (Topics)	Table of Contents for a Book Introducing Christian Theology
Week 1: What is Theology?	Section One: Key Figures
Week 2: The Identity of God	(The vast majority of whom would be white European men.) [*e.g. Kant, Hegel, Schleiermacher, Nietzsche*]
Week 3: Jesus Christ	
Week 4: Creation	Section Two: Key Events and Movements
Week 5: Salvation	(All of which take place in Europe and/or North America) [*e.g. Enlightenment, Liberalism, Romanticism*]
Week 6: Holy Spirit	
Week 7: Church	
Week 8: Sacraments	Section Three: Doctrines
Week 9: Eschatology	(Repetition of the Weeks 1–10 of the syllabus)
Week 10: Theology and Science	Section Four: Approaches to Theology
Week 11: Liberation, Feminist, Womanist Theologies (Post-Colonial and Post-Modern Theologies)	(An inexplicable mixture of denominational and contextual positions on theology now designated as "independent" approaches to theology, e.g. Anglican, African, Evangelical, Feminist, Black, Roman Catholic)
Week 12: Theology and Ecology	
Week 13: Theology and Pluralism	Section Five: Contemporary Issues in Theology
	(Here we get feminism, ethics, environmental issues, race and gender, culture, science, pluralism, violence, war, etc. as important concerns for theology.)

There have been and continue to be many challenges and defenses of this schematic. But the power of this schematic (of both the syllabus and the book) is not only in its framing of options for reflection but in the options through which one may channel subjectivity. If the teacher follows the schematic outline, what process of identification will they perform: *when*, *where* and *how* will they enter (to borrow from Paula Giddings's powerful theme)?[9] In one sense, the answer to the question of entrance is already established by being the teacher of the course or the writer of the textbook. There are, however, multiple possibilities and problems for performing visibility or invisibility with this schematic. If the teacher of marked body follows the logic of this schema, they would need to decide whether they are or are not present in the part of the architecture that designates marked bodies. If they "blow up" the architecture, have they destroyed aspects of

9. Giddings, *When and Where I Enter.*

what Charles Foster called "signature pedagogy"?[10] That is, have they rejected a pedagogical practice honed over time that yet proves productive in overcoming perennial problems of teaching content? These questions only magnify the problem.

The teacher within this schematic enters an architecture that serves and reinforces whiteness and white invisibility. Moreover this architecture orientates us toward the naturalness of the dual authorization. It is, of course, the right of a teacher to determine what matters require isolating focus, holding back other details that would detract from the clear communication of aspects of a subject matter. Yet this dual authorization is broader than the use of a pedagogical technique because it not only establishes *when* and *what* bodies become matters of consideration in real space and time, but also angles intellectual work toward a particular historical trajectory of disembodiment, one that linked didactic authority to gestures of white invisibility.

Here we must grasp what it meant "to speak as a white man" as a stabilized subject bound to the subject position of teacher. Such authorized speech when joined to the content (of a course or a discipline) rendered unnecessary any thick account of identity in relation to the discursive performance of the teacher/scholar.[11] The particular realities of this teacher/scholar folded into the content. Such an enfolding bequeathed a perceived naturalness of the linkage between white male identity and the dissemination of content. This linkage produced not only styles of confidence but also a sense of normalcy that the presentation of the subject matter was in its proper hands and thereby self-justifying. It is this trajectory of disembodiment that women and people of color have needed to press against, yet the entanglements here are far more complex than have often been appreciated, because they cannot be and have not been easily undone.[12] If white male identity bound to content yielded not only an invisibility enfolded in the content itself, but also the power of the invisible narrator, then content placed alongside marked bodies yielded its opposite. It yielded a visibility that demanded new compelling accountings of this new teacher's authentic connection to the content.

10. Foster et al., *Educating Clergy*

11 Bhabha, *The Location of Culture*, 66ff. Said, *Culture and Imperialism*, 97ff.

12. Bass and Dykstra, eds., *For Life Abundant*. Jones and Paulsell, eds., *The Scope of Our Art*. Both of these fine edited volumes capture many senses of the way disembodiment distorts theological education and the vocational identity of the theological teacher, yet they do not reach into the racial history of disembodiment in modern Western education, especially theological education.

We are referring here to economies of display and not primarily the credentials, training, or background of the minority and/or female teacher. Every teacher who steps into this pedagogical architecture must negotiate the complex optic and discursive currency that historically flowed from this naturalized linkage. How does one function within, yet alter, economies of display deeply shaped by white male hegemony within the presentation of content and one's engagement with a discipline? There are constant struggles within this negotiation. On the one side, it is not simply a matter of making visible what was invisible. White invisibility in relation to the content of theological education has always been instrumental and not simply spectral. That invisibility is energized through the continuation of discursive practices that angle content toward disembodiment and pull away its connective tissue. In addition, the visibility of the teacher with a marked body is always at play standing over against content marked with the echoes of its nameless invisible narrators. This means that the marked visibility of the female and/or minority teacher is already connected to white invisibility (bound to content) such that the teacher is automatically caught up in a messy process of trying to make visible an invisibility that can draw life from the very content of a course or curriculum *and* the marked visibility of the teacher. This means that making visible white invisibility can sometimes actually strengthen its power of narration.

On the other side, these same teachers are also caught in economies of display and must secure their authority in relation to the content and its long history of interpreters. This is especially the case in theological education where even newer fields of inquiry are encircled by a constellation of traditional areas of study that remain the foundation of curricular paradigms (i.e., Bible, theology, ethics, history, etc.). Yet how do minority and/or female teachers secure their authority in relation to course or curricular content and their disciplines? They must enter into the difficult work of teasing out and repeating time-honed and honored pedagogies from racial or gender mimicry. They do this while also negotiating the styles of confidence originating from the naturalized linkage of white men with the content of theological education.

This difficult work yields yet a third site where we can see troubling subjectivities, and that is in the chaos of evaluation. We need to distinguish evaluation in this sense from processes of assessment, whether institutional or classroom. This reality of evaluation grows out of the economies of display and brings the minority and/or female teacher into a space where they must intercept the interpretive strategies that flow in and around their bodies in relation to the content of their subject matter. These are not *their* interpretive strategies but the ones constituted by the architecture, of content *cum* students *cum* the teaching practices and learning processes that have been historically associated with the institution or the course. Even if the teacher is teaching a new course for the institution or the curriculum, interpretive strategies are in play. This is especially the case if the instructor is teaching something in minority or feminist/womanist studies. The difficulties of being a marked body in the traditional classroom have been well documented, but what is yet to be fully appreciated is *the intensity of its evaluative character.*[13]

The teacher in this regard enters a world where they must reconcile their own work in their chosen discipline with the work that has gone before them. Every teacher stands within particular traditions of scholarly inquiry. Yet the teacher of marked difference is often severely pressed against questions of alignment with those traditions. Are they following their field's tradition of scholarship in ways that honor that tradition while also challenging the identity markers normally associated with its presentation? What is the nature of their intellectual departure from what they perceive as the wrong direction, detrimental elements, unhelpful procedures, or flawed assumptions or conclusions at work in their discipline? Will their conceptual departure be received as a new direction within the field and not something destructive to its tradition of inquiry? Will their engagement with the discipline be interpreted as a contribution to it and not as a concern external to it? These are the kinds of concerns that swirl around their engagement with the content of their courses and their discipline.

This does not mean that every female scholar and/or scholar of color is or should be a revolutionary to their discipline. Indeed some scholars find no greater joy than simply inhabiting a field's prevailing axioms and intellectual agendas. Such scholars not only understand their work to be wholly inscribed within particular scholastic contexts, but they also imagine their contribution as faithfully carrying forward the greatest *shared* contribution their field makes to the overarching goals of educational institutions. Yet it is precisely the notion of contribution that is haunted by questions of alignment. Shared contributions require acknowledgment— institutionally, professionally, and interpersonally—and it is exactly such acknowledgments that are often delayed or denied scholars of marked difference. Thusly, they find themselves in the odd position of waiting for what they should not be waiting for, a sense that they share in the impact of a field of inquiry on an institution's educational endeavor.

This is a self-evaluation. As such it carries aspects common to any process of self-evaluation for anyone staring down at the content of their

13. Ropers-Huilman, ed., *Gendered Futures*; Smith, et al., eds., *The Racial Crisis.*

courses. This self-evaluation for a teacher marked by difference, however, has already been caught up in a racial and gender calculus the strength and speed of which will be determined by the field and its collegium, the teacher's particular institution, the curriculum, and the course and its history. This is, in effect, much more than a self-evaluation because the self at play here is also one constituted in questions. The scholarly inquiry of the field has been turned on and into an inquiry into the status of the scholar in ways that may even challenge the scholar's own self-narration. But who is doing this? Who is pressing these teachers hard against a wall of cross-examination? If, on the one hand, this is an exaggeration to distortion of the kind of customary self-evaluation any teacher might have as they engage their field, then on the other hand it is made all the more chaotic through the classroom ecologies where student and institutional expectations flow inside the economies of display. If, with the first kind of troubling subjectivity, these teachers are faced with a prison house of exaggerated accountability, then with this third kind of troubling subjectivity they are faced with a swirling mixture of harsh winds of self- and site-evaluation.

Any minority and/or woman who enter academic space unaccustomed to their presence understand the complexities of evaluation within classroom ecologies. These complexities are never captured on evaluation forms, or on formal exit interviews with students or faculty colleagues. These complexities of evaluation flow through the measurements of discursive performance, scholarly output, and course materials and expose expectations impossible to pin down. These teachers are measured against simulacrums, images of white male teachers, images of what women teachers ought to be, images of what minority teachers ought to be, and assumptions about which ideas and concepts should matter to women and minorities and which ideas and concepts are the proper domains of white men. It is very often the content of the courses displayed in such artifacts as syllabi, reading assignments, guest lectures, and writing assignments that weave together these simulacrums into convoluted impressionistic evaluations of the course and the professor, and thereby lead to the drawing of a hard evaluative circle around perception and banishing reality to the margins of interpretation. Faced with this chaotic reality of evaluation, many teachers are forced to spend enormous amounts of time and energy simply trying to move through this chaos as they prepare courses and function in the classroom. This is why for some women and minority teachers their syllabi resemble academic administrative fortresses to protect them from as much of the chaos of evaluation as possible.

RETHINKING THE ARCHITECTURE OF PLEASURE IN CONTENT

An empty house is an invitation to dream, yet the architecture of the house could press that dreaming in directions that lead to unsatisfying rest and even nightmares. Our central point thus far has been that women and minority teachers face struggles with teaching the content in theological education, given its architectures. When moving into a house, choices have to be made for the sake of survival and human flourishing. My concern is with the range of those choices and whether in fact we have positioned ourselves in ways that illumine new possibilities, new wine and new wineskins. A starting point for reassessing choices returns us to the power of dreaming. If one is in the blessed position of not being homeless, and is able to get an apartment or a house, then one enters a space between the habitation of those that have gone before you and your own hopes of life in that space. A wise homemaker will draw deeply into two logics: the logic of those who inhabited that space before the new homemaker, and the logic that informs the new homemaker's dreams for the space and for their own future in it. Here then we have the interplay of two logics of habitation.

A logic of habitation comprises (i) the structural design of desire, (ii) the design of desired structures, and (iii) the demand for structural success. These elements build from one owner or inhabitant of a space to the next, moving from the originating logic of the architect and builder to subsequent generations. The *structural design of desire* in its most positive sense are the ways in which materials have been set in place to capture and generate hope, facilitate pleasure, and overcome despair. These are the structural designs intended to restore and rejuvenate us. The *design of desired structures* are those material elements that bring us sheer pleasure by their existence, things of an aesthetic character and inspirational quality that fulfill their purpose by simply being in our lives. They may be understood as decorative and/or functional, or filled with the promise of help in time of need or emergency. The *demand for structural success* reflects the ways things must be designed for survival, recognizing the many past failed structures and the dangers that lay ahead. This demand will also include the desire to capture compelling appeal such that future generations will welcome the structure as applicable to their hopes and dreams and not detrimental. In effect, we always have to do with many logics of habitation building from the originating architectural endeavor. However, the crucial gesture in making a place a home is to engage, as best as possible, these logics of habitation. To what end?

Here we want to recall the quote from Botton with which we opened—a house is a "... psychological sanctuary ... [and] ... a guardian of identity."[14] At heart, every teacher who has decided to enter a discipline and the honorable space where it will be taught to successive generations commits to spending a considerable amount of their life energy in that space. It is indeed a shared space, a communal space. It is precisely this communal sense that should draw us deeply into the logics of habitation and toward new ways of imagining both sanctuary and identity. I would suggest three lines along which we might imagine the teaching of the content of theological education as sanctuary and identity.

CAPTURING THE DESIGNS OF DESIRE

As we consider these lines of engagement with teaching the content of theological education we should keep in mind three basic ways one may use the word "architecture." It may mean (i) the art or science of designing and erecting buildings, or (ii) buildings or large structures, or even (iii) an ordered arrangement of parts, or a structure.[15] So the first question we should ask ourselves is how might we gain a sense of the desire of the architecture? Here we seek to grasp some sense of the desire embedded in the inherited designs (of course or curriculum) given to us. We are not going after a Freudian reconstruction of the psyche of past designers, modern or ancient. We are interested in the ways in which we can think backward and forward from the desired results of any aspect of pedagogical design. What problems will be overcome if students learn this content following this particular format? What newness did this design hope to create in students? Who does this design or this aspect of the design imagine the student will become after they experience knowledge, understanding, enlightenment, or transformation from it? Sometimes these matters can be clearly seen. Sometimes we can only tease out elements of desire from inherited designs. The point here is that entering the arena of desire opens up new ways of conceiving accountability, justification, and evaluation. Here the teacher is primarily accountable to desire, not design. This does not make one dismissive of inherited design. It does, however, demystify design as fundamentally artifacts of desire.

This approach summarizes the content of theological education as constellations of desires materialized in designs and artifacts of designs. If designs could be analyzed so could desire. How might we engage an ancient

14. de Botton, *The Architecture of Happiness*, 11.
15 *The American Heritage College Dictionary*, 4th ed., 74.

desire for a particular way of thinking about a theological matter with a more modern desire that moves in the opposite direction, and then with our own desire for the ways students might think about matters? This approach is not simply about analyzing something like pre-modern forms of mimetic thinking over against modern forms of critical thinking, or phenomenological forms of reflection (thinking about the ways people have thought about what they believe) over against theological forms of reflection (thinking about right ways of believing). Rather, engaging desire embedded in design may in fact allow us to tease out points of productive interface with our desires for particular outcomes in teaching. This kind of approach would lend itself to reaching for richer accounts of designers and inhabitants of particular designs and their life stories, including their own encounters with the desires of their own teachers. At all points, we should seek to humanize the processes of theological education by laying bare its hopes and dreams embedded in all its designs, including even those that seem most oppressive.

ASSESSING DESIRED STRUCTURES

We should seek to grasp the beauty and elegance that others see. Christian intellectuals in general, and those involved in theological education in particular, rarely speak of the beauty or elegance of curriculums, course outlines, paradigms, course syllabi, and assignments, because such language often is not deemed appropriate when thinking about designs or conceptual structures we find to be problematic or even supportive of oppressive regimes. Yet if we wish to see how desire embeds itself in design, one of the most fruitful places to locate it is precisely in structures held up as time-honored and essentially compelling. This location is less a matter of discerning the differences between orthodox and heterodox frames of thinking or even less a question of correct or incorrect designs. It is about capturing a view of what designers and inhabitants view as beautiful or elegant according to their working definitions of those terms. In systematic theology, for example, grasping beauty and elegance would be something like identifying elements in systematic structure that someone finds important and even pleasurable in the way they exist or work to accomplish some learning goal.

This line of engagement searches for the conceptual fetish. This fetish is a structure or a way of structuring that its user believes conjures aesthetic qualities like coherence, elegance, clarity, or symmetry. Staying with systematic theology, one example would be the doctrinal formulations emerging out of various scholastic periods, Catholic or Protestant, and the use of Latinized designations for making visible different shades of doctrinal articulation, (e.g., *fides qua creditur* as opposed to *fides quae creditur*). *Fetish* in this regard is not a pejorative term; rather it implies the continuation of a stylistic line of argumentation, or conceptuality that is believed either to do real work in solving problems or simply makes pedagogical matters more pleasurable. If we cast light on these fetishes, then we open up important questions about not only their continuation but also why and if they might be compelling to us.

Theological education is replete with conceptual fetishes in every field of inquiry's pedagogical practice. Whether someone wishes to argue for the essential permanence of a given structure is a separate but related question to the *desired necessity* of it. Desired necessity indicates imagined beauty. Women and/or scholars of color entering the content of theological education have entered into someone else's imagined beauty, and entering into the imagined beauty born of white male hegemony is, in point of fact, a central aspect of the aesthetic struggle of the Western world. Yet someone's imagined beauty need not be a prison, but instead can be a place that we might innovate or renovate depending on the social and political stakes. Equally important, exposing fetishes does not require we dismiss them, but rather brings us into the freedom to question them, and to work with them without simply giving over our creativity and agency to them.

I have no idea what he is talking about!

GAUGING THE DEMAND FOR STRUCTURAL SUCCESS

What does it mean to design a space to succeed? This is one of the most enduringly interesting questions of architecture. Success might be defined as supreme utility that could serve known and unanticipated functions. Success could also mean permanence in the sense of durability and/or aesthetic eternity—forever sublime, forever inspirational. Does the demand for success come from the hopes and dreams of the architect, or from those who called for the building? Certainly we can, in most cases, see both sources of demand for success working together. Indeed an architect may imagine a design that would contain in itself infinite possibilities of utility and also be able to capture a sense of infinity itself so that the design is able to hold the imaginations of generations of people.

Such desire, however, while appropriate, could also border on incredible hubris and narcissism if architect and builder impose on a given space a design and a building that creates no respectful conversation with its environment, disrupts ways of living that promote flourishing, and facilitates oppressive social, political, or environmental practices. Such situations mark the imperialist legacies of quite a bit of Western architecture placed on colonialist sites. There one finds beautiful and impressive buildings that show master artisans who have learned their craft often in the ancient manner of years of meticulously tracing the drawings, prints, and architectural outlines of great European buildings. Yet the success of the design is a wholly self-referential determination with no input from its place or native inhabitants. The demand for success and the metric of it in this example are in part external to the actual lived reality of the built environment. We could add that the building's durability will also be a measure of success, yet that hoped-for permanence of the building will be due to maintenance forced out of indigenes who, in many cases, would be taught to love the very building that helps to establish their subjugation.

A successful space, therefore, can be defined through a sense of coherence internal to the logic of the design/building itself. It follows a tradition, maintains particular standards, embodies a series of structural advances, and makes faithful uses of particular kinds of materials. A successful space could also be defined through a sense of coherence with its wider environment and inhabitants, where it continues and enhances the conversation with its landscape, promotes customary ways of flourishing, and opens up new possibilities of pleasure and joy. These visions of successful design could exist either in utter contradiction of each other or in mutual reinforcement. Something similar attends the visions of success in teaching the content of theological education. Yet the dynamic women and/or people of color face in teaching would be similar to that of a native inhabitant who is now an architect/builder. How do we define a space to succeed?

It may not be true for every teacher, but for many teachers the first and foremost sign of structural success of teaching a course is surviving it. The syllabus held, the assignments worked, we handled the intense chaos of evaluation, and students learned something(s) we desired them to learn. Yet while this may be a central gauge for many teachers of marked body and other educators, attending to wider questions of success holds the possibility of entering more deeply into the pleasure of its demand. Why imagine pleasure with this demand? Here we should remember that the work of designing draws us into the power of creativity and the realities of conversation with past and present. Creativity and conversation hold the promise of bringing these two visions of successful design into productive tension. This tension challenges visions of purity that would contort the agency of the teacher, driving out any sense of the sheer newness of their life in the space of a teacher.

Success in this approach is rooted in honoring the newness of the teacher to the space of design and the designed space. The coherence of a tradition of design and the coherence of its intended space both pivot around the living reality of the architect/builder. *New* in this sense is not primarily a teacher new to the craft of teaching. This newness is the freshness of each day, every time one enters upon the work of crafting content, or enters the classroom, or entertains how one will inhabit the curriculum. Both demands of success—either of coherence within a tradition or of coherence to the given environment and peoples—could be not only pedagogically oppressive, but also could lead to constant missed opportunities to enhance life. Yet if both are drawn together in imaginative gestures of communion, then successful space within teaching content could open up new ways of imagining home as a blending of the familiar with the foreign.

Such a possible blending returns us to the point about styles of confidence. Sensing the demand for success can become the greatest drain of a teacher's confidence in teaching the content. If one is aligned with a tradition of coherence such that the metric for success always comes from the imagined voices of the past whose designs one seeks to faithfully perform, then confidence and comfort become bound up with an unrelenting mimeticism that gives life to constant troubling subjectivities for so many. Yet if one is captivated by the need to find coherence with one's environment, institution, and/or a constellation of immediate concerns, then newness of one's own agency might be compromised. The point of blending here is to open up styles of confidence that emerge from being in between these two kinds of demands, neither fully within the controlling reach of either, yet open to conversation with both.

CONCLUSION

These lines of engagement with teaching the content of theological education build from one simple premise: Our newness to the architecture of theological education is a great gift. *Gift* in this sense moves in two directions: first, we are a gift to the architecture and second we are new inhabitants of a space that might be made into our space. New forms of subjectivity are possible for all those who teach in theological education, especially for those who were once envisioned as the primary conveyors of pedagogical mastery. So I imagine these strategies to be available inclusively to all teachers, not just those of marked body. All this depends however on whether, in fact, we are ready and willing to press more deeply into the logics of habitation in hopes of creating new more inviting spaces for both those who will be taught the traditional lines of content in theological education and those of us who stay between the lines.

7

Thoughts on Curriculum as Formational Praxis for Faculty, Students, and their Communities

ELIZABETH CONDE-FRAZIER

I WRITE AS A Latina practical theologian who has spent thirty years of her life working at providing theological education for pastors and lay leaders in the Latina/o church in some form or another. The scope of this work has included working in denominational bodies, seminary Hispanic programs, Bible institutes across the nation and Puerto Rico, and more recently working at a Christian community college located in North Philadelphia, one of the top ten poorest counties of the United States.[1] I have also been a founding member of the Association for Hispanic Theological Education (AETH), a Protestant organization that brings together individuals, groups and institutions—including seminaries and Bible institutes—involved in the endeavor of education and formation of clergy and lay leadership.

It is from this perspective that I write about curriculum and what we teach. The realities of this context and experience have had, at their center, the question, "What shall we teach in order to produce pastors who can carry out effective ministries?" Much of my and others' advocacy within the formal educational structures has been about what we teach. The work

1. Bible Institutes are pre-collegial training centers for clergy and laity.

I have done with AETH and independent church bodies of the Hispanic church has been as a result of having to circumvent and/or supplement and complement the curriculum of theological schools accredited by the Association of Theological Schools.

DEFINITIONS AND UNDERSTANDINGS ABOUT CURRICULUM

Before going further I will define curriculum. In this part I will draw from the writings of Robert Pazmiño, a Christian educator/scholar who has written thoughtfully about the subject over the last three decades; his definition gives a broad and overarching understanding of curriculum. I also draw from the work of Michael Schiro, who defines curriculum from the perspective of ideological frameworks in American society. This is helpful as it gives more context to our discussion. I then include the more particular scholarship of practical theologians as they write about curriculum in the context of ministry.

Pazmiño sees curriculum as including the experiences of the students, the written courses of study, and the learning activities that are guided by the professor with the learning outcome that is desired as a result.[2] Usually when asking what we should teach we think about knowledge, understanding, values, and skills. These in turn have a purpose or a desired outcome that may be related to particular tasks, efficiencies, or modes of thinking and attitudes that we wish to see our students being able to participate in. However, I tend to start thinking about my curriculum by asking, "Who am I teaching?" This is because this question sets the tone of teaching for me, since teaching is a highly relational endeavor. The fabric of the relationships I wish to weave in the classroom is important to the environment I create and what then can happen in that place.

This question also leads me to the context of the students: Where is our teaching taking place? Location affects our expectations, resources, and limitations. The socio-economic, cultural, and political circumstances in which we teach form our goals differently. For example, when I was in Kazakhstan I had to learn much about the history of the people and the history of the church there. I had to understand how the language worked and how culture gave shape to language. Speaking with men or women changed the language and the way we engaged the topics because it changed the expectations of the conversation. The history also changed the symbols that would

---

2. Pazmiño, *Foundational Issues in Christian Education*, 213–32.

be effective or impose barriers to my teaching. The past political climate had shaped the parameters of teaching and the relationship between teacher and student. I had to find ways to facilitate questioning and critical thinking in a place where these activities had been forbidden for seventy years. This meant that my methods and strategies were informed by the politics and history of the land.

If I ask "Whom am I teaching?," I am also asking, "Who is teaching?" The longer I teach the more I am aware of the fact that I teach who I am. My own struggles and what I have garnered from these as I reflect on them, the places where perhaps I am not yet empowered, the strengths of my life, my knowledge and approach to the discipline I teach from, the things I integrate, my preferences and reasons why they are preferred (many times communicated in my attitudes), the way that I learn and apply information, the passions of my heart—these are the very things that make up the curriculum. My social location, gender, race, and ethnicity are all at the root of many of these aspects and very much form the curriculum.

I am aware of the fact that I speak with the language of expression, and therefore my gestures, intonations, inflections, vocal volume, manner of pacing, and the many different looks I give my students while I speak or listen to them speak, are a great part of how I communicate content as well. In all of my evaluations students will speak of the embodied dimensions of my teaching, signaling to me that the texts and the theorists we discuss are not the only content of my teaching curriculum, although why I choose those theorists is also a part of my embodied reality as a second generation Latina who is bilingual and bicultural. How I dress becomes a part of the curriculum especially as students then interpret why I teach what I teach. They look for information about me to figure this out, and how I dress becomes a part of the information that they consider in answering that question. Is she professional enough, is she too uncovered or too covered, is she fashionably dressed, what does this say about her socio-economic reality and therefore about her experiences and about what she is going to "push" on us in the classroom or how she can relate to our reality . . . This then informs the teaching and learning dynamic in my classroom and how students prepare to resist or to be open to what I teach. At the same time the resistance they bring also informs what I teach and how I teach it—my teaching strategies. The relationship between teacher and student makes the curriculum much more than texts and tests.

The curriculum is also informed by what holds it all together. "What serves to provide unity, integration, and culmination to the educational experience in terms of planning, implementation and evaluation?"[3] This leads us to look at the philosophical, theological, and/or biblical elements that inform the theoretical underpinnings of our teaching.

Theorists in the area of curriculum have named three types of curriculum: the hidden, the explicit, and the null curriculum. The explicit curriculum is that which usually appears on the website about the courses taught at an institution. The hidden curriculum is about the contexts of education, some of which have been named above. To add to those we can name the architecture, the classroom arrangement, the processes, and policies operating that socialize us in the educational environment. I teach in an undergraduate environment where most of the students are the first generation going to college. During orientation we discuss a glossary of terms that those of us who understand the college system take for granted, but which are completely new to these incoming participants to this educational culture. Things such as syllabus or FAFSA, which refers to the economic dimension of education, are totally foreign. As students become versed in this new jargon they become citizens of the college world and they begin a process of figuring out how invested they wish to become in this world. What are the benefits of becoming immersed and what are the costs to their lives and their family's lives?

Other elements of the hidden curriculum beg more questions: What is the distance that professors take from the subject they teach? How do our evaluative measures nurture collaboration or competition? What is the make-up of the board that formulates and decides on the policies of the institution? What values are inherent in their decisions? This curriculum is a powerful one. As a dean at my teaching institution I am well aware of the fact that the nature of the relationships that we have with one another as staff, professors and administration is felt by our students and it teaches them an entire content about power and powerlessness, class, gender, and race relations.

The null curriculum is composed by the things we choose not to teach and asks: What is it that we teach by what we do not teach? What we do not teach affects the options one teaches students to consider or not consider. It can create biases. Maria Harris points out that ignorance or the absence of something is not neutral and it eliminates perspectives that help us to see.[4]

Curriculum is influenced by the structures of our institutions. The accrediting agencies and academia inform curricula greatly. The beginning of the nineteenth century saw the forging of a relationship between higher

---

3. Ibid., 235.
4. Harris, *Fashion Me a People*, 122.

education and the legitimacy of social power in American society. The middle class was developing, and professional structures established standards for licensing and education necessary for the practice of the professions. Universities developed degrees, fields of study, and processes for mastery of these systematic bodies of knowledge.

The ministry was also professionalized during this time so that the matter of ordination based on the profession of ministry became a class issue. Theological education did not take into consideration the financial realities of working and lower class ministers, and it became inaccessible. It was no surprise then that its curriculum catered to those who had the means to attend institutions of higher learning and often had gaps or pockets of irrelevancy for those who came from blue collar neighborhoods. This was part of the historical context of theological education. This context of professionalism influenced the denominational and educational structures of the church. Middle class professional values informed theology as the priesthood of all believers was de-emphasized and the image of the one expert/professional pastor took precedence. This shift then informed the structures of the church, turning its preference to a professional paradigm with intellectualized understandings of calling. The educational philosophy became that of social efficiency. The sense of the priesthood of all believers and the charisms for ministry diminished.

It is this socio-economic, historical context that informs curricula in theological education today. Professors must demonstrate skills and knowledge in their fields of study the same as any other professors at any school. They must give evidence of their expertise, which implies then that they must turn their attention to academia and its foci. This is in tandem with a scholar/academic ideology.

I have mentioned two different curricular ideologies above, the scholar academic and social efficiency. I wish to provide a summarized definition of these along with a third ideology, that of social construction. I will show examples of this one later in the essay.

The scholar academic ideology of curriculum stems from the perspective of the academic disciplines. The curriculum is therefore grounded in the purposes of the distinctive discipline. It reflects the styles of intellectual inquiry of that field of study, sets forth the "history and tradition of the discipline, determines the key concepts, and sets forth the instructive character of the discipline."[5] This approach may divorce itself from how it is that the knowledge is to be applied in a context of ministry or any other context that is not the promotion of the knowledge of the discipline itself. In

---

5. Schiro, *Curriculum for Better Schools*, 34.

this ideological paradigm, knowledge "derives its value and claim to being knowledge from its ability to contribute to the extension of an academic discipline" and is linked with the skills of inquiry in the discipline.[6]

We will note that in this ideological mode one needs to include diversity through the scholarly voices of texts, through other scholars brought into the teaching/learning environment, through the voices of the students, and through the sources of inquiry. It is in these places that we need to be intentional about bringing in other voices and about making sure that when we open the space for them we give them a place of equal authority by how we value them.

When I have to teach in this mode due to the structure of the institution or the program, I make sure to include the other voices as authoritative voices by introducing them into our midst in ways that will help persons listen to these voices even when they have never had the opportunity to listen to them before. I may even introduce voices that my students are resistant to listening to. In this case I set up the voice and the content of the voice. I connect it with the topic of the day and with the things we have said in class. I recognize the resistances and name where they may be coming from or allow the students to reflect on where they believe them to be coming from. It is important and effective to help persons find their own way to something new. My questions to them help participants listen to this in themselves, after which I invite them to something new, introducing at the same time the hope and potential of the new to our learning. My perspective, my spirit in the invitation and the way I set it up, lets them understand that one must bring respect to the encounter. I model the respect. I build the appreciation of that voice. I do not simply bring in a new voice as a part of a dry bibliography; that style is very impersonal and distant. It does not build a relationship or a positive expectation in the learning process. As a part of this introduction I am responsible for helping a student interpret the canvas of the diversity of the voices so that the student feels comfortable entering this space. I am a guide.

Part of introducing the student is the process of helping them to see the methodologies of the other voices and the reasons for those methods. It then becomes a moment for critical thinking, for giving consideration to the different perspectives an author may bring and how these are constructed and shape knowledge.

Curriculum is controlled by the powers in the institutions that validate it and that are themselves sustained by it. In this case, the institutions that benefit from this type of curriculum are those that gain prestige within the

6. Ibid., 59.

academy as a result of it. Research institutions with doctoral programs make sure that professors are engaged in the academy through the particular guilds of their disciplines and require them to participate in these bodies by contributing in ways that expand the body of knowledge of their discipline. The discourse of these disciplines has traditionally promoted and maintained the interests of the metanarratives of the dominant culture. Minority perspectives brought to this discourse may not be well received or considered "scholarly enough." This is reflected in who then is able to continue to be a part of the "club" and whose perspectives are placed in journals and texts that then are engaged by students. Such protection and perpetuation of the dominant culture narrative is the reason that we have so few scholars of color in our schools.

Social efficiency is a different ideology. It derives its values from the skills mastered for performing specific tasks and activities, such as, in this case, the ministry. The purposes and experiences of learning are all derived from this goal of bringing about performance behaviors. To be able to preach, to do a funeral, to do good exegesis are all objectives that are congruent with this goal. Part of the curriculum is to create learning opportunities to help persons gain the "ability to practice the kind of behavior implied by the objective."[7]

The practices of ministry take place in a great variety of contexts and the theories and assumptions that inform these cannot be the same. However, the curricula of many schools treat them as if they could. The practice, doing, and action of a ministry setting become a teacher. Many minority students come to theological study after having been in ministry for a while. They are no longer novices but are seeking to go to a different level of practice. The curriculum of their experience must be taken seriously and engaged in the classroom as part of the curriculum. Experience and practice are part of the knowledge to be engaged in the classroom. Theory from the discipline alone will not be sufficient to fully engage the goal of these students. One must engage the "doing" of their ministries for it shapes the knowing of their ministries. This is where the knowledge that a professor brings to the curriculum is lacking if it is only informed by the discipline. The curriculum must be more integrated. Perhaps bringing those who are proficient or experts in their own practice of ministry who could serve as mentors alongside a professor would make for a richer curriculum. The valuing of this type of expert within the hierarchy of the institution is an important topic of a conversation that needs to be had.

7. Ibid., 88.

Social reconstruction is for educating persons to become aware of the oppression around them, and it prepares them to take action that improves or eventually transforms their communities by overcoming the problems and social crises in their midst. The primary method of educating is dialogue and group discussion so that teachers and learners are both learning and teaching simultaneously. The outcome of this dialogue involves shared participation of the group towards the goal of changing and/or improving their quality of life. The dialogue begins with the problems or difficulties experienced by persons.[8] Liberation theologies are a part of this curriculum, as are those who have participated in prophetic action. The work of faith-based non-profit organizations is a text of this curriculum, as are the different methodologies that engage communities with the purpose of facilitating this type of awareness and action for empowerment and improvement of life. Some of these methodologies are: ethnographic studies, narrative approaches, and participatory action research.

In theological education, practical theologians have redefined curriculum as content and processes.[9] They name the vertical curriculum, which is defined as moving from introductory to more advanced studies. Horizontal integration is the relationship and impact that the different parts of the curriculum have on one another so that the student is making connections between subjects and disciplines. Finally, diagonal curriculum is the "integration of the unintentional processes of life events . . . and events in society which are then integrated into one's identity, practice and theological knowing."[10] This is a more fluid and unpredictable curriculum. It is present in one's classroom and will emerge on its own, or our awareness of it in our midst may prompt us to engage it in an invitational manner so that persons are aware of the fact that it is valued as a part of the learning discourse. It is here, in the diagonal curriculum, that privilege or discrimination experienced by a person or the impact of oppressive forces on their lives becomes a part of the teaching and learning. A professor must be able to facilitate a valued interaction with these sources of knowledge and must be able to create an environment where the connections between these and the other elements of the curriculum cross-fertilize each other.

While teaching on the West Coast at a school where students came from many different countries and cultures, I was often surprised by the experiences that my students brought to the classroom of oppression, war, torture, and hate. These were expounded on with passion or great suffering.

8. Ibid., 271.
9. Cahalan, "Integration," 389.
10. Ibid., 390–91.

These students taught the rest of us how theologies of suffering that come from the West do not begin to adequately engage the depths of the problems that they will need to address upon returning to their contexts of ministry. The questions they brought and the critical thinking process we employed debunked the theoretical reasoning of the West.

As teacher I was forced to change the readings of the class midstream in order to keep up with the reality of the discourse of my classroom. Rituals of reconciliation and healing became a regular part of the classroom exchange. These were carried out by all of us at different times as expressions of embodied knowledge and connection with one another, and of the new voices of scholars and ministers in our midst through the students and the research presented. They were practices of ministry that we experimented with and rehearsed for the practice of our actual ministries. I also used drama to facilitate deeper reflection of the impact that the oppressive forces had had on our lives, and for problem solving.

Drama also served as a way to help students confess how they were implicated in different forms of hate and discrimination of their own. Drama facilitated repentance and imagining practices of redress and/or ministries of reconciliation. This was a much more effective way than if I had required that they read and write a paper on racism explaining how they saw themselves implicated in the structures of racism. The resistive defenses that usually emerge when discussing this subject had been eliminated by the curricular resources of the experiences of persons.

As I reflect on this I am aware of how my training with the theater of the oppressed, and my own sense of wisdom or practical reasoning for reading the contexts and persons, inform the curriculum. However, my own personal work of self-reflection on the places of my woundedness due to experiences of discrimination, powerlessness, and coming to power through depression, anger, and forgiveness has also become a source of knowledge for equipping me to teach in this manner. The diagonal integration of my life became an important part of the curriculum.

Charles Foster names two types of pedagogies that are a part of the curriculum for theological education: pedagogies of performance and pedagogies of formation. The first is the way in which we teach the practices for ministry.[11] The very nature of a practice requires that it be observed, imitated and rehearsed. We learn a practice by practicing it. This changes the setting for learning to communities of faith or other places where viable ministry is taking place for those who are lay ministers. These may be

11. Foster et al., *Educating Clergy*, 156–86.

community organizing or faith-based non-profits, charter schools, or other work in the context of the broader community.

The second pedagogy focuses on spiritual and professional identity. Formation takes place outside of the classroom as well where one experiences worship, prayer, spiritual practice and service.[12] Cahalan points out that spiritual formation is the way "that students appropriate changing religious vocation."[13]

CURRICULUM FOR NON-TRADITIONAL STUDENTS IN ALTERNATIVE SETTINGS

Both of these forms of pedagogies take place outside of the traditional classroom. I would like to share a few examples of alternative contexts that can be engaged or created for this type of curriculum. Each of these engage non-traditional students of theological education: the bi-vocational pastor and lay leader of an ethnic minority community.

In the Latina community there are many different realities that have forced clergy in that community to engage in a variety of new types of ministry practices. They often embark upon these as a response to survival needs, and have little time to reflect theologically about their practices much less to articulate the theology that emerges as a result of these practices. The Esperanza Capacity Institute provides opportunities for this to take place. The Institute is designed for leaders of community and faith-based organizations. Community organizations and churches that are responding to the needs of their community through feeding programs, job training, housing, counseling, health, education or other forms of assistance and empowerment attend this Institute. It is leadership training for teaching participants current best practices in non-profit management and service delivery.[14]

As a part of the two-day training, ministers and lay leaders attend a workshop where they reflect theologically on their practice. They look at how their work is a part of the tasks of the church: proclamation, teaching, service, fellowship, social justice, and worship. They then engage in a discussion that helps them to do a social analysis of the needs of their community. The social analysis includes the historical, economic, political, psychological, educational, and cultural roots of the problems in their community. They also do an asset-based assessment. The next step explores the

---

12. Ibid., 100–126.

13. Cahalan, "Integration," 391.

14. See www.esperanza.us.

theological and biblical sources of the church for doing the ministry they are already engaged in. At this point they describe the practice of ministry they are involved in, including the outcomes desired and forms of evaluation. Participants name the theological basis for their praxis of ministry. The question remains: How will they communicate this praxis to the larger congregation so that all can own it and become more intentional in participating in it? This brings them to the different tasks of the church with the purpose of using the tasks to communicate the theology that they have articulated.

Worship is a major focus of the church. Much energy is invested in its forms. This is where the artists and musicians of the church collaborate with the ministers to bring attention to the theology through the arts: drama, music, art, and liturgical dance. These will generate theological symbols to be incorporated in the worship and songs that will now go beyond the theology that they have embraced. The collaborative process becomes a communal moment of reflection. This is called "teologia de conjunto," a collaborative theology. It is a theology done as a community where persons seek to define God, themselves, and their purpose in the world as a community and not as individuals. It is also a pastoral theology in that it stems from the church and its purpose is to serve by denouncing the injustices of the socio-political structures.

This theology includes a social political dimension. It is theology as community building, an expression of empowerment. It begins as a people apply their faith to the process of initiating solutions to social problems in order to create a link between faith and social and political involvement in their communities. Theology that is caught and not taught is theology that is sung. The musicians now become theologians.

This curriculum serves as a way of creating an organic and relational association of ministers with a common practice of ministry. It is a teaching space that is accessible and within the rhythms of the reality of bi-vocational ministers that incorporates experiential and theoretical learning in a particular situation. The teacher in this setting is a practical theologian or a pastor/activist/scholar who serves as facilitator of this process. The teacher integrates the practice of ministry with the theological method that is birthed from the Latina context by Latino/a theologians and makes it accessible by way of a method of doing theology that includes a community reflection. The teacher is also the people, who are participating in the reflection of their practice of ministry. Their insights are part of the content of knowledge.

In this case the persons engaging in this curriculum are open to the process because it refers to a practice they are already involved in. However, if one were to seek to foster a critical consciousness in persons that in turn would lead to a redefinition of ministry for the betterment of their communities, what would such a curriculum look like? The teacher in this situation would want to empower persons to redefine their practice of ministry, not to prescribe a practice.

I want to describe a transformative method of teaching where church leaders, both lay and clergy, who are recent immigrants are invited to reflect on their practice of ministry. This approach is taken from my work with Bible Institutes. Ministers are asked to reflect on three areas: the personal, the ministerial, and the interaction between the church and the community. While this reflection takes place, notes are taken on newsprint. We begin the discussion with the lived experiences of persons. The participants then speak of their daily experiences beginning with their first reactions upon arrival in the United States. They identify how life has changed for them: their family roles and routines, their frustrations and disappointments, and how they have overcome these. They speak about language and the education of their children, about finding employment and housing, and about their hopes and dreams and how these have been redefined since they first arrived. Persons are then invited to analyze the list of things they have mentioned. What do they see in it? What issues repeat themselves? What does this mean? What categories emerge for them? What issues are prevalent? What creates this situation? What forces do they see operating? How does this compare with situations of persons in the congregation? What does this say about all of our lives?

This procedure is repeated with the second area, the ministry. Now persons are asked to share their goals and tasks of ministry along with their frustrations and conflicts experienced, and the strategies they have used to overcome. When they examine this area they discuss the theology that informs their ministry, the causes of their frustrations and conflicts, and reasons for the effectiveness or lack of effectiveness of their strategies. Participants look at the different models of leadership that are carried out. Persons talk about the denominations they belong to. Many of these are controlled by leaders of the dominant culture. The policies regarding Hispanic churches are formed by persons who are not Hispanic and do not understand the context. These policies shape the budgets that affect the Hispanic faith communities as these determine the resources made available for their ministries. They reflect on the support or lack of support received from these bodies and how their denominational relationships enhance or obstruct their ministries.

The next step is to correlate the two areas. What does one have to do with the other? How do they inform and affect each other, if at all? What are the time management issues? What areas of personal experience are addressed by the ministry and why? What areas are not addressed and why not?

Finally, we discuss the interaction between the congregation and the community and ask persons to describe the communities in which they minister and the relationship the congregation has with the community. What are the needs they see in the community? How do the ministries of the congregation engage the community either directly or indirectly? What sources inform the nature of this involvement? How do they think the community sees the congregation in its midst? If they have a community ministry, they are asked to describe how this came about and what the ministry entails. How do both the members of the congregation and the community participate in the program? In what ways has this ministry impacted the life of the community? What other congregations are in the community? What is the relationship between these? Are there any ministerial alliances or associations and what are the purposes of these? How do these relate to the issues of the community?

One more time the teacher will correlate all the areas discussed and ask questions that guide persons in making links between the three. We may ask: How does the congregation see its ministry in relationship to these issues?[15] How does our theology address these? Are there biblical passages that address these areas? As we examine these passages, do they take us beyond the parameters of our theology? What should we do with that? What are the structures of the church already in place that can be used to address these issues? What resources and/or skills do we need? What picture of ministry emerges as we look at this? What biblical/theological/denominational models have we drawn from? What new models are we creating?

This method identifies the sociopolitical and economic issues in the present experience of persons. The questions facilitate the naming and analysis. This part of the process also points out how the ministry of the church relates to the dimensions identified. Discussion and further analysis of this area lead to a rereading of the scriptures and reappropriations of them for the purpose of redefining the practice of ministry. This is a communal process of discernment whereby participants seek to discover how the scriptures address their context and inform their concept of "mission."[16] The curriculum is closer to that of social construction, and makes use of the different pedagogies aforementioned. The setting is non-traditional

15. Some of the common issues that emerge are discrimination, racism, housing problems, and the most discussed issues are problems in the schools attended by their children and immigration laws.

16. Conde-Frazier, *Hispanic Bible Institutes*, 133–35.

and makes education accessible to communities that are not served by the current structures of theological education.

Curriculum takes shape within an institutional structure and serves to cultivate an institutional culture. A culture socializes us into the way things are by defining the framework for worldview. Language, symbols, and norms are a part of how these are communicated. These norms are fashioned by the beliefs of a faith community and these are encapsulated, fostered, and promoted by the knowledge validated by the institution of learning and its policies. These shape the curriculum.

What do we do when the institutional structure expounds a set of values that claim inclusivity but the curriculum does not? To address this question I will draw from the wells of multicultural education. Multicultural education has been an evolving term. Over the years however there is a core set of values and characteristics that has emerged as its definition.

Christine Bennett uses a comprehensive definition that is useful for theological educators: ". . . an approach to teaching and learning that is based upon democratic values and beliefs which affirms cultural pluralism in an interdependent world. It is based on the assumption that the primary goal of public education is to foster the intellectual, social, and personal development of virtually all students to their highest potential."[17] The first part of the definition recognizes the increasing pluralism in the world, while the second part affirms the values of social justice needed in the realm of education in order to promote democratic values. In theological education, social justice is a valued goal. Many schools include it in their mission statements. It is a dimension of the *basileia* of God.

Preparing persons for a variety of ministries in a pluralistic world no longer means equipping minority persons for ministry in their particular communities. If the world is interdependent and multicultural, then everyone needs to have knowledge about each other's histories and theologies as well as the competencies for addressing common issues in a pluralistic context of ministry. These are best presented as a part of the whole, showing the interdependence of the church throughout its history rather than representing a curriculum that is an expression of the fragmentation of our society and of the forces and metanarratives of dominance in the church. To seek such a direction would move theological education toward the goal of "equity, curriculum reform, attention to the process and skills of becoming interculturally competent, and the commitment to combat prejudice and discrimination, especially racism."[18]

17. Bennett, *Comprehensive Multicultural Education*, chapter 1.
18. Ibid., 11.

Equal education has two dimensions: the first is the right to retain one's heritage. The second is the right to extend one's ways of thinking and learning so as to include the views of the culture/theology of others. While these may seem like ideals that one could easily assent to, Linda Gibson points out that cultural ideologies are embedded in our everyday activities. As such, educational ideologies are defined by our social group. She argues that when we work out of the ideology of the dominant social group, we reinforce that group and we define as "deficient" those who do not exhibit competencies or characteristics as prescribed by this ideology.[19] This applies not only to the students we teach but to the criteria we use to select the content we teach. It results in the promotion and expansion of inequality in an educational system that reflects the nature of our dominant system and not the capacities of all students or the contributions of all cultures and segments of the full church. The education we provide meets the needs of the student who fits into our dominant categories and fails to provide quality theological education to other students, while also depriving dominant culture students from becoming interculturally literate.

An ongoing intentional discussion about these matters among faculty is needed in order to move in new directions. However, the conversation around how to diversify curriculum to address multiculturalism too often is met by silence among theological faculty. Those who seek to open up such discussions are usually minority faculty.

Why have we not engaged in these discussions more frequently and fully? Systems theory tells us that institutions gravitate toward homeostasis. The silence of the faculty around such subjects serves as a way of maintaining the status quo while voicing a more progressive rhetoric that is more socially accepted and in line with our theologies and ideals for the church.

To understand at a deeper level what this silence means and does in relationship to multiculturalism, I find Elizabeth Allan's definition helpful: silence is "the failure to acknowledge or articulate the advantages of privilege."[20] Robin Gorsline addresses the failure of the theological academy to speak to issues of racism by presenting an anti-racist or anti-white supremacist theology or ethic. She asks: "Why is it that despite the good intentions of many, and actual attempts by a few, to combat white supremacy within the theological academy and the church, . . . white scholars and ministers find it so difficult to make white supremacy a central concern in our work?"[21] Gorsline defines white supremacy as "the operation of social

19. Gibson, "Teaching as an Encounter," 360–71.
20. Allan, "Bringing Voice," 3.
21. Gorsline, "Shaking the Foundations," 34.

practices by individuals and institutions, including political and economic mechanisms, to achieve and maintain the political, social and economic dominance of white people and the subjugation of peoples of colors."[22] She places white supremacy within a matrix of structures, attitudes, and behaviors that maintain the dominance of those at the top in spite of the challenges offered by both peoples of color and those in alliance with them.[23]

Gorsline claims that maintaining this practice, keeping it in place, does not require the help of anyone, for it is self-perpetuating and not self-correcting.[24] The reason for this is that the practices and mechanisms of this form of dominance are invisible to those who carry them out. It is a social construct whereby knowledge of the world is filtered through the lens of whiteness. As such, it makes up the world of white persons and becomes the norm. As the norm it therefore makes up the world of others as well. One inherits the construct as a process of socialization that teaches one to adapt to and fit into it as one makes meaning of life situations. Talking about this process makes visible its power to structure society, in this case theological institutions. Therefore, white supremacy depends on silence for its self-perpetuation.

A culture of conversation, on the other hand, could lead to white supremacy's demise through organized and consistent efforts. I will discuss how this might take place with curriculum. As teachers we bring our interpretations, perspectives, and intentions to our disciplines. These influence not only what we teach but how we perceive the needs of students. This is part of the curriculum. Multicultural efforts have tended to focus on curriculum by directing attention to changing the readings, the student, and not the teacher. In order to understand the cultural perspectives of the students in our classroom we must first look critically at our own worldview. Educator Terry Ford suggests that we ask ourselves questions such as: "Why do I believe this? What in my experiences has shaped and formed my views?"[25]

This process of critical self-reflection on the part of the teacher is how becoming multicultural begins. Another educator, bell hooks, refers to this as a self-transformation necessary for being able to accept equally the reality interpretations of all in the classroom.[26] Attempting this equality implies a dialectical exchange where we engage in listening, hearing, and trying to see the experiences of others with the purpose of sharing and negotiating

---

22. Ibid., 36.
23. Ibid.
24. Ibid.
25. Ford, *Becoming Multicultural*, 196.
26. hooks, *Talking Back*.

personal meanings so that new social perspectives might be constructed. Asking and answering questions is a part of this dialectic. Ford points out that there are two exchanges taking place at the same time. The first is a self-critical reflection and the second is a social interaction with one another in the classroom where knowledge is shared primarily through conversation.[27]

Pedagogically, different methods of teaching need to take place. The lecture halls are a symbol of the normative means of dictating and transmitting knowledge, where discussion takes place within the parameters of the metanarratives already established. However, connected knowledge, where a teacher engages in authentic conversations with her students and with the possibility of constructing shared perspectives, is what hooks suggests is the challenge to love.[28]

It is this exchange that confronts the ministry of teaching in the church and in theological institutions. It is where the content of our disciplines intersects with the different perspectives garnered from the experiences of our students and the issues and problems of their communities. Here is where a pastoral imagination begins.[29] It is a place of struggle, a critical pedagogy, where we plan for and expect discomfort, tension, and conflict to take place on the way to transformation.

In order to discuss these issues, a climate of personal trust with one another as faculty is necessary. The power differentials among a faculty group may create a perception of lack of safety. This may then create a different level of silence that would hold back the discussions about the consciousness one comes to regarding privilege and the classroom. As a result, the creative directions that could be explored are never realized. Meaningful dialogue requires going past our fears so that we might be empowered to trust and to take risks. Dialogue and trust become a part of the curriculum of the institution when faculty members are able to engage one another in this fashion.

The goal of the discussion of the faculty is to gain perspective regarding the experience of those different than ourselves. Decentering our own worldview could then sustain the focus of seeing difference in relation to our dominant view and its link to oppression.

Allan offers some viable suggestions for constructing the lens and sustaining the focus for faculty and students who are privileged. Some of these are: focused reading, discussions, and writing that promote understanding

27. Ford, *Becoming Multicultural*, 196.

28. Ibid.

29. For further reading on teaching practices and pastoral imagination see Foster et al., *Educating Clergy*.

about the concept of privilege, incorporating self-reflection with a focus on privilege in order to avoid the pitfalls of intellectualizing the discussion, unraveling discourses and epistemologies that can reinforce the denial of privilege through ideologies such as the myth of meritocracy or Cartesian dualism, acquiring grants that will require accountability as a way of developing extrinsic reinforcement, making presentations at conferences or denominational forums about intentional and visible efforts made (to promote intrinsic reinforcement), and focusing on what can be gained by acknowledging and working to dismantle unearned advantages.[30]

Karin A. Case adds theological dimensions to the tasks identified by Allan. Her insights include confessing our complicity in white supremacy and seeking to understand it with the purpose of changing it.[31] This is the work of repentance. Such work must be shared in order to create a new web or matrix of resistance leading to change. Gorsline insists that there must be a critical mass of inter-connected writing and teaching about white supremacy and the silence that permits it to thrive.[32] However, the purpose of this research and professing is to change the thoughts, behaviors, and attitudes that promote it; this is the epistemology and the praxis of such a work. It entails working to change our consciousness—coming to an awareness of the mechanisms of white supremacy, and joining persons of different cultures to think and work creatively for a better future.

What might be the manifestation of change? Moving from resistance to respectful and humble listening to those who have been victimized by white supremacy or learning to know and value other cultures could be such manifestations. Case also highlights the importance of seeking to form "intimate connections" with persons who have been targets of racism, that one might come to knowledge of what that feels like. This takes us to an epistemology of connected knowing, where not only the cognitive dimensions are engaged, but where we also gain emotional knowledge of the harms of racism.[33]

In order to maintain a momentum toward change, accountability is necessary because most of us experience both privilege and disadvantage in different aspects of our lives, which causes such experiences to blur and then hides the presence of privilege from our consciousness and discourse. As a female minority professor, I could become more conscious and versed in my understanding of disadvantage. However, by virtue of being

---

30. Allan, "Bringing Voice," 10.

31. Case, "Claiming White Social Location," 68.

32. Gorsline, "Shaking the Foundations," 56.

33. Case, "Claiming White Social Location," 79.

a professor, I realize that I have the power in the classroom and, therefore, power to choose the type of struggle I want to engage. The power to choose is a privilege which, if not made visible, can implicate me in the oppression of others. In like fashion, a white female professor may be able to identify and speak to gender discrimination while being unable to see herself as a participant in the discrimination of others through how she uses her white privilege to create the syllabus and classroom environment. Discussion that is accompanied by accountability helps us grow beyond our blind spots of privilege.[34]

The dynamics of privilege and disadvantage are experienced differently by minority faculty. I will explain how this experience may also work towards our own complicity in the compact of silence. Our educational process involved socializing us into appropriating and functioning within the socially correct knowledge of the privileged group. Some of us had mentors at some point of our lives or support communities that kept us accountable throughout this educational process and who taught us to critique this knowledge. If we found the space in our doctoral program and the courage in ourselves, we may have sought an intercultural hermeneutic that gave us the accepted tools for offering a critique of the socially correct paradigms of knowledge.

Securing a position in a faculty has given us a new level of privilege. We must reflect on what this privilege means: how it influences our perspectives, our classrooms and our decisions at institutional levels. We possess the knowledge of being a minority and the insights of survival and suffering at the margins alongside the socially accepted knowledge. This "bilingualism" characterizes our professional identity. We also live two realities: the reality of privilege in the institution and the reality of the continued disadvantage of our identity in society. At times, the latter means that dominant cultural students may discriminate against us, albeit in subtle and passive-aggressive ways, because we have power in the classroom. In the midst of these double realities, as we come to understand the reach and limits of our influence due to our privilege, we too must make choices between solidarity with the dominant social group of which we have become a part or an interactive dialogue among faculty and between faculty, administration, and students that facilitates the breaking of the silence, and the movement toward equality of all persons in the educational system.

Silence fosters a language of evasion, whereas breaking out of silence begins when we formulate a voiced reflection.[35] We must find the words to

---

34. For further discussion see Wildman and Davis, "Language and Silence," 50–60.

35. The work of Ruth Frankenberg shows that we evade by "partial description,

describe our experience of privilege and disadvantage so that we might become committed to the practice of voiced reflection and emancipatory praxis rather than the practice of the compact of silence already present in theological education. It is this practice of voiced reflection that will provide a vocabulary for breaking the silence regarding the issues of privilege.

As we return to the pedagogy of performance mentioned above, we realize that, for students to find themselves in a teaching/learning community that extends and renews its own traditions of theological education, we must engage with students in discussions that challenge the common assumptions we bring to our teaching in light of diversity. This is an example of a pedagogy of empowerment that would become a dimension for the revitalization of congregations. As students, faculty, and administration live out a pedagogical practice that creates an ethic of justice, we acculturate students in the practices of justice.

Religious educator John Westerhoff speaks of enculturation as a way for a community of faith to represent its systematic and intentional efforts to shape the knowledge, skills, and attitudes of its members. In the process, both teachers and students are active respondents.[36] Our ways of teaching and reflecting, and of including and excluding content, become the hidden curriculum. The ethos that this hidden curriculum may reinforce is empowerment for social justice, or possibly a contradiction to our well-intentioned instruction in the lecture halls and seminars. When this is the case, we teach for the maintenance of the status quo, silencing an action-reflection dialectic that could be disempowering not only to students but to the contexts of ministry they will be going to, as it creates habits and competencies for silence.

The silencing of a conscientization process for faculty results in the silencing of our students and potentially of the faith communities and other contexts of ministry that the students go to. Silence of this nature becomes formational for a praxis and cycle of disempowerment. On the other hand, to create a climate for reflection about privilege and disadvantage, and a dialectical action for equal education at institutions where we teach, is to learn with one another, in humility, the human limitations and strengths for a praxis of empowerment toward a more just society. This enculturation in turn becomes a formational dimension in the theological educational experience of our students, with the potential for becoming embedded in their

---

euphemism, and self-contradiction. See Frankenberg, *White Women, Race Matters,* 156–57.

36. Westerhoff, *Will Our Children Have Faith?,* 49, 80.

own commitments and style of leadership. We will have created a culture that strives towards becoming interculturally competent.

8

Teaching Disruptively

Pedagogical Strategies to Teach Cultural Diversity and Race

BOYUNG LEE

FROM A SPECIFIC TEACHING CONTEXT

WHERE RELIGION MEETS THE world! Click the webpage of the Graduate Theological Union, where I serve as a core doctoral faculty member, and the above tagline immediately catches one's attention. My school, Pacific School of Religion, is a member of the Graduate Theological Union, which is the largest theological consortium in North America. Commonly known as the GTU, its reputation for diversity is reflected in its composition of five mainline Protestant seminaries, three separate Catholic schools affiliated with different religious orders, and eleven academic centers inclusive of Greek Orthodox, Buddhist, Islamic, and Jewish studies. This diversity is also reflected in my classroom, where it is not uncommon to have students from various religious affiliations and denominations. For example, one year my Introduction to Christian Education class had students from approximately twenty different religious affiliations: most major mainline denominations, several different evangelical non-denominational churches, various New Thought and emerging churches, diverse branches of Paganism, different Catholic orders and dioceses, and one Buddhist tradition.

Although the students come from such diverse religious and denominational backgrounds, the majority of them come from white middle-class contexts. Almost all of them identify their worldviews as liberal or radical, coupled with a professed commitment to social justice work. However, from my Asian American point of view, the students' approaches to social justice, especially around the issue of race, are White American centered. Students vocalize a willingness to invite others to their privileged center, but the inviters always control the forum. In this context I constantly wrestle with two major tasks: 1) helping students to see the pitfalls of their antiracist gestures based on white privilege; and 2) educating them to become agents for a culturally diverse and racially just world.

Classes in which I pursue these two tasks can be considered disruptive at times because conflicts often erupt which may require my intervention. They also may be disruptive considering that I design my classes to intentionally disrupt students' worldviews. Furthermore, interactions in my classes may not flow smoothly or they may be methodologically resisted. Yet I have learned, as have other educators who teach from an antiracist and social justice perspective, that resistance, confusion, and disruption are necessary reactions to social justice pedagogy.[1] In the following sections, I would like to share some of the practical pedagogical principles and strategies I employ in my teaching to disrupt.

PEDAGOGICAL PRINCIPLES FOR DISRUPTIVE TEACHING

Robert Kegan, a constructive developmental psychologist and educator, suggests that through an ongoing (evolutionary in Kegan's term) interaction with others and with our physical/cognitive/cultural environments, human beings develop an authentic sense of who they are and construct their truth accordingly.[2] Kegan suggests a three-way meaning-making process: Confirmation, Contradiction and Continuity.[3] "Confirmation" occurs when a particular environment corresponds and supports peoples' already existing meaning-making systems. When new experiences, events, and opinions conflict with these existing worldviews, people are challenged to transform their current meaning-making system. Kegan calls this "contradiction." When people face contradictory events and contexts, they either emotion-

1. hooks, *Teaching to Transgress,* 39.
2. Kegan, *The Evolving Self.*
3. Ibid., 113–32.

ally isolate themselves to maintain their existing framework, a process which Kegan deems unhealthy, or they incorporate new meaning through conjoining both "old" and "new" realities. Kegan labels this process of incorporation "continuity." People have a more mature sense of who they are once they achieve this incorporation, which is often called "transformation."

This three-fold dynamic provides significant pedagogical insights for theological education for a culturally diverse and racially just world. Antiracist pedagogy, or more broadly social justice pedagogy, aims at transformation of the person—the agent working to build a just world. Bearing that in mind, antiracist educators hope that students will live a just life and move beyond mere knowledge acquisition concerning social justice issues. I have learned from my own experiences that an antiracist, or social justice, pedagogy that transforms people often requires Kegan's 3C processes: Confirmation, Contradition and Continuity. I have developed these three categories into the following eleven pedagogical principles and practices.

CONTINUITY

In Kegan's dynamics of continuity, the stage of transformation, students integrate their old and new worldviews and cultivate a new meaning-making system. In a theological class designed to build a culturally diverse and racially just world, students, personally and pastorally, commit to building a culturally diverse and racially just world and to living antiracist lives. For such transformation, I suggest the following three principles.

Principle 1: Teach Race as an Integral Part of Your Class Subject

In the syllabi of many of my colleagues who work toward racial justice, I have observed that racism and other social justice issues are only included as separate units. Although having a unit or two is much better than nothing at all, such an approach gives the implicit lesson to students that race and social justice issues are not central to theology. They are subjects that students can study, that is, if they want to. Many faculty members from the dominant culture who operate out of tokenism misuse this approach. If a similar approach is taken by racial and ethnic minority faculty members, those students, who resist to engage race itself, often misunderstand as if professors are imposing their own agenda on students.

As many contemporary theologians such as liberation, contextual, feminist, and postcolonial theologians have proven, "all theologies are contextual."[4] Theologies as contextual disciplines invite people to be compassionate Christians and work for justice. The Bible, Christian doctrines, and Christian practices are products of their own contexts, and therefore, critically examining their culturally and racially biased contexts is a just and appropriate way of teaching them. Having discrete units on race and social justice issues would be effective only when those subjects are addressed as an integral part of the class throughout the semester. Whenever I argue for this first principle, some of my colleagues complain that there are not enough textbooks in their theological disciplines that deal with race matters. For people like my colleagues, I suggest the following two pedagogical principles.

Principle 2: Expand Your Boundaries of Textbooks[5]

It is only a recent phenomenon that racial ethnic minority theologians' published works are readily available. However, situations vary depending on theological disciplines. For example, in the field of religious education, except for a handful of excellent books by African American colleagues, there are not many religious education books that reference worldviews other than those of white middle-class heterosexuals. This is not because there are no non-white religious educators who work out of their own racial and cultural contexts, but, rather, there is a lack of awareness of that reality in some religious education venues, particularly in market-driven publishing worlds.

As there are so few education textbooks written about non-white religious settings, my task as a teacher is to complement, pragmatically, traditional textbooks' templates. In my Introduction to Christian Education course, for example, I emphasize critical analysis of students' own social-cultural locations and assumptions. Students are asked to produce reading reflections, short papers, research papers, curriculum design, and other assignments that elicit critical analyses of students' own culture and ministry contexts. Without knowing one's own social-cultural assumptions and worldviews, one can easily (mis)appropriate others' cultures and experiences.

Concurrently throughout the semester, students also work in small groups on shared projects that focus on learning and teaching a religious tradition other than their own. Foci have included Greek Orthodox, African

---

4. De La Torre and Floyd-Thomas, eds., *Beyond the Pale*, xxiii.

5. This principle is an excerpt from my own article, "Broadening the Boundary of 'Textbooks' for Intercultural Communication in Religious Education."

American, Asian American, Hispanic, and Queer approaches to Christian religious education. In other words, through small group work students are expected to learn about the religious education of an *other*; they are to think out loud about some tradition whose rich and long-lived wisdom is not widely available in printed form in the North American religious education field. After studying the traditions and practices of religious education of a different cultural group for a semester through participatory observation (including conversations with community members and reviewing available literature), each group presents what they have learned to the class.

However, since the class challenges students to engage race and antiracism as an integral part of the class throughout the semester, it is unsurprising that there is struggle with or resistance to this methodology. Genuinely learning about and from the *other* requires my students to become aware of their own biases and assumptions, which can be a humbling experience. Notwithstanding this, every year I witness group presentations that include "coming out" stories, including students' realizations of their own privileges and racism, intentional and unintentional ignorance of other traditions, and students' awareness of their resistance to genuine conversations with their neighbors. Frequently, students list the small group work as the best learning experience of the class in their course evaluation. If my students have to learn about a particular cultural group's approach to religious education only through a few available books, articles, and my lectures, they could easily become the privileged beneficiaries of theological tokenism.

I do not intend to say that my students are completely transformed by my class and their small group work within a semester. However, they at least learn that there are great traditions with which they need to be in conversation and from which they can learn. More importantly, I hope that they learn the critical necessity of antiracism work for their ministry and how to pursue it. Critical analysis of one's own contexts and assumptions, and learning about and from others, are only some of the ways to expand the boundaries of our traditional concept of textbooks. Finding appropriate ways to expand your "textbooks" will require a thorough needs assessment of your students and local resources in your area, and I will address this subject in *Principle 5*.

Principle 3: Pay Attention to Your Implicit Curriculum

Recently I visited an Asian theological school that has only one woman on its faculty. Unlike my expectation that the woman faculty would be the most loved and respected teacher by students, as she might practice feminist pedagogy in a male dominant Asian theological school, students secretly complained to me that in fact she was the most patriarchal and authoritarian teacher. Some students even said that if being feminist means becoming such an authoritarian teacher, they do not want to be feminist. There must be justifiable reasons for her reputation. Whether her characterization is true or not, her students' evaluations on her pedagogy challenge us to think of our own pedagogical practices: Whether our explicit and implicit curricula resonate with each other.

In his book *Educational Imagination*, Elliott W. Eisner, a noted curriculum theorist, introduces broadened concepts of curriculum and offers a comprehensive definition of curriculum. Discussing the subject of curriculum in public educational contexts, Eisner says that each school offers students three different curricula: the explicit curriculum is the one that is the actual content, consciously and intentionally presented as the teachings of the school; the implicit curriculum is the one that, through the school's environment, includes the way teachers teach and interact with students; and the null curriculum are those ideas and subjects in educational programs that are withheld from students.[6] By leaving out options and alternatives, the school narrows students' perspectives and the range of their thoughts and action. Thus the explicit curriculum, which is often regarded as the entire curriculum, is only one facet of teaching. In fact, Eisner points out that the implicit and the null curricula might have more influence over students than does the explicit curriculum.[7]

Beneath the complaint of the students about their only woman professor is a complaint signifying the discrepancy between her explicit and implicit curriculum. She may be an excellent scholar of feminist theology, however, in her pedagogical practices, she seems to contradict feminist pedagogical principles: facilitating democratic and liberating classroom process, respecting students' experiences and stories as much as textbooks, generating knowledge through a communal process, etc.[8] As Eisner states, no matter how liberating our explicit curriculum—the content of our teaching—is, if our implicit curriculum—the way we teach—is not liberating, our teaching for justice is not as effective as hoped.

Then what are the good antiracist pedagogical practices that theological educators need to embody so that students learn not only from our explicit teachings, but also from the ways we teach? First we need to understand the nature of antiracist and social justice pedagogy. Antiracist and

6. Eisner, *The Educational Imagination*, 378.
7. Ibid.
8. Shrewsbury, "What is Feminist Pedagogy?," 6.

social justice pedagogy tries to build an egalitarian society in which no one is discriminated against on the basis of race and any other hierarchical and discriminatory categories. Next, the classroom should also be egalitarian. In the classroom, the teacher is not only an expert of knowledge who teaches, but also a learner who has the humility to learn from students, who bring with them rich wisdom and different life experiences. Paulo Freire lists the following characteristics of non-egalitarian classrooms,[9] and challenges us to reflect on our own teaching practices:

a) the teacher teaches and the students are taught;

b) the teacher knows everything and the students know nothing;

c) the teacher thinks and the students are thought about;

d) the teacher talks and the students listen—meekly;

e) the teacher disciplines and the students are disciplined;

f) the teacher chooses and enforces his/her choice, and the students comply;

g) the teacher acts and the students have the illusion of acting through the action of the teacher;

h) the teacher chooses the program content, and the students (who were not consulted) adapt to it;

i) the teacher confuses the authority of knowledge with his or her own professional authority that she or he sets in opposition to the freedom of the students; and

j) the teacher is the Subject of the learning process while the students are mere objects.

Freire names the above pedagogical characteristics as "banking education," which considers humans as adaptable and manageable beings. Teachers who use the banking education model treat students as if they are the passive recipients of knowledge deposited by teachers. Such knowledge often has nothing to do with the pressing issues and situations that students wrestle with in their lives and communities. He warns, "The more students work at storing the deposits entrusted to them, the less they develop the critical consciousness which would result from their intervention in the world as transformers of that world."[10] In other words, no matter how hard we work to bring antiracist and social justice commitments to our teaching, if our pedagogy looks more like the above descriptions of a non-egalitarian

9. Freire, *Pedagogy of the Oppressed*, 73.
10. Ibid.

class, we are basically teaching our students not to be antiracists and not to take social justice commitments seriously; this is the (mis)power of implicit curriculum.

Principle 4: Create a Physical Environment that Embodies Antiracist and Justice Pedagogy

Every spring I teach Introduction to Christian Education as a required course for the Master of Divinity degree. The school registrar assigns a sizeable classroom capable of holding thirty to forty students. The room typically has forty-plus desks and chairs lined up facing a white board with a tall podium in front of it. Before each class my teaching assistants and I spend a chunk of time rearranging the room, i.e., arranging the chairs and desks into a big circle and removing the podium from the room. I do this tedious work every week to embody some of my pedagogical assumptions, namely: 1) the professor is not the only teacher from whom class members receive new information for I also am looking for new insights from students; 2) students are practice teachers with one another and with me; and 3) more precisely, we not only study the subject matter through written texts, but also through "living texts" such as students' wisdom, insights, life experiences, cultural backgrounds, and critical analysis. Thus, I practically highlight the importance of social justice and democratic pedagogy in that students' own reflections, reading, speaking, and writing about their ministerial contexts are integral to our pursuits.

Let us imagine for a moment that after I share such assumptions, I do not embody them in our learning environment. Although I present myself as a non-authoritarian teacher who respects students' opinions, imagine if students are not allowed to speak in the class; that there are no conversation opportunities for students. My students would think that the social justice pedagogy I promote is just talk. Students may be encouraged to participate in class discussions and activities, but if the physical environment of the classroom hinders it, the social justice pedagogy is less effective. Students will not trust what I say about antiracism and social justice because I do not practice them in my own teaching. When goals, pedagogy, and physical environment are compatible with one another, students better understand social justice issues so that good ideas and good experiences, theory and praxis, congeal.

CONFIRMATION

Kegan's dynamic of confirmation suggests that it is critical for educators to meet their students where they are and to acknowledge their current meaning-making system. This means that in antiracist and social justice classrooms, it is important to be sensitive to and patient with people's dis-ease and resistance to the topics of race and antiracism work. If educators rush to contradiction, emphasizing deconstruction of their racist framework of mind without affirmation and analysis, many students will perceive the educational event itself as criticism of their own being and culture. To support the process of confirmation, I suggest the following principles.

Principle 5: Do Your Needs Assessment

Kegan's dynamic of confirmation is a principle that is affirmed by most adult education scholars.[11] For example, Jane Vella, a prominent adult education scholar and activist, provides twelve principles for adult learning. Among those principles, she lists needs assessment as the first principle.[12] However, unlike common perceptions that needs assessment is knowing what our students want to know, she defines it as "participation of the learners in naming what is to be learned."[13]

Assessing students' needs is often confused with assessing what they want. Needs assessment can include what students want to learn, but what they want is not necessarily the same as what they need to learn. Often, in antiracist classrooms, we are confronted by students who do not want to engage the race issue at all. Some confrontations occur because of the dis-ease that the subject matter creates, and others because some students do not want to give up their privilege and comfortable status quo. Still others acknowledge its importance, but do not consider antiracist work as relevant for their contexts. For these students, antiracism and social justice work is not what they want to learn, but from a teacher's perspective, it is what they really need to learn. Therefore figuring out effective and appropriate ways of teaching the subject is crucial for the success of antiracism and social justice pedagogies. This process of discernment is what Vella defines as needs assessment.

11. Gupta et al., *A Practical Guide to Needs Assessment*, 13.

12. Vella, *Learning to Listen, Learning to Teach*. Vella's twelve principles are: Needs assessment; Safety; Sound relationship; Sequence; Praxis; Respect for learners as decision makers; Learning with ideas, feelings, and actions; Immediacy; Clear roles and role development; Teamwork; Engagement; and Accountability.

13. Ibid., 4.

According to Vella, needs assessment is specifically listening to the voices of both teachers and learners: "adult learners must take responsibility to explain their context; the teacher must take responsibility to contact learners in every way possible, see them at work if possible, and be clear about what she can offer them."[14] From the teachers' perspectives, this means that teachers listen deeply to students' stories and teach from where they are. In this sense, it is understandable why Vella defines needs assessment as the "participation of the learners in naming what is to be learned."

Needs assessment as deep listening is also the key pedagogical method of Paulo Freire. Freire, when he was a beginner teacher, tried to teach people how to read using traditional literacy methods, i.e., equipping people with the skill of literacy in a non-reflective, non-conscientizing way such as making them memorize alphabets; but he was not successful.[15] Through his failure, Freire realized that learning to read and write in a way that was separated from people's reality would not work. He was convinced that learning "must lead to a critical comprehension of reality."[16] His new literacy program was based on conscientization and on making a connection between learners' situations and the subject of learning. With this new program, he was able to teach 300 illiterate sugarcane farm workers to read in forty-five days.

Freire's literacy education program consists of four phases.[17] The first phase is a deep listening period—a needs assessment time. This was the phase before the official start of the literacy education program, during which Freire and his team spent extensive periods of time in the village where their learners lived. Participating in informal conversations with residents, observing their cultures, and listening to their life stories, the team identified the vocabularies of the communities: the words and themes that the people were most emotionally attached to and repeatedly used. Later those words and themes were presented in symbolic ways, e.g., pictures, to those villagers so that they could read their own realities by analyzing the elements of the scenes. Typically each scene portrayed conflicts found within the community for people to recognize, analyze, and attempt to resolve as a group. The group was then asked why things were that way, and that naturally led them to critically analyze their realities in the larger social contexts. Only in the last phase were the learners presented discovery cards, the learning cards that contained the researched vocabularies from the first phase.

14. Ibid., 5.

15. Gadoti, *Reading Paulo Freire*, 7.

16. Freire, *The Politics of Education*, 24.

17. Freire, *Education for Critical Consciousness*, 37–51.

The above Freirian approach to literacy education demonstrates the importance and methods of needs assessment. Spending time with our students through formal and informal contacts, talking with them in a school cafeteria, learning about their life circumstances, identifying their fluency in antiracism and social justice work, assessing their learning styles, listening to their pressing issues and concerns, worshiping and praying with them, and so on are all possible ways of assessing their needs. Through these contacts, we can identify why certain students are resistant to antiracist pedagogy and what will be the most appropriate ways and intensities to teach them. However, the reality of North American theological faculty life, especially for racial and ethnic minority professors, makes it difficult for us to spend as much time as we would like with our students. Therefore, I suggest that needs assessment be incorporated as a part of the class. Moreover, even if we do the initial needs assessment through formal and informal contacts with our students, it is important for us to assess our students' needs on a regular basis during the course. The ongoing needs assessment allows teachers to adjust their curriculum according to the changing situations of the class.

As incorporated ways to assess students' needs, I suggest the following methods adopted from Jane Vella.[18] All of them should be done at the beginning of the semester.

- Shared Survey: In the beginning of the semester when the teacher has a full list of the registered students in the class, via email the teacher asks a set of three or four questions that are later forwarded to the entire class. In a class that deals with race and social justice issues, you can ask students to describe 1) their involvement in antiracism work; 2) their hopes for learning after reading the syllabus; and 3) a recent situation where they designed or taught issues related to antiracism.

- Learning Biography: In the early part of the semester invite your students to reflect on their best learning experiences in antiracist and social justice work, particularly experiences that helped them to move in a new direction.

- Vision Building: Invite your students to describe what their lives will look like when they have learned antiracism and social justice work in the class. Vella emphasizes that, at this point, it is important for teachers to share how they are engaging their commitment in their own lives.

18. Vella, *Learning to Listen, Learning to Teach*, 247–49.

Principle 6: Assess Needs and Create a Safe Learning Community through a Liturgical Rhythm

Occasionally, I am visited by students who claim that they do not feel safe in my or another colleague's class and, therefore, they cannot learn. Whenever I hear such cries for help, I hear two different things. Some students mean that they do not feel physically or psychologically safe due to the presence of a fellow student in the class, due to past traumatic memories triggered by something in the class, or due to the authoritarian teacher. Other students mean that the class is academically too challenging for them and thus they feel left behind and unsafe. Their cries or complaints appear to be two very different things, however, Vella says that they are closely related to each other.[19] The principle of safety enables the teacher to create an inviting setting for learners. People are not only willing to learn but are eager to learn when they feel safe. Although safety does not reduce or take away difficulties and challenges involved in learning, it supports learners' efforts to stay.[20] In others words, safety and creation of a learning community are in a reciprocal relationship. Vella particularly emphasizes the importance of creating a safe learning community if the learning experience has transformation as a part of its intentionality; i.e., race and social justice issues.[21]

There are many ways to create a safe learning community. Firstly, I strongly emphasize paying attention to the implicit curriculum of your class and especially your teaching style as described above in *Principle 3*. Secondly, I suggest devotional rituals led by the professor and students. In a class that integrates antiracism and social justice issues, two very difficult subjects, it is critical for teachers to set a tone that does not blame certain groups for every wrongdoing or describe others only as victims. Even if there is some truth to such claims, dichotomized blaming does not help students to have authentic and open conversations. Opening the class with a devotion can help to set the tone. Moreover, unlike other typical graduate schools, theological schools have many second or third career students who come to us after giving up much better paid jobs, and some of them even sell their homes for their educational expenses. Although they are not seeking their professor's affirmation, when it happens, their motivation for learning is increased. As Vella says, the feeling of safety emanates from the trust that students have in their teachers and colleagues, and thus in the learning

---

19. Ibid., 71–84.
20. Ibid., 8.
21. Ibid., 4.

process.[22] Building trust without affirming their journey, which sometimes involves personal and familiar sacrifices, is not easy, yet I personally find that providing such affirmation in a worshiping context is powerful.

Typically, I lead the first devotion of the class, in which I share stories from my personal journey as a theologian and teacher that are related to the subject matter of the class. Since race and social justice issues are integrated into every class I teach, my sharing is specifically about my journey as a postcolonial feminist religious educator. During the first devotion, I also invite students to name, briefly, their experiences and goals in the class by asking: "What is your one-word image of religious education that you experienced?" "What is your one-word goal that you want to achieve after you take the class?" These are needs assessment questions that invite students to name their own learning, as Freire and Vella emphasized. Student sharing is recorded and I try to frequently refer back to the comments throughout the semester (Vella's Principles # 4: Sequence and Reinforcement). In a devotional context, the class also creates a class covenant including principles such as keeping confidentiality, respecting introverts and ESL students, acknowledging humans' physical needs, etc. Obviously, the goal of creating the covenant is to help the class to create a safe learning community.

Subsequent opening devotions are led by an individual or group of students. Devotion leadership, which should take no more than ten minutes, is a course requirement. Students can be creative in terms of the format and style of their devotion. The only two instructions that I provide are 1) the devotion should reflect students' own contexts—racial, cultural, social, and religious; and 2) their devotion should make a connection to the subject of the day that requires students to have read and critically reflected in advance on course materials for the day. Through their devotional rituals, I assess their past and current experiences that influence their learning and their level of understanding of that week's readings and subject matter.

Principle 7: Multiple Intelligences are Kith and Kin to Antiracist and Social Justice Pedagogy

Howard Gardner's theory of multiple intelligences[23] is no longer new for theological educators. Many of us make intentional efforts to utilize different intelligences in our classes. Notwithstanding that, I would like to reiterate

---

22. Ibid., 9.

23. Gardner, *Frames of Mind*. His nine intelligences are linguistic, logical-mathematical, spatial, bodily-kinesthetic, musical, interpersonal, intrapersonal, naturalistic, and existential intelligences.

their importance in antiracist and social justice pedagogy, not just because using them is a good pedagogical practice, but because it is a matter of justice. Among nine intelligences that Gardner proposes, *linguistic* intelligence and *logical-mathematical* intelligence have dominated the traditional pedagogy of western societies.[24] The problem here is that the standards for excellent linguistic and logical-mathematical intelligences are closely tied to race and class in Western society and its education. For example, the language people use in everyday conversations both reflects and shapes the assumptions of a certain social group, i.e., white middle and upper class heterosexual male.[25]

According to Basil Bernstein, a prominent British linguist and sociologist of education, to be successful in a class-based society like the U.K. or the U.S. means that one is able to use what Bernstein calls the restricted or elaborated language code.[26] As an educator, he was interested in finding reasons for the relatively poor performance of working-class students in language-based subjects compared to their counterparts from middle and upper-middle classes. Among many reasons, he concluded that, in working-class families, people use mostly restricted language code, but at school elaborated code is taught as the norm, a communication style to which working-class people lack access. In other words, through education, western societies have promoted the ideology of a particular group as the objective norm, and thus have been able to keep the status quo. Therefore, in antiracist and social justice pedagogy, it is inevitable for teachers to intentionally use different intelligences.

Principle 8: Help Students to Learn Through Praxis

Racism, antiracism, and social justice are not subjects that one can learn through mastering knowledge. Subject fluency requires each participant's commitment, involvement and ongoing efforts toward the transformation of the society. Therefore, teaching a class that integrates antiracism and social justice in classroom contexts alone has its limits. There needs to be a way for students to engage in antiracist and social justice work or projects, and I specifically recommend small group projects.

---

24 Campbell, "Multiple Intelligences in the Classroom," *In Context*, 12.

25 Littlejohn and Foss, *Theories of Human Communication*, 178.

26. Bernstein, *Class, Codes and Control*. Elaborated code is a communication style that is complete and full of detail. Restricted code is shorter and condensed, and requires background information and prior knowledge.

One key characteristic for almost every racial and ethnic community in North America is the sense of community.[27] Traditionally, in these communities, learning and teaching were done in communal contexts. For example, George DeVos, who has compared American and Japanese science classroom processes, reports specific cultural differences of individualistic and communal education.[28] In an American class, the teacher gives assignments and elicits divergent ideas and proposals, but does not try to arrive at a conclusion or consensus. There are implicit understandings and expectations that individuals may have diverse thoughts about what is observed. In a Japanese classroom the situation is almost reversed: the class starts with children's various views and most of the class time is taken up with students' discussing or changing their position. The teacher gradually focuses upon the major issues involved in understanding the subject, asking questions until the students form a consensus about the subject or about the meaning of what they have observed. In sum, even in a science class, American students learn that the central goal of their education is the development of individual autonomy in thoughts and actions, but Japanese students learn the centrality of community with common ideas. In individualistic American classrooms, an educated individual gains knowledge as private property and in communal Japanese classrooms knowledge is gained as the community's.[29] Therefore, beyond the fact that humans are communal beings, we as teachers need to teach our subjects, particularly race and social justice, in a way that respects racial and ethnic community's communal culture. We need to help our students learn how knowledge can and should be generated through a communal process.

Through engaging a small group praxis project, our students can learn ways to implement race and social justice issues in their own pastoral contexts concurrently. Instead of solely learning theories and praxis in a classroom setting, or learning theories in class and later practicing what they learn in their own contexts, students engaged in a small group project can immediately apply what they learn in their presentation to their classmates.

CONTRADICTION

Kegan's dynamic of contradiction suggests that educators need to create moments for students to critically reflect on their current meaning-making systems. In antiracist and social justice education, challenging students to

27. Hui and Trandis, "Individualism-Collectivism," 225–48.
28. DeVos, "Dimensions of the Self," 149–50.
29. Watt, *Individualism and Educational Theory*, 138.

revisit ideological foundations of their current views of race is critical. For this I propose the following two principles; one is on the institutional level and the other is on the faculty teaching practice level.

Principle 9: Ask "Why Questions" Regarding Your School's and Your Own Curricula

Antiracist and social justice education in theological schools cannot be achieved by one concerned faculty member's teaching. Without changing the entire institution's ways of operating and curriculum assumptions, our work is only partially done. There are three major schools of thought in the field of curriculum studies: traditionalist, conceptual-empiricists or re-visionist, and re-conceptualists.[30]

Traditionalism and conceptual-empiricism are dominant approaches to current education. These approaches endorse that education and knowledge are value-free and objective. Traditionalists believe that the purpose of education is to deliver good knowledge to the coming generations, and hence once students master certain level of knowledge, the goal is achieved. In the traditionalist approach to curriculum design, there is no room for students' experiences and ideas. Educational institutions and experts decide everything. The conceptual-empiricists or revisionists question how to deliver that knowledge appropriately to students. They integrate the research of psychology and other disciplines to determine how certain age groups of students learn better. Utilizing developmental psychology, they organize certain activities to help students to learn according to their age capacity. However, students' experiences still do not find a home here. The purpose of considering other disciplines is to produce generalized results for all, and thus, educators can predict the effects of education.[31]

Unlike these two schools, re-conceptualists believe that education often reflects the social structure and ideologies of the dominant groups, and thus they ask "why questions" in each stage of curriculum development. They believe that education that does not ask (whether intentionally or unintentionally), "Who is being benefited and who is being left out in our current system?" becomes the main tool of status quo maintenance. I believe that it is crucial for marginalized communities to ask "why questions" as well as "what and how questions" of our educational system. Among these three schools, it is obvious that antiracist and social justice pedagogy is in sync with the re-conceptualists.

30. Giroux, *Curriculum and Instruction*.

31. Ibid., 14.

So, on an institutional level, how can theological educators ask the "why questions" in our curriculum? Pacific School of Religion, where I teach, requires every faculty who teaches required courses to submit their syllabus to the entire faculty for discussion and approval. The school's stated mission is "serving God by equipping historic and emerging faith communities for ministries of compassion and justice in a changing world."[32] One of the key commitments of the school in achieving this purpose is through advancing racial justice. For this to happen, the school voluntarily requested to be audited for institutional racism, and the students, the staff, and the faculty have been engaging in antiracism work for a long time. As a part of their antiracist work, the faculty agreed that our individual courses should also embody the school's commitments, which resulted in this decision for syllabus review. When the faculty reviews each other's syllabus, we particularly pay attention to how antiracism work is done in the class and whether the scholarship of racial and ethnic theologians is respected, particularly in the choice of textbooks and other reading materials. In regard to this practice, some colleagues from other theological schools wonder if this is a violation of academic freedom. It may be, but the faculty of PSR believes that advancing racial justice work cannot be done on an individual level, and we all need each other as checks and balances for the communal work. This type of practice is only possible when deep trust exists among the faculty. Therefore, each theological school will need to figure out together the best practices for antiracism work in their school's context.

Principle 10: Practice Problem-Posing Teaching Methods

As a concrete teaching method for antiracist and social justice pedagogy, I find Paulo Freire's problem-posing method used in his literacy education program extremely insightful. As briefly described in *Principle 5*, in Brazilian literacy education, Freire used picture cards that portrayed the reality of the learners; particularly conflicts in the community. Then, learners were asked to read the reality by asking "why questions." Through this process, the learners were able to analyze their reality in connection to the larger systematic issues in their society. This process of conscientization eventually led people to be the agents of the change that they wanted to see.

Based on the needs of the students we assess, antiracist teachers need to identify a medium through which we can help students read the reality of racism in which they themselves consciously and unconsciously participate.

---

32. The direction statement of Pacific School of Religion. http://www.psr.edu/direction-statement.

Being mindful of utilizing multiple intelligences will help us to find a creative medium. That medium can also be lecture. Many people seem to misunderstand that if they are committed to non-banking education, they should not lecture any more. However, as long as your lecture engages students' realities, Freire states that it can be a good problem-posing method.

> We have to recognize that not all kinds of lecturing is banking education. You can still be very critical while lecturing . . . The question is not banking lectures or no lectures, because traditional teachers will make reality opaque whether they lecture or lead discussions. A liberating teacher will illuminate reality even if he or she lectures. The question is the content and dynamism of the lecture, the approach to the object to be known. Does it critically re-orient students to society? Does it animate their critical thinking or not?[33]

The goal of antiracist pedagogy is not to persuade our students through our opinions and thoughts, but, rather, to transform reality through listening and being influenced by others, and changing ourselves. Both our students and we can be agents of transformation for each other through genuinely listening to each other and reflecting and processing with each other.

Principle 11: Think about Evaluation before You Teach and Use Focus Groups to Qualitatively Evaluate Your Class

When we think about evaluation, we typically consider it as the last thing that happens in teaching or something that we do after we finish teaching. However, in antiracist and social justice pedagogy, I suggest that we think of it even before we teach. Evaluation should be thought of alongside needs assessment. Based on our needs assessment, we set and adjust our goals of teaching. Our needs assessment provides a picture of where our students are, what they need to know, and how. Next, we should think about how to assess their learning and transformation. The shared survey, learning biography, and vision building statement that were introduced in *Principle 5* can be redistributed to each student. Students then can be asked to provide some sense of how they would evaluate their own learnings based on the statements they created in the beginning of the class.

In antiracist and social justice pedagogy, our evaluation should also consider the different needs of our diverse student populations. What typical white middle-class students need is probably not the same as what our

---

33. Shor and Freire, *A Pedagogy for Liberation*, 40.

racial/ethnic students need. For this, I suggest using focus groups.[34] If possible and in order to get a balanced evaluation, having three different groups will be ideal: a white student group, a racial/ethnic student group, and a mixed one. Using open questions from the needs assessment, a group of about three to eight students, depending on the size of the class, can meet for about an hour. To create an honest conversational environment, it might be better if a TA or a student facilitates the group. If possible, videotaping the conversations for a later review by the professor would be ideal.

Another method that I find effective is using Survey Monkey to send a few open-ended questions to every student in the class. Because students can choose to be anonymous, some students may feel that they can be truly honest about themselves, their own learning experiences, their classmates, and the professor. Including questions about the class's implicit and null curricula will provide a helpful resource for the professor to use to reflect on his or her teaching practices and to revise the class for the future. The accumulated Survey Monkey evaluations will illuminate certain student patterns which in turn will provide us with insights for (re)designing our courses.

In evaluating our courses, I also strongly advocate for teacher's self-evaluations. Some of the topics that we need to critically reflect on are: whether our explicit and implicit curricula are resonating; whether we intentionally left out certain subjects and students; how we dealt with resisting students; what creative teaching methods utilizing multiple intelligences were used; and whether our own relationship with our TAs embody egalitarian leadership. As Paulo Freire says, we are not only teachers, but also learners[35] who need to be transformed by antiracist and social justice pedagogy. Without critical self-reflections, at some point our growth as teachers may cease.

NOT SO DISRUPTIVE TEACHING FOR TEACHING DISRUPTIVELY?

I titled my chapter, "Teaching Disruptively." Teaching for a culturally diverse and racially just world is disruptive in nature because it challenges the status quo. However, the disruptive teaching methods that I have described are not so disruptive. They are only disruptive in the sense that they are faithful to the original meaning of education in a world where the original meaning is often lost or dismissed. The etymology of the English word *education*

34. For detailed guidelines for using focus groups for evaluations, see Krueger and Casey, *Focus Groups*.

35. Freire, *Pedagogy of the Oppressed*, 68.

teaches us that education is to lead out or to draw out.[36] Education is to help people find a truth that is already within them. It is not just a teacher transmitting knowledge to the young, but, rather, it is helping learners to be the subject of their own learning, and thus to be transformative agents in the world. If every teacher is faithful to the original meaning of "education," then no matter what we teach, our education will disrupt the world that is so complacent with the status quo.

In this chapter, I have allotted more pages to the Confirmation section than Continuity and Contradiction. Disruptive teaching methods start from deeply knowing our students. In my own teaching practices I have experienced that once I do a thorough needs assessment that leads to establishing a safe learning community, about 60 percent of my teaching is done. From my needs assessment I get insights for appropriate teaching methods, content and evaluation. Through my initial and ongoing assessments, I am provided opportunities to establish genuine relationships with my students. As I conclude this chapter, I would like to reiterate the importance and centrality of Confirmation for all teachers. Without knowing our students we cannot help them to be the agents of transformation for a culturally diverse and racially just world. May we both—teachers and students—become partners for mutual transformation for the reign of God on earth: *"Thy will be done on earth as it is in heaven."*

---

36. Groome, *Christian Religious Education*, 5. *E-ducare* (to draw out); *E-ducere* (to lead out).

9

A Pedagogy of the Unmasked

"Unheard but Not Unvoiced, Unseen but Not Invisible"[1]

JULIA M. SPELLER

INTRODUCTION

From the early 1820s in North America, "black face" was introduced as a common feature. In these routines, white men darkened their skin with burnt cork, accentuated their lips with white makeup, and performed songs and skits in "Negro" dialect. By the mid-nineteenth century, this evolved into the popular form of entertainment known as minstrel shows when performers sentimentalized the nightmare of slavery in the South with crude caricatures of the black population as shiftless buffoons.[2] Also among these performers were black men who wore this same costume in their comedy routines, in spite of the demoralization it incited. Bert Williams was one such performer. This actor and comedian, hailed as a genius at his craft, was the first of his race to integrate the world-renowned Ziegfeld Follies. But the irony is that he was only able to break the color line of white mainstream vaudeville by wearing a distorted mask of blackness. It is no wonder that

1. Cannon, "Structured Academic Amnesia," 21.
2. Toll, *Blacking Up*, 51.

the young W. C. Fields called him " . . . the funniest man I ever saw and the saddest man I ever knew."[3]

The truth behind this comment points to the tragedy of being invisible, but for Williams invisibility was not simply a matter of physical nonexistence. It echoed the experience of Ralph Ellison when he said, "That invisibility to which I refer occurs because of a peculiar disposition of the eyes of those with whom I come into contact."[4] In each case, invisibility was a required element of identity, determined by those who refused to see Ellison and Williams as totally human. Their black bodies, whether covered in burnt cork or not, were masks that hid their authentic identities with demeaning stereotypes that justified their existence in a disempowering world.

In many ways, this same reality exists for too many racial-ethnic minority scholars, teachers, and professors in seminaries, schools of theology, and religious studies programs who experience a culture of invisibility. Because the number of full-time faculty of color in theological education is only about 20 percent of overall faculty,[5] an environment of isolation is created where they are disrespected, underemployed/over-used, and directly challenged by students.[6] In the latter example it is very difficult to employ pedagogical approaches that prepare students for ministries of justice and activism because of the way in which these teachers are devalued. In this instance, their black, brown, yellow, and red bodies are masks that extend the racialized, sexualized, and gendered identities of society into the academy. This calls into question the truth of their lives and the validity of the wisdom, knowledge, and expertise they bring.

I believe an important part of the answer to this dilemma is that these educators of color must engage in the task of "unmasking." Using different language but conveying the same sentiment, Katie G. Cannon charges black women to tell their stories,[7] denouncing disempowering images, perceptions, and interpretations of their experiences—unmasking the old and replacing it with the new. She asserts that this task is deeply embedded in the agenda of Womanism as it encourages black women to fully embrace their

---

3. Snow, "The Smile Above the Tragedy," 8–9. Bert Williams's career spanned the years 1898–1922 and included a major role in the all black production, "In Dahomey" that was performed at Buckingham Palace.

4. Ellison, *The Invisible Man*, 3.

5. Association of Theological Schools, "White and Combined Racial/Ethnic Faculty."

6. Turner and Myers, *Faculty of Color*, 105–9.

7. Cannon, "Structured Academic Amnesia," 19.

truth, though some view it as a lie,[8] and live with power and integrity. This is not a simple task, particularly for those in the academy. It is here, she continues, that "structured academic amnesia" renders them invisible through presuppositions that ignore the soundness of their epistemology, question the veracity of their methodology, and dismiss the relevance of their experiences. Despite this perplexing predicament, she affirms that they may be "unheard but not unvoiced, unseen but not invisible."[9]

Similarly, teachers and scholars of color must participate in the task of unmasking by rejecting the caricatures and stereotypes they have inherited from society. They must know that they are richly endowed with "embodied reasoning,"[10] which includes the depth of their experiences and the breadth of their worldview that enhances and expands the academic and scholarly knowledge they have acquired. Thus, I submit that when racial ethnic scholars and teachers truly "unmask" they bring an authentic identity to the teaching/learning environment, which offers the kind of engaged and transformative pedagogy that enriches and empowers students as they prepare for effective ministry in a culturally and racially diverse world.

To that end, this chapter will identify self-actualization as an essential virtue in the pedagogy of minority racial/ethnic teachers and scholars, in an effort to reverse their marginality as they prepare students for ministries of justice and inclusion. It will explore the complexities of sustaining a healthy self-concept in institutions where bodies of color are "marked" and worn as "masks" that distort identity, minimize expertise, and challenge authority. Finally it will outline a pedagogy of the unmasked using insights from Womanist thought that are instructive for teachers and scholars of color as they support engaged and transformative pedagogy in their classrooms.

KNOWING THE WHO AND WHERE

In the book *The Courage to Teach: Exploring the Inner Life of Teachers*, Parker Palmer asserts that self-awareness is an essential element toward authentic connections for teachers who guide learning and shape lives. He transgresses conventional assumptions that cite the beginning of effective teaching in techniques, methods, and content, and states, "Technique is what teachers use until the real teacher arrives." For him, real teachers are those that have the courage to bring their entire being, with all its gifts and challenges, to the teaching/learning experience. He argues that the quest

8. Ibid., 21.

9. Ibid.

10. Ibid., 27.

for self-knowledge is not a narcissistic endeavor and in any authentic effort, teachers will discover "secrets hidden in plain view"[11] that are instructive in cultivating and sustaining effective pedagogy. He goes on to say that while "secrets" reveal both the strengths and weaknesses of teachers' styles and practices, they become important points of self-evaluation for those who wish to grow and develop as educators. As an advocate of educational reform, Palmer also raises concern about the perennial questions that inform the teaching/learning enterprise and notes that teachers often rely too heavily on the *what*, the *how* and the *why* questions of teaching at the expense of the *who,* as he asks, "Who is the self that teaches?"[12]

Stephen D. Brookfield, in *Becoming a Critically Reflexive Teacher,* echoes a similar sentiment regarding the value of self-knowledge. He states that the investigation of autobiographies of educators as both teachers and learners is the first step on the critical path to being self-reflective in the classroom. This level of awareness taps into their formative educational experiences, helping teachers put themselves in the role of the "other," thereby revealing assumptions, perspectives, and dynamics that abetted or hindered their own learning process.[13] It allows teachers to become aware of the assumptions they bring and how they shape their overall pedagogy. Brookfield goes on to discuss the role of critical reflection as a way to "hunt" assumptions that inform teaching practices that define teachers' beliefs and values about themselves and the world as taken-for-granted norms that reveal "hidden dimensions" in a teacher's pedagogy. He asserts that teachers committed to critical reflection of themselves and their practices possess a valuable tool for uncovering deeply set "hegemonic assumptions" that support structures, ideas, and actions that perpetuate tradition on one hand and concretize layers of oppression on the other.[14]

In each of these examples, Palmer and Brookfield highlight and affirm the virtue of self-knowledge for educators. They also identify the presence of *hidden* or *invisible* elements within the teaching/learning exchange that become the places where hard questions are asked and internal transformation takes place. Thus, knowing the "who" that is teaching and courageously employing a critical reflexive lens in the process are essential tools that sustain self-actualization in the classroom. With skillful use, teachers are equipped to excavate the deep terrain of their experiences uncovering perceptions, assumptions, and attitudes that have been suppressed for years.

11. Palmer, *The Courage to Teach,* 3–5.
12. Ibid.
13. Brookfield, *Becoming a Critically Reflective Teacher,* 29.
14. Ibid., 14–15.

More importantly, through courageous employment of a critical reflexive eye, teachers are prepared to honestly examine and interpret the ways in which universally normalized contexts and pedagogies have shaped or mis-shaped, educated or mis-educated them, creating the *selves* that they bring to the classroom.

While digging deep to explore unanswered questions is only the first step of self-actualization, it is also necessary to understand and interpret the connection between the *who* that is teaching and the *where* that teaching takes place. For Palmer and Brookfield, enhanced self-knowledge and reflectivity in the teaching process clearly strengthens their pedagogy. However, when we consider their *who-ness* as white male teachers in traditional educational institutions, we see how their experiences of identity and authority in the classroom differ from teachers and scholars of color. In reality, the social locations of Palmer and Brookfield parallel, and in many ways complement, the dominant culture framework of knowledge production that has been in place for centuries. As helpful as their pedagogical tools are, they must be reconsidered when examining the *where* of teaching for the educators of color.

In the essay, "Engaging Diversity in Teaching Religion and Theology: An Intercultural, De-colonial Epistemic Perspective,"[15] Michael Elias Andraos expresses concern about the limited attention given to the relationship between the *what* (content and knowledge) and the *how* (pedagogy) in culturally diverse contexts of theological education.[16] He references the growing number of international students in theological institutions affiliated with the Association of Theological Schools, the greater complexities their diversity brings to the classroom, and the critical need for an education that prepares students for encounters with difference. This preparation is much more than awareness of various cultures. It involves a serious examination of how the dominant educational structures use power and control knowledge to restrict and silence difference. He cites his own experiences as a student and teacher in a variety of educational institutions, describing a context based on

> . . . a hierarchy of systems and sources of knowledge, with the Western perspectives at the top of the pyramid, that is consistently affirmed in subtle and sometimes unsubtle ways as universal. This hierarchical relation shapes students' approach to "academic" knowledge, their relation to other students who

15. Andraos, "Engaging Diversity," 3–15.
16. Ibid., 6.

come from *different* places, and to professors, the authority figures representing "academic" knowledge.[17]

He goes on to focus on diversity and the value of intercultural conversations in theological education, noting the impact of "colonial differences" in
the classroom and the way dominant frameworks of knowledge shape both
content and pedagogy. He then describes how the hegemonic structures and
rigid epistemic categories have defined values and pedagogical approaches
in the academy that continue to colonize minds and educational systems
alike. The result has been "a dominant academic cultural consensus, silent
and subtle,"[18] yet unrelenting in its power to stifle any form of knowledge
that remotely moves toward transformative pedagogy. I submit that in this
context, teachers and scholars of color must bring a new affirmation of self,
honestly recognizing how they have been shaped by this context, but also
enthusiastically affirming how this context is reshaped by their more authentic presence.

For most teachers and scholars of color, the marks of the dominant
culture are constant reminders of the emotional, spiritual, and physical toll
of their educational pursuits. As the "only" or one of a few persons of color
in a graduate classroom or on a faculty, how do polite (or not so polite)
rebuffs of their comments and insights chip away at their self-confidence?
What pressures on their self-awareness are felt when they become the
resident "expert" on their cultural experience? What happens to their self-
concept when their experiences are interpreted as too subjective? How often
do they border on insanity when their truth is countered with one deemed
more relevant and powerful? How many times do they wonder if the entire
pursuit of scholarship is worth all the trouble? The answers to these questions form the "hidden and invisible elements" that shape their pedagogical
practices—consciously or unconsciously. In far too many cases, they reveal
doubts and insecurities fed by the structures and systems that support the
dominant paradigm and stifle authentic self-affirmation in teachers and
scholars of color. The result is a pedagogy that is robbed of its transformative power in the classroom.

There is another side to this coin, however, that speaks to the tremendous potential for change that educators of color bring to the classroom, but it requires intentional and sustained self-actualization. Like the
mythic Sankofa bird[19] that takes an intentional turn backward to retrieve

17. Ibid., 7.

18. Ibid., 7–8.

19. This symbol from the Adinkra writing system of the Akan people of West Africa
means "return and get," and emphasizes the important way that learning from the past

the wisdom of the past before it flies into the future, faculty of color must retrieve and affirm the strengths and values of their respective heritages and experiences as they enter the challenging waters of academia. This strong action helps them recall sustaining experiences and perspectives that form new questions to ask within the established educational systems and equally important, in the classroom. These questions in turn disrupt traditional assumptions, rearrange categories of knowledge, and critique power structures in ways that create discomfort for all. It is within these places of uneasiness, however, that transformation occurs, when teachers and scholars of color honestly confront and reflect upon their own "hidden secrets" and use this process to strengthen and empower their pedagogical practices. The resulting change can be as simple as a restructured syllabus or the introduction of a new course that invites a new version of long established truth. But as both Palmer and Brookfield affirm, it is the level of self-actualization, confidence, and creative energy that teachers bring to the pedagogical task that makes the difference.

In her book *Teaching to Transgress,* bell hooks says, " . . . teachers must be actively committed to a process of self-actualization that promotes their own well-being if they are to teach in a manner that empowers students."[20] For her, this is an important part of engaged pedagogy, which is a process that fosters critical thinking skills, cultivates the ability to develop one's own knowledge, and creates an educational environment where teacher and students experience a "radical openness" as they dialogue and interact.[21] In order for educators of color to invite radical openness among students, they must courageously bring their full selves to the classroom. It is important for them to remember that the well-being they cultivate in themselves and model for their students opens new opportunities for engaged learning for all. I believe this provides the framework for the next step toward transformative pedagogy that moves beyond critical inquiry toward broader social issues that support concrete actions. Therefore, the task for teachers and scholars of color in the current academic context is to know that they bring a tremendous wealth, and that this wealth is a gift to the teaching/learning experience.

Through intentional affirmation of their full selves—the gifts as well as the "hidden and secret"—these educators provide essential elements that help reimagine pedagogical practices in the classroom and challenge systems and structures in the academy. This is a great undertaking for educators of

---

illuminates the future.

20. hooks, *Teaching to Transgress,* 15.

21. hooks, *Teaching Critical Thinking,* 10.

color who have been marked invisible by those who refuse to acknowledge their full humanity and choose instead a masked caricature that is easier to manage and exploit. The good news is that masks can be removed but this requires a consistent and sustaining level of self-actualization. It is in this heightened state of positive self-awareness that teachers and scholars of color are reminded that while their voices may be "unheard," in all their richness, they are not "unvoiced" and though the truth of their presence is "unseen," they are not invisible.

REMOVING THE MASK, SUBVERTING THE GAZE

Masks have been worn throughout human history as cultural objects that convey a variety of symbolic meanings. Whether in social or religious contexts, masks were intended to hide or conceal one's basic identity in order to establish another. In some religious contexts, they forged a link to the spirit-world and the wearer, while in a trance, assumed the attributes of a certain spirit. It is noteworthy that mask-makers not only selected materials and created designs, but also determined the meaning and interpretation of the masks.[22] Whether used during religious ceremonies or cultural festivals, or as an accouterment of war, masks have been full of meaning for many peoples throughout the world. In most of these instances, the wearer removed the mask at the end of the event to assume his/her normal identity, until the next time, but Paul Lawrence Dunbar reveals another reality.

> We wear the mask that grins and lies,
> It hides our cheeks and shades our eyes,
> This debt we pay to human guile;
> With torn and bleeding hearts we smile,
> And mouth with myriad subtleties.
> Why should the world be over-wise,
> In counting all our tears and sighs?
> Nay, let them only see us, while
> We wear the mask.
>
> We smile, but, O great Christ, our cries
> To thee from tortured souls arise.
> We sing, but oh the clay is vile
> Beneath our feet, and long the mile;
> But let the world dream otherwise,
> We wear the mask![23]

22. "Masks," *Encyclopedia of World Art*, 520–70.
23. Dunbar, "We Wear the Mask."

In this poem, he describes the centuries-old plight of Africans in the Americas as they lived with the physical, emotional, and psychological terror of invisibility. The masks they wore were their black bodies, born of natural material but reinscribed by the mask-maker with a meaning that dismissed their pain and suffering, hiding them beneath masks that would reluctantly "smile" and "sing." But unlike the religious masks described above that rendered the wearer unconscious during spirit possession, Dunbar laments the predicament of a people who were conscious of the objectified identity their masks represented. They knew their role in society was to wear the mask, despite the humiliation and pain, to allow the world to remain in its "dream." For them, removing the mask and subverting the gaze presented great risk as it challenged, destabilized, and disrupted dominating structures and relationships. Throughout the history of Africans in the Americas, this simple act has caused the loss of life for those brave enough to try, leaving a strong warning for others foolish enough to attempt the same.

In many ways, educators of color, with marked bodies in the academy, live this dilemma. For some, their physical presence alone is the *raison d'être* that visibly fulfills institutional obligations and requirements. While they bring solid academic preparation that broadens and deepens scholarly discourse, the unspoken but loudly proclaimed expectation of the academy is that they wear the mask that hides these gifts. So what are "marked" teachers to do? Consciously "smile" and "sing" as they bear the pain and shame of their objectified identities or exist in an academy-induced trance that numbs the pain? For those who remain committed to engaged and transformative pedagogy the answer is simple—affirm their worth, remove the mask, and subvert the gaze.

In her essay, "Visible/Invisible: Teaching Popular Culture and the Vulgar Body in Black Religious Studies," Carol B. Duncan explores the experiences of black women scholars and teachers, and problematizes the intersection between their black bodies and the teaching of black religious studies.[24] She draws from personal classroom experiences when students with sexist and racist assumptions challenged her identity and authenticity. She notes, that in many instances, students who were unaccustomed to or had never been taught by a black female teacher gave verbal and non-verbal responses to her based on gendered and sexed stereotypes. These points of reference were used to manage the cognitive dissonance triggered by her black body and became the mask that those students needed for her to wear as they engaged in the learning process.

---

24. Duncan, "Visible/Invisible," 7.

One of the masks that was operative for her students was the "expert on all things black,"[25] that assumed that her body verified her ability to expound with in-depth knowledge on a variety of topics related to black culture, history, and tradition. While this could be interpreted as a way to honor or acknowledge her presence as teacher and scholar of color, there is a level of naiveté (or calculated intent!) that does two things to tighten the mask. First, it presupposes a static and monolithic reality of the black experience rendering it broad, vague, and lacking in relevance and vitality. It casts all persons of African descent into the same circle regardless of cultural, linguistic, geographic, or religious locations and it colonizes the black experience, further objectifying black presence and identity in society. Second, it shifts the role of teachers and scholars from one that has mastery and expertise in a specific subject to one that dispenses footnotes on people of color in a world of non-color. For Duncan and others, the mask of the racial/ethnic expert diminishes pedagogical authority and credibility and positions teachers as a less threatening presence to the dominant cultural worldview. While interesting, the information they give is viewed as incidental and inconsequential to the learning process, allowing those in the class who wish to, to "dream otherwise."

This experience in the classroom points to a widely accepted understanding in those who affirm a textual approach to cultural studies that identifies the body as text. In reality the physical body is the first text of the class, before any readings or other assigned materials. Addressing this pedagogical issue in "Reading the Signs: The Body as Non-Written Text," Anthony Pinn asserts,

> In an epistemological twist, the body as source of information trumps secondary information as more readily acknowledged texts. Furthermore, the materiality of the body in various ways serves to bring into focus unstated meaning in the written texts.[26]

Whether acknowledged or not, the body by its very presence carries on a dialogue with written/secondary texts that impact the teaching and learning process in unseen ways. This occurs because of the social, political, economic, cultural, and religious realities of daily life that the body brings to the dialogue. The perspectives and assumptions that rise from these realities are often informed by uncritical emotions and experiences that bring varying levels of confrontation and heated debate to the classroom. It is within

25 Ibid., 4–5.

26. Pinn, "Reading the Signs," 88.

this tension-laden context that transformation can occur for both teacher and student as new and difficult questions are asked and deeply engaged dialogues take place.[27] The challenge arises, however, when teachers of color, because of the realities their marked bodies represent, are rejected as reliable, credible, and relevant sources. As the first non-written text, their marked bodies become masks that distort content and prevent the objective acquisition of knowledge for many students, preventing any significant experience of transformative pedagogy.

Pinn asserts further that bodies worn as masks in this context allow a "sympathetic exchange," and create a hiding place where self-disclosure is selective and controlled. While he acknowledges some benefit in masking as it creates a place to gather and assess information about the other at a safer distance, he also cautions that there is little "pedagogical value," in this position.[28] Indeed, for teachers and scholars of color, engaged and transformative pedagogy requires an ability to critically reflect and courageously imagine action responses, but this is an impossible task if they remain cloistered within the safety of a masked environment. Hence, if the goal is to provide a full, self-actualized presence in the classroom by unmasking, it is important to also recognize the tensions that emerge in the process of self-disclosure.

Erica Lawson, in "Feminist Pedagogies: The Textuality of the Racialized Body in the Feminist Classroom," acknowledges the value of feminist pedagogies that challenge positivist approaches to knowledge production that center on universal objectivity and patriarchal hierarchy.[29] She addresses the challenges faced by women of color due to their embodied presence in the classroom, through feminist pedagogies that advocate multiple voices in the teaching/learning experience. This form of unmasking acknowledges the inherent tension in a teaching/learning experience that attempts to welcome multiple voices that encourage the level of vulnerability necessary for critical dialogue. This more democratic classroom also creates a dilemma, particularly for teachers and scholars of color, whose embodied presence already invites a challenge to authority. In her teaching, Lawson struggles to reduce a top-down authoritative presence in the classroom while retaining some level of authority to counter the reduction of her power-presence as a contested body.[30] She considers the risks involved for teachers in this context and states that she carefully distinguishes between those personal

27. Ibid.
28. Ibid., 86–87.
29. Lawson, "Feminist Pedagogies," 108.
30. Ibid., 113.

narratives that invite voyeurism and those that serve as a "critique of structural inequities."[31]

This dilemma is not unlike those of other educators of color in their efforts to live out their truth by unmasking and subverting the gaze. In this dual action, a power play is ignited in the classroom when teachers are faced with reluctant and dismissive students. This act of disrupting the dominating discourse held many risks for Williams or Dunbar. Standing toe-to-toe and eye-to-eye with the oppressor in their contexts was interpreted as the ultimate expression of disrespect that challenged the structured and systemic norms and threatened their lives. For scholars and teachers of color in theological education today, reluctance or refusal to remove the mask and subvert the gaze is itself a self-instigated death. In the classroom, it reduces the possibility of engaged and transformative pedagogy by living out the caricatured identities that reinforce old methods and use outdated paradigms. In the larger academy, it allows the hegemonic structures to continue to colonize minds and dominate knowledge production. In total, the failure of teachers and scholars of color to remove their masks and challenge the dominant discourse underscores the negative impact of the academy on their identities and denies the giftedness they bring to the classroom. However, when they are able to courageously embrace and celebrate all that they are, a drastic realignment of power occurs, making their invisible presence a visible reality, as uncomfortable as it may be. I submit that as they intentionally and continually affirm self, remove the mask, and subvert the gaze, a renewed power and purpose will emerge and loudly proclaim that they are no longer unheard and unseen, but are fully voiced and fully visible!

TEACHING WHILE UNMASKED

So how do self-affirmed and empowered teachers and scholars of color sustain their identities in contested classrooms that are defined by hierarchical structures and hegemonic systems? How do they create an environment for engaged and transformative pedagogy in institutions that perpetuate the coloniality of minds and the marginalization of differences? How do they genuinely adopt and sustain a pedagogy of the unmasked? I submit that valuable insights are found in Womanist thought. First defined in 1983 through the prose of Alice Walker, Womanism became the foundation for thirty years of scholarship and it remains a vital platform of protest and renewal for black women. Moving beyond white feminist dialogue that centers on gender justice and equality, Womanist thought expands the focus

31. Ibid., 111.

to include the holistic realities of black women's experiences through race, gender, and class, but many argue that this tripartite oppression is incomplete without also addressing the difficult issue of sexuality as well.[32]

It is important to note then that Womanism is far more than a movement of liberation. It is an epistemology that seeks to dismantle the legitimized knowledge production of the white patriarchal academy[33] by broadening the discourse to include the ethical commitments, the methodological approaches, and the theological interpretations of black women. Four tenets of this epistemology have been identified: radical subjectivity, traditional communalism, redemptive self-love, and critical engagement.[34] While each of these could speak to different challenges faced by teachers and scholars of color who acknowledge a pedagogy of the unmasked, I contend that two are most informative for this discussion. The first, radical subjectivity, reinforces earlier insights about the *who* within the teaching enterprise and the value of self-affirmation on the part of teachers. The second, traditional communalism, informs the *where* as it outlines the attitudinal conditions and relational interactions that enrich the classroom. In each case, these tenets of Womanist epistemology are essential and instructive for educators of color committed to a pedagogy of the unmasked as fully voiced and fully visible partners in the teaching/learning enterprise.

In general parlance, subjectivity—which relates to the feelings, thoughts, and temperaments of the subject—focuses on individualism that views self-interest as the goal of human action. It upholds a notion of responsibility that honors autonomy and independence but also motivates and sustains a single-mindedness that easily moves from focused self-interest to egotistic self-absorption, which isolates and negates others. The expression of subjectivity espoused by Womanist thought, however, is grounded in the quest for self-determination that emerges in the midst of multiple layers of oppression. It becomes radical as it dares to retrieve and rename the self by "subverting forced identities and hegemonic truth claims."[35] It is, thus,

> . . . a process that emerges as Black females in the nascent phase
> of their identity development come to understand agency as
> the ability to defy a forced naiveté in an effort to influence the

---

32. Douglas, "Twenty Years a Womanist," 152. Also see Cannon, "Unctuousness as Virtue," 91ff.

33. Floyd-Thomas, "Writing for Our Lives," 3.

34. Ibid., 7.

35. Ibid., 8.

choices made in one's life and how conscientization incites resistance against marginality.[36]

Radical subjectivity then acknowledges the importance of self-affirmation as the first step toward empowerment. It is essential for black women in the academy to critically assess and challenge "forced" images, perceptions, and interpretations of their lives in order to move from the margins into the center of dialogue and action. For educators of color, I believe this Womanist tenet models authentic unmasking by advocating a heightened self-understanding that dismisses stereotypes and caricatures that perpetuate fear and self-doubt, which keep educators of color on the fringes of the academy. This fortified emphasis on the *who* of teachers requires a level of radicalism that courageously and continuously re-appropriates their truth in light of the "structured academic amnesia" enacted by students and institutions.

In the classroom, radical subjectivity is a starting point for educators of color who attempt to teach unmasked, but in order for engaged and transformative pedagogy to be possible, students must unmask as well. It is in this tension-ridden classroom space that unveiled teachers and students risk vulnerability but it is also the place where change happens. In this context, teachers and scholars of color are prompted to creatively partner the academic content, the richness of their interpretive truths, and the experiences of the learners into teachable moments that provide alternative pedagogical lenses. The goal of this approach is to demonstrate multiple ways to name and reassess the personal bias and misconceptions of students as well as structural inequities in society. It also focuses more attention on the dynamics of the educational process and less on reacting to the fears and insecurities of students. From a starting point of radical subjectivity, fully voiced and fully visible educators of color employ a pedagogy of the unmasked that will create over time a more just and inclusive educational experience for teachers and learners.

Communalism in the broadest sense is understood as loyalty to a particular group based on a common affiliation such as religion or ethnicity, and it endorses shared personal, economic, and spiritual *capital* for the good of the whole. Critics interpret this lifestyle as closed and restrictive, placing higher value on the interests and commitments of the group to the exclusion of others. In counter distinction, Womanist scholars understand the integral link between communalism and the traditions of solidarity inherited from generations of Africans across the Diaspora, through

36. Ibid., 16.

... the affirmation of the loving connections and relational bonds formed by Black women—including familial, maternal, platonic, religious, sexual and spiritual ties [through] Black women's ability to create, re-member, nurture, protect, sustain, and liberate communities . . . by acts of inclusivity, mutuality, and reciprocity.[37]

For Womanist scholars, traditional communalism is an essential step toward sustaining the empowered identity that emerges from radical subjectivity, and its real strength lies in the reality of relationships. Attention to this tenet, in the spirit of Womanism, helps educators of color focus on the importance of relationality in light of the inevitable conflicts that will come as they strive to create relational bonds that will help sustain students during difficult and painful moments. I believe it introduces an ethic of care into the classroom that is not sentimental and over-emotional but provides a level of genuine concern that cultivates a less toxic space for encounters with difference.

In the classroom, traditional communalism is a useful tool for educators of color committed to fully voiced and visible teaching because it values the relational dimension of the learning process. It was noted earlier that within the autobiographical accounts of a teacher's journey are valuable experiences that shape her/his pedagogy. Each of these experiences occurred within relational exchanges, and whether they were positive or negative, learning took place. This means the goal of the educational experience should not be the avoidance of conflict that results from differences but rather the manner in which those exchanges are used to educate. Thus the cultivation of relational bonds, as fragile as they may be in the beginning, has the capacity to shift the atmosphere within the classroom from distrust to trust, making it crucial for educators of color to make every effort to teach unmasked—fully voiced and visible. While the desire of a totally safe classroom is an illusive goal, the introduction and modeling of communal values anchored in the Womanist tradition of mutuality, inclusivity, and reciprocity will begin to lower barriers and invite more engaged and transformative interaction in the classroom.

CONCLUSION

Surviving and thriving as racial-ethnic minority scholars, teachers, and professors in seminaries, schools of theology, and religious studies programs is

37. Ibid., 78.

not a task for the faint-hearted. It requires the audacity to make their voices heard by those who refuse to listen and the tenacity to make their presence visible to those who choose not to see. This presents a peculiar dilemma for those committed to preparing students for ministries of inclusion and justice because the structures and systems that frame the educational enterprise stifle pedagogical approaches that acknowledge the richness of authentic and critical dialogue across cultures. Ironically, educators of color bring important contributions to this process but they are packaged in marked bodies that render their expertise unsound, questionable, and unauthorative. Hence the challenge for these teachers and scholars is to find ways to remove the masks that portray a false identity and to live and teach as fully voiced and fully visible educators.

In this chapter, the work of selected pedagogues has revealed the importance of self-actualization for all teachers, highlighting the value of authentic self-critique and its impact on pedagogy. Yet the reality for educators of color, whose marked bodies are too often read as distorted text, challenges the sustainability of any level of self-affirmation attained. The challenge they face is to remove the mask and return the gaze in full acknowledgement of the power that comes from authentic self-knowledge and it is this action that moves them toward full voice and visibility. This pedagogy of the unmasked finds wisdom in the practices of radical subjectivity and traditional communalism as understood in Womanist epistemology. These tenets born from the womb of black women's experiences reflect the pain of marginality and the isolation of invisibility familiar to many scholars and teachers of color. They each affirm the need to transgress established norms and introduce alternative paradigms that honor different voices and experiences. More important to this discussion, however, is the commitment that they share in moving women and men toward more responsible and ethical action in the world through the disruption of outdated and oppressive models of theological education.

So what is the next step for fully voiced and fully visible teachers and scholars of color as they reverse their own marginalization while preparing students for ministry? How do they remain unmasked and uphold the power of their truth to create and sustain an engaged and transformative pedagogy in their classrooms?

The bad news is that despite any degree of growth and enlightenment they experience in their *who-ness*, the *where* of the educational enterprise remains unchanged, leaving the classroom as a contested space. Conversely, to end this chapter with a concrete list of strategies to reverse the trends and correct the problem is naïve and impossible. As long as the hierarchical structures and hegemonic systems remain in place, the realities of invisibility for teachers and scholars of color will still make it difficult to unmask and teach as fully voiced and fully visible partners in the educational enterprise.

The good news, however, is that through an ongoing commitment to a pedagogy of the unmasked grounded in an unapologetic belief in and embrace of the value of their presence and gifts, educators of color have the tools needed for engaged and transformative pedagogy. In their full voice and visibility, they affirm the experiences, interpretations, and analyses that they bring as often different but not deficient; they critically assess the formative educational experiences that have shaped and informed their pedagogy, for better or worse; and they apply the insights learned from these encounters to challenge, empower, and prepare students for ministries of inclusion and justice in the world.

10

The Vocational Cycle to Support Institutional Justice

A Pathway for Scholars of Color to Transform Institutional Life and Governance

MARY HINTON

If you are here unfaithfully with us
You are causing terrible damage.

~RUMI

THIS CHAPTER SEEKS TO address how faculty and administrators of color engage institutional life and governance to create and sustain racially just institutional cultures. Critical to the discussion is understanding how personal vocation can be used as an agent of change, moving institutions of higher education towards greater racial justice. While the topic is being engaged at the institutional level, the central thesis of the chapter is that when electing to serve an institution and committing to creating a more just institution, one must discern, be faithful to, and promote personal vocational aspirations and allow them to drive the daily work that shapes the institution. The notion of using vocation to shape an institution, and allowing the institution to shape vocation, is described as a Vocational Cycle to Support Institutional Justice. This cycle was developed in response to my analyses of my experiences in higher education as a person of color. It is only by understanding and acting upon this cycle between the institution and the individual that institutional justice can be achieved.

Several questions will be addressed in order to demonstrate this critical cyclical dynamic. First, it is important to situate the premise of the chapter within the context of its author. The situational context is important not only to understand the basis for the argument and how it might be applicable beyond a single individual, but also to create a broader understanding of how people of color impact, and are impacted by, higher education institutions. This section will also discuss institutional climate using a series of three dialectics experienced by scholars of color in higher education. Next, the chapter defines the Vocational Cycle to Support Institutional Justice, exploring how engaging vocation enables one's work to transform the institution. This section also demonstrates that, as vital as vocation is in shaping one's work, the work of institutional justice is best achieved when the institution also shapes vocation. Finally, the chapter concludes by exploring the implications of this cyclical relationship for increasing racial justice in higher education.

PERSONAL CONTEXT AND INSTITUTIONAL CLIMATE

How one understands, engages, responds to, and shapes institutional life and governance is quite heavily shaped by personal context. Therefore, there are two goals for this section. I first seek to explain my own personal context and situate myself within higher education. Once personal context is revealed, the commonality of that experience in higher education is discussed. This section asserts that there is remarkable similarity across the variety of roles people of color experience in higher education. In fact, due to the paucity of numbers of people of color in higher education, the similarity between roles is far greater than the differences. A series of three dialectics are identified and explored as a means of describing the institutional climates that scholars of color dwell within. These dialectics are used to support the premise that institutional climates with regard to racial justice, while varying across institutions and their missions, share some significant commonalities. These dialectics also help frame the need for, and potential impact of, the Vocational Cycle.

Personal Context

Given the fact that this chapter is being written from the perspective of the author, it is imperative to say a word about the role of perspective and bias. The experiences that I bring with me not only fashion how I interpret my personal experience in higher education, but they are the lens through which I understand and interpret the institutions I have been, and continue to be, a part of. Therefore, my lens informs not only what I say and do, and what opportunities and challenges I identify, it also frames how I understand other responses to those words, thoughts, and actions.

Identifying personal perspective is important in understanding the lens through which I view and understand higher education and how the story of my experience has shaped the proposed cycle. Mary Elizabeth Moore writes, "Stories bear meaning in themselves. They do not need commentary; yet analysis amplifies life narratives by uncovering layers of hidden wisdom. Analysis enriches knowledge, but never exhausts or replaces the richness of stories, which inevitably carry a surplus of meaning."[1] This chapter, though grounded in experience and supported by analyses and empirical evidence where possible and appropriate, is, primarily, my story.

It is important to note that while I believe my experiences to be typical of what many women of color face in the academy, I cannot unequivocally state that my experiences are either universal or exclusively unique. Rather, my institutional experiences have been influenced by my context. Thus the offerings of this chapter must be situated and understood within that context. Hayes writes, "Today I recognize that my words are heard in different ways by different people. They are heard in one way by those who seek to oppress and are seen as threatening and divisive; they are heard in another way by those engaged with me in the struggle for liberation of humanity, hopefully as affirming and liberating. I am a Black woman, for some, a symbol of nothingness, but for myself and many others, a sign of liberating faith."[2]

I am a black woman. Euphemistically, I come from humble beginnings. As a student, and early in my career, I would have been labeled as "disadvantaged" or of low socio-economic status. As I began to own how I am defined and create my own definitions, I would describe myself as black woman who views the world through a womanist lens. Broadly, I am using womanist to mean an African American woman who recognizes and embraces all of the complexity that dwells within those three small words:

---

1. Moore, "Stories of Vocation," 219.
2. Hayes, *Hagar's Daughters*, 45.

African. American. Woman. "To be a womanist," Hayes writes, "is to be made whole—to be the continuation of the Black past and builders of the Black future. It encompasses the theological, yes, but also the political, cultural, social and economic traditions of Black being in the world. It is a way of keeping the faith, of renewing that faith, and of passing on the faith of Black folk to the strong Black women and men who keep 'a comin' on."[3]

Specifically, a womanist acknowledges the historical influence of a heritage that extends back to Africa. How deeply one embraces that heritage can vary greatly among womanists, however, none would deny the influence of that origin and how it shapes their self-understanding. A womanist also readily acknowledges the complexity of American heritage as well; a heritage that wants to deny and lessen your role in its creation and maintenance; a heritage that seeks to place you into a clearly defined box within which you do not, and cannot, fit. Though not in an externally proscribed manner, but in each womanist's own way, she battles against imposed definitions and seeks to live out her own meaning of what it means to be a black woman in America. A womanist is one of deep and abiding faith, though not one who unquestioningly accepts the constraints thrust upon her by religious doctrine. Rather, a womanist has faith in God because she recognizes that her strength, and very survival, is a reflection of God's faith in her. It is this reciprocity of faith between the womanist and the divine that gives her the ability and fortitude to continue her struggle. A womanist is living a complex mix of ancient heritage, American experience, and divine engagement, defining herself by the way she responds to each element of who she is.

This self-definition was shaped, in part, by my experiences in higher education. My first introduction to higher education was as a student at a highly selective, majority white, liberal arts college in New England. I was then a student in several other contexts, including a comprehensive research university in the Midwest and a large, private, Catholic university in metropolitan New York City. My experience as a professional in higher education has been less diverse as I have only served at small, Catholic, liberal arts based institutions in the northeast. However, I have held positions as faculty, student affairs staff, and as a junior and senior administrator.

While my personal experiences may be considered diverse for an individual, they do not represent the totality of the types of experiences possible in higher education. However, the consistency of my experiences in terms of the situations I have observed, and how individuals have responded to me as a black woman, is notable. Further, that consistency is reflected regardless of the role occupied in higher education: student, faculty, student affairs staff

---

3. Ibid, 54.

member, or senior administrator. Given the consistency across institution type and the consistency across roles it is legitimate to draw some conclusions about institutional climate in higher education. The conclusions may be limited to my context as a black woman, however, I believe the experiences will resonate with other scholars of color as well.

Institutional Climate

It is reasonable to posit that higher education is consistent in its treatment of people of color because the landscape of higher education regarding people of color looks similar across institution type. According to *The Journal of Blacks in Higher Education*,[4] in 2011, black students made up nearly 14 percent of the enrollment in higher education. While this number varies across institutions, the highest average is 24 percent, which is found in private, for-profit colleges and universities. State-run and private colleges and universities reflected enrollments of 12.7 percent and 11.5 percent respectively. While these statistics reflect great improvement regarding access, we know that of those black students enrolled, only 45 percent will graduate from college, compared to 64 percent of whites,[5] indicating ongoing issues and challenges facing black students with regard to persistence in higher education.

Like students, faculty of color are also rare. Currently, 12 percent of faculty are people of color.[6] Within this group, only 5 percent are African American.[7] In terms of success within the professoriate, only 9 percent of full professors are minorities.[8] According to a study of highly ranked colleges and universities in the United States, "At the current rate of improvement, it will be a century or more before the black percentages of the faculties of these institutions mirror the black percentage of the American work force."[9]

For administrators, the numbers are more difficult to verify because how administration is defined can vary widely and there is limited research available for review. However, we know that 10 percent of administrators are Black/African American, with Black women slightly outnumbering black men in academic leadership roles (53 percent vs. 47 percent).[10] Some

4. Anonymous, "Nearly Three Million Black Students," lines 1–10.

5. Anonymous, "Black Students Show Solid Progress," 46.

6. Humphreys, "Faculty Recruitment in Higher Education," para 8.

7. Anonymous, "Black Faculty," 24.

8. Humphreys, "Faculty Recruitment in Higher education, para 8.

9. Anonymous, "Progress of Black Faculty," 78.

10. Ibid., 13.

may argue that "success" in administration is becoming a college president, of which only 9 percent are minorities.[11]

It has also been found that blacks enter into administrative roles earlier than their white colleagues.[12] While this may appear to be of benefit to the individual, it is actually a complex phenomenon. Entering academic administration early may contribute to the lower tenure rates and lower number of peer reviewed articles by people of color. In turn, these two factors may contribute to the inability of blacks to attain the most senior level positions in higher education.[13] While all of these numbers can vary widely by institution type, evidence shows that black students, as measured by graduation rates, and faculty and administrators, as measured by tenure status, attaining department head positions and having academic leadership roles are most likely to be successful at liberal arts institutions.[14,15]

The above data indicates, quantitatively, that higher education has significant room for growth with regard to supporting the success of people of color. With that backdrop in mind, what are the experiences of people of color in higher education? Or, what is the institutional climate within which students, faculty and administrators of color dwell? Whether as a student, faculty member, staff or senior administrator, my experience was often one of balancing competing forces. Specifically, I have found that, as a black woman, I was faced with dialectics that required a careful negotiation in order to be successful. Three specific dialectics will now be explored: unrealistic power vs. powerlessness; underutilization/low expectations vs. being overworked; and engaging authentically vs. hiding the authentic self to attain and maintain a place at the leadership table.

Negotiating Dialectics in Higher Education

The first dynamic, unrealistic power vs. powerlessness, takes different forms depending on one's position in higher education, though it is active regardless of role and status. At times, institutions ascribe great power to people of color. The power is not, however, the type that can facilitate change. Rather, the person becomes the universal representative of their demographic. For

11. American Council on Education, "Leading Demographic Portrait of College Presidents," para 3.

12. Association for the Study of Higher Education, "Status of Ethnic and Racial Diversity," 30.

13. Ibid.

14. Ibid.

15. Anonymous, "Black Faculty," 82–83.

example, regardless of my role, whether as a student or a senior administrator, there were moments when I represented to those in the room the totality of their experience with black women. I held the power to define their image of black women and how they would respond to black women in the future. I became the universal black woman and my words were viewed as representing all black women or, at times, all black people—an individual whose words and actions carried unrealistic, albeit heady, authority. There is, on the surface, great power in this dynamic. Hayes notes that black women in academia, "Have been marginalized, yet, at the same time, strangely empowered, given authority we have not sought to speak for all Black women and, indeed, all Blacks."[16]

However, the power quickly becomes burdensome and morphs into feelings of powerlessness as one recognizes that they are not heard for their unique opinion or ability to facilitate change, but only in terms of how well they align with perceived notions of their demographic. In contrast to feeling powerful, the opposing dialectic occurs when people ascribe to you the characteristics that *they* want, based on their prior experiences with black women, and you are powerless to shape those perceptions. At its worst, you are shaped and perceived by the negative prior experiences: any misdeed caused by a black woman can make those around you perceive you suspiciously. Being unable to define oneself is the very definition of being powerless.

The burden of this dynamic is particularly acute. At times, the power of representing an entire demographic is overwhelming and fashions one's behaviors and responses beyond the realm of authenticity, a dangerous position that will be discussed in detail later. Equally burdensome is the lack of power, and the subjection to someone's delayed response to experiences that they had with folks of similar demographics previously. Therefore, the initial dynamic, one that was uniformly experienced at each level of higher education, regardless of role, is an often repeated dynamic and the one most likely to resonate with other scholars of color.

The second dynamic that has shaped my personal experience is that of underutilization versus being overworked. It is well understood that women and minorities often feel the need to outperform their colleagues in order to achieve even modest recognition. Again regardless of role in higher education, for some, a black woman is a novelty. As such, there may be an assumption that key concepts and tasks will elude them. Whether this experience happens at the student or senior administrator level, the belief is that because of your demographic you cannot be given leadership tasks.

16. Hayes, *Hagar's Daughters*, 5.

The other side of this dialectic is a powerful desire to over-perform in order to prove one's ability. This over-performance is generally not limited to high level tasks, but often happens with tasks of varying levels of importance, resulting in the student, faculty, and administrator of color risking burnout because of taking on excessive amounts of work to prove their value. Of course, the argument can be made that all new employees work extra hard to demonstrate their value. While true, the initial power dialectic heightens, and extends, the need for people of color to prove themselves, thus leading to and emboldening this dynamic.

Patitu and Hinton[17] suggest that faculty of color, in particular, had powerful narratives surrounding this dynamic. They reported faculty descriptions of feeling isolated, being subjected to different standards, and having feelings of being "watched" and having to repeatedly demonstrate their value, especially as they were on the tenure track. Further, the secretive nature of the tenure and promotion process exacerbated the need to over-achieve to receive professional recognition. Underutilization vs. overwork, like unrealistic power vs. powerlessness, has as much to do with those surrounding the scholar of color as they do with the scholar themselves. The dialectic is triggered by the reaction of those surrounding the scholar. The scholar then has to determine how they want to react to the dynamic and how they will resolve the resulting tension.

In no dialectic is the scholar's reaction more important than in the last one, which leads directly to the Vocational Cycle to Support Institutional Change. The final dynamic is that wherein one has to balance being one's authentic self and advocating as needed, versus maintaining a place at the leadership table, at times by hiding one's authentic self.

While the power dynamic and the utilization dynamic were consistent across roles, the authenticity dynamic is much more acute as one rises through the ranks of higher education. In part, this is due to an increased level of access to the decision-making structure of the college. As that level of access increases, one has to be more intentional in deciding which issues, in the universe of issues, to explore and advocate for and against, and the dynamic becomes more critical. Further, as real power, not the perceived power discussed in the first dynamic, increases, this dynamic becomes increasingly fraught.

Charisse Jones and Kumea Shorter-Gooden explore black women's struggles with authenticity in the professional world at great length and find that in an effort to support and comfort others, black women often suppress and silence their own authentic needs:

17. Patitu and Hinton, "Experiences of African American Women Faculty," 79–93.

> Our research shows that in response to their relentless oppres-
> sion, black women in our country have had to perfect what we
> call "shifting," a sort of subterfuge that African Americans have
> long practiced to ensure their survival in our society . . . Black
> women are relentlessly pushed to serve and satisfy others and
> made to hide their true selves . . . From one moment to the
> next, they change their outward behavior, attitude, or tone . . .
> And shifting has become such an integral part of Black women's
> behavior that some adopt an alternate pose or voice as easily
> as they blink their eyes or draw breath—without thinking, and
> without realizing that the emptiness they feel and the roles they
> must play may be directly related.[18]

In addition to shifting, some scholars and administrators of color in the
academy may choose to disengage at critical times as a means of self-pro-
tection. Evans and Herr suggest African American women, who are subject
to both racial and gender discrimination, may well materially disengage
from their professional lives as a survival strategy: "In order to avoid a negative situation, a person may decline to participate in a particular activity,
modify life-styles, or redirect ambitions and goals. It seems reasonable to
assume that African American women, who perceive themselves as victims
of double discrimination and prejudice, might use some of these techniques
in their attempt to avoid the probable thwarting of their aspirations in the
labor market."[19]

Everyone, men and women, majority and minority, at times determine
when to speak up and when to maintain silence. However, this dynamic
may be more pervasive for scholars and administrators of color given the
dialectics discussed earlier. At the highest levels of academic administration, decisions have wider-reaching impact and may provide the best opportunity for improving campus climate. Scholars of color must determine
how much of their authentic selves to reveal in order to support change.
With the increased importance, the obligation to carefully negotiate this
dynamic is vital.

How one resolves this, or any, of the dialectics is not proscribed. Instead, one has to be awake to, and aware of, the dynamics at play. To successfully challenge institutional culture, one must name the dynamics, help
others to see and acknowledge them, dwell in the tension of how to resolve
the dialectic and then go about authentically addressing and learning from

---

18. Jones and Shorter-Gooden, *Shifting*, 7.

19. Evans and Herr, "The Influence of Racism and Sexism," 132.

the dynamic. Most importantly, the need to negotiate the final dialectic sets forth the rationale for the Vocational Cycle dynamic.

VOCATIONAL CYCLE TO SUPPORT INSTITUTIONAL JUSTICE

In this section we engage the central thesis of the chapter: that it is by employing the Vocational Cycle to Support Institutional Justice that scholars of color can support and bring forth institutional justice. This cycle was created based on my personal context, experience with the dialectics, and attempts to engage in institutional transformation. The cycle appears as follows:

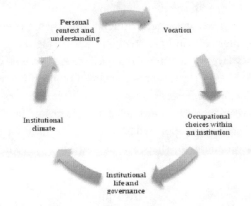

The chapter will briefly address each element of the cycle in turn and conclude by describing the importance of the continuous nature of the cycle.

Personal Context and Understanding

As established earlier, personal context and understanding are powerful, shaping forces. Not only do they fashion how one experiences the world around them, personal context and understanding shape how one responds to the world and impacts it. In higher education, the context is shaped by experiences as a student and continues to be shaped as one progresses through higher education professional culture. Without repeating my personal experience, it is important to review contextual themes identified in the literature as recurring in African American women's experiences.

Moore's[20] qualitative research found that women often live out their professional lives utilizing and capitalizing on the following qualities: fac-

20. Moore, "Stories of Vocation," 218–39.

ing unexpected turns; trusting spiritual-intuitive knowing; analyzing and responding to social contexts; standing for justice; committing to make a difference; helping others be who they can be; building bridges; practicing hospitality; valuing women's communities; caring for self; and practicing humor. Given the diversity of Moore's sample, it is reasonable to assume its applicability to women of a variety of demographics. Further, research surrounding the personal context of African American women in higher education yields additional insights. Patitu and Hinton write that for black women, "To cope and survive in these environments, some of them retreated, some worked harder and smarter, some relied on support networks and faith in God and used prayer and spiritual development, while others invoked laughter and recalled pearls of wisdom from other black African American women, grandmothers, and holy scripture."[21]

What is clear is that women's contexts force them to develop a number of strategies, internally and externally, which enable them to address the challenges they face and continue to move forward, both professionally and personally. Further, African American women's context often involves being empowered by and empowering others. Therefore, the personal context of African American women is one that capitalizes on and leverages a number of skills to engage and support self and others. The need for, and utilization of, these skills undoubtedly shape vocation, the next stage in the Cycle.

Vocation

Clearly, context frames vocation. Vocation, or insight into divine direction for life, is often a powerful factor in the lives of religious and theological scholars. For many, vocation is not merely a clear career path. Rather, it is viewed as a divine fashioning of one's energies. Clarity about vocation is achieved through a process of discernment, wherein one must align their context, experiences, and potential and submit them to divine shaping.

Surely the commonalities of personal context provide some insight into vocation for women of color. Moore, Patitu and Hinton, and others have articulated the many common factors that women employ as they approach and engage their vocation. For African American women, race and gender are also undoubtedly active forces shaping vocation. Further, according to Hayes, for womanists, vocation may include elements of "mothering": "Mothering thus requires an ability and willingness to maintain traditions while reshaping them for future generations—discarding that which is not

---

21. Patitu and Hinton, "Experiences of African American Women Faculty," 84.

nurturing and upholding while incorporating that which is."[22] Therefore, for many African American women, vocation includes those activities that serve to bridge the past and future in powerful ways and in ways that facilitate and maintain justice for future generations, especially those that are marginalized.

The premise of the cycle is that institutional justice is impacted by, and impacts, the vocation of the scholar. Black women seeking to shape a racially just institutional life and climate will acknowledge their vocational call in support of institutional justice and make occupational choices directly aligned with this vocation.

Occupational Choices within an Institution

If authentically living into vocation, one's occupational choices—both immediate and long term—will maximize personal context and vocational choices and capitalize on them. To be successful in supporting institutional transformation, these choices must be driven by the desire to serve an institution fully and in ways that allow vocation to positively transform the institution. To make choices that are not in alignment with vocation is to do both professional and personal damage. Therefore, when occupational choices, whether daily decisions or long range occupational planning, run afoul of vocational choices, one is, in many ways, denying personal context and the individual becomes divided. Parker Palmer notes that we live a divided life when choices are made that are not in alignment: "I pay a steep price when I live a divided life, feeling fraudulent, anxious about being found out, depressed by the fact that I am denying my own selfhood . . . How can I affirm another's integrity when I defy my own? A fault line runs down the middle of my life, and whenever it cracks open—divorcing my words and actions from the truth I hold within—things around me get shaky and start to fall apart."[23] Undoubtedly, the dynamic Palmer articulates is heightened for people of color in higher education, as the dialectics discussed previously increase susceptibility to feeling anxious and on shaky ground. If occupational choices to resolve the dialectics and to enable true vocation to shine through are not made, then the fault lines Palmer describes can surely engulf scholars of color. Therefore, it is imperative that the occupational choices scholars make must serve their own vocational needs in order to truly serve the institution and move it towards justice.

22. Hayes, *Hagar's Daughters*, 25.
23. Palmer, "A Life Lived Whole."

As an example, recall that many minorities enter into administrative roles earlier than non-minorities. This might well be attributed to the fact that there is a belief that institutional change can happen more readily at the institutional or administrative level than at the classroom level. This is not to argue the veracity of that belief, but rather to acknowledge that perhaps many professionals of color elect the administrative route because it enables them to live into their vocation. Similarly, those who remain in the classroom, squarely focused on the personal development of their students, may be doing so in order to live deeply into their vocation and transform institutions in that way. In either instance, faculty and administrators of color are making occupational choices that support vocation and have the potential to shape and transform institutions.

Institutional Life and Governance

As indicated earlier, personal context, especially for African American women, often includes mothering, bridge-building, humor, mentoring, caring for, and nurturing others and self, drawing on history and a commitment to improving the future for others. Therefore, how these strategies are carried out in occupational choices and behaviors will drive how one engages institutional life and governance. These strategies, often dismissed as soft, are the very characteristics needed to drive and support institutional justice. It is only by actively employing these strategies that institutional life and governance are influenced.

While the institution is the level of discussion, higher education institutions are merely a collective of people, seemingly working together towards the same mission. If a scholar of color is going to move their institution towards greater racial justice, it is only by approaching each person, task and challenge with their most authentic selves and employing these strategies that transformation will take place. We must bring our full vocational aspirations not only to the occupational choices we make but to the ways we dwell within our institutions and engage governance. Palmer writes, "In fact, when we live by the soul's imperatives, we gain the courage to serve institutions more faithfully, to help them resist their tendency to default on their own missions."[24] The missions of the majority of colleges and universities speak, explicitly or implicitly, to the role of education in creating a more just society. It is the collective of people within the institution who are charged with carrying out that mission. This can only be done when our interactions in institutional life and governance structures are driven,

24. Ibid., 3.

first and foremost, by our ability to authentically relate to one another and remain focused on mission. Institutional mothering means that we explore the governance and institutional structures that have historically sustained institutions, but we do so with a critical eye that enables us to reshape those structures so that they are more just, and supportive of future generations regardless of demographics.

Institutional Climate

If one is authentically engaging institutional life and governance using voca-tion, and *de facto* one's personal context, then the institutional climate will undoubtedly shift. Institutional climate is the primary point of impact in terms of transforming our institutions. Therefore, all that we bring to bear in our personal context and vocational discernment has power to shape the climate. Our vocational choices inform how we engage the governance structures and how we address justice across the campus as opposed to in our own siloed areas. We are open about our desire to have a unified, as opposed to divided, experience on campus and to seek ways to allow others the same. When we enable our personal context to shape the institutional climate, when we "rejoin soul and role," it becomes impossible for institu-tions to perpetuate injustice. The challenges cannot be ignored and change left as something hoped for. Rather we embrace what brought us to this point, positive and negative, and use that to change the climate.

Return to Personal Context and Understanding

The shift in campus climate, then, immediately circles back to impact per-sonal context and understanding, thus bringing us back to the beginning of the cycle. A changed institution has new needs and new opportunities for progress and transformation. The institution shifts the context within which we dwell. As agents of change, we then need to determine how best to re-engage the institution to continuously facilitate change. It is when the in-stitution is allowed to impact our context that we can review and re-engage our own vocation, providing us with the skills and temerity needed to make the necessary occupational choices to impact institutional transformation. Michael Jinkins, writing about teaching and writing and their relationship, articulates the importance of willingness to being shaped by external forces.

> The courage to make oneself vulnerable is the common point
> for the vocations of teaching and writing. When we say that

good teaching and good writing call us beyond ourselves into relationships that can transform us in ways we never imagined, we must also confess that the changes we face may inspire dread as much as joy. If we are unwilling to risk transformation at the hands of our students and colleagues, our readers, editors, and reviewers, we are unlikely to enjoy either of these vocations very much. However, if we can deliver ourselves into the hands of others, and learn to respect not only the others, but the disciplines and the risks our vocations entail, perhaps we can become good teachers and good writers, and maybe even good people.[25]

While Jinkins specifically references teaching and writing, the work towards institutional justice equally demands being vulnerable to critique and influence. The Vocational Cycle to Support Institutional Justice requires constantly exploring and engaging our context so that we are energized to do the work of institutional transformation. The cycle, like our institutions, should never be satisfied. We must constantly explore, and re-explore, personally and institutionally, what we are called to do (our vocation) and be prepared to indicate if we are fully living into that vocation and, if so, are living it justly.

FACILITATING CHANGE USING THE VOCATIONAL CYCLE TO SUPPORT INSTITUTIONAL JUSTICE

With the cycle as a driving force, two recommendations are proffered in this section to move towards more just institutions. First, one must be authentic in one's approach to the work and, second, the institution must be engaged at multiple levels to facilitate transformation. Again, we will turn to personal experience and opportunities to positively engage change and transform an institution as evidence of the cycle's value.

For many scholars of color entering academia, there is a tendency to try to replicate the model of what success looks like in colleges and universities. Unfortunately, that model does not fit me, as a black woman, and is unlikely to fit many other underrepresented populations. Like others, though, I tried mightily to fit that mold. What I eventually realized, however, was that the higher education model was not designed for me. I concluded that my success would be in spite of, not because of, the current model of higher education.

25. Jinkins, "The Professor's Vocation," 64.

In fact, it was not until I recognized that what I had to offer was not my ability to be the same and mirror what higher education offers that I was able, instead, to see that it was my "difference" that would contribute to my work and help me fashion the institutions I cared very deeply about towards greater justice for all. In 2010 I wrote, "We have to explore those exclusionary traditions that hinder students from learning. We must stop trying to fit students to match a system that was never created for them and was, in fact, intended to discard or constrain them. Unless we begin to identify and reconfigure colleges and universities, we will continue to see large disparities between students because they are having largely disparate experiences. If we fail to rethink higher education, we will continue to replicate its inequities in increasing proportions."[26] While these statements were written to support *student* success in higher education, the same principles apply to our institutional life and governance and the success of scholars of color who comprise our institutions. We have to look at the patterns and dynamics in higher education that exclude our personal contexts, that demand we separate our "soul and role" and that fracture our humanity and care for one another, and be willing to stand up to those structures and refuse to be a party to the injustice. Scholars of color may, like students, have disparate experiences from their majority colleagues because the institutions were not designed with them in mind. Unlike students, however, it is our *obligation* as professionals to impact those institutions in powerful ways, to not only benefit ourselves but to benefit students as well. This impact can only be realized when we acknowledge the strength our context and vocation brings to our institutions. It was only when I was willing to embrace my "difference" and live authentically that I was able to truly engage colleagues in the work of diversity. It was the implementation of the Vocational Cycle to Support Institutional Justice that empowered me to make positive institutional changes. Whether through the development of curriculum review to support diversity, professional development to support diversity, or reviewing and implementing policies to support diverse hiring practices, this work was only accomplished successfully when I authentically engaged my institutions and allowed the cycle to unfold.

The second recommendation demands that scholars of color use the vocational cycle to engage the institution at multiple levels. Perhaps the clearest explanation of how to engage the institution at multiple levels can be found through Eisner's three curricula. Eisner[27] posits that there are

---

26. Hinton, "In Need of a Newer Model," 43.
27. Eisner, *Educational Imagination*.

three curricula at play in educational institutions: the explicit, the implicit, and the null curriculum.

The explicit curriculum, what a college explicitly teaches, is perhaps the easiest point of engagement. There are multiple opportunities to engage and improve the curriculum. Texts, pedagogical practice, and course offerings are but a few elements of the explicit curriculum that can readily be examined and where change can be made to support institutional justice. Again, it is easiest to engage institutions on this level as curricula are often open to debate and inspection. When making occupational choices scholars of color can choose to have a significant impact on the explicit curriculum.

The more challenging and, arguably, more important point to transform the institution in support of racial justice is the implicit curriculum. The implicit curriculum is that which teaches because of how it is structured. The implicit curriculum might broadly be thought of as the culture of the institution. For example, it is within the implicit curriculum that we find the dialectics at play as they emerge based on patterns of interaction, not because of an explicit plan of action. This is also the curriculum where changes to governance structures may best be addressed. While governance structures are explicit, their existence is often the result of implicit assumptions and needs. Scholars of color must always question if those implicit assumptions remain valid and if those same assumptions support diversity.

It is in the implicit curriculum that change for racial justice is most difficult and complicated, because what needs to be addressed is not always clear. Rather it is here that African American women can call on their skills for engaging others to facilitate change. Changing the implicit culture of an institution is long-term and sensitive work. It requires the full engagement of the vocational cycle to see change happen. Though challenging, change at the implicit level is both lasting and powerful.

The final curriculum Eisner addresses is the null curriculum. The null curriculum teaches through its absence. In this area, a scholar must ask what topics are not being addressed. What ideas, people, and activities that create and sustain institutional justice are missing from the culture? The scholar must then begin to name and address those activities throughout the vocational cycle and especially when making decisions that impact governance and institutional climate. If the institution maintains a commitment to diversity in the curriculum but never addresses diversity in the practices of its human resources office, then decisions in the vocational cycle must be made to address this null curriculum. By using the vocational cycle to address the explicit, implicit, and null curricula at the institution, it is possible to proactively facilitate more just institutions.

CONCLUSION

Use of the Vocational Cycle to Support Institutional Justice is imperative if we are going to bring about justice on our campuses. First, we must recognize and own the context that brought us forth and enable that context to shape our vocation. By being faithful to our vocation we are able to make occupational choices that support institutional justice. These choices allow us to build on, learn from, and, when needed, challenge institutional life and governance structures. By bringing to bear the full weight of our vocation on these structures, we can refashion them in ways that positively and powerfully impact institutional climate. That transformed climate then reshapes us, further enabling us to move forward with our work.

It is difficult to overstate the importance of being faithful to institutions and their work to create more just institutions. It is important not only so that people of color have equal employment access; it is equally important because it supports the hopes and dreams of the students on campus. Patitu and Hinton write: "The experiences of African American women in administrative and faculty roles is important because enrollment and persistence toward degree completion of African American students is linked to the number of African American faculty and administrators on predominantly white campuses. When minority students see African American and other minority faculty on campus, they believe that they can also succeed and hold professional positions."[28] Being faithful to the institution and its governance, therefore, is not only about being faithful to oneself, but also being faithful to the future.

---

28. Patitu and Hinton, "Experiences of African American Women Faculty," 80.

11

Institutional Life and Governance

*Realities and Challenges for Racial-Ethnic
Leadership within Historically White Theological
Schools*

DAVID MALDONADO JR.

THEOLOGICAL SCHOOLS HAVE HISTORICALLY reflected their social, religious, and political environments, including the nature and conditions of race and ethnic relations in society. During the pre-civil rights era when open and legal racial/ethnic segregation was the norm, theological institutions reflected the separation of races and ethnic groups. Among historically white institutions, such racial separation involved no access or limited racial/ethnic access to participation at all levels of institutional life, including student bodies, staff, trustee boards, and especially presidential or decanal leadership. Unfortunately, even after fifty years since the civil rights movement and anti-discrimination public legislation, historically white theological institutions continue to be products of and reflect the historic and shameful period of segregation and separation. Since the civil rights movement, these institutions have struggled to address such a history and overcome the results of such institutional formation and practices.

Today, the struggles continue. Given the demographic changes in which the people of color are becoming the majority population and white mainline congregations and denominations struggle to survive, the challenge to historically white theological institutions has become more critical and even urgent. The struggle is how to be more relevant and effective in the transformed social environment. The traditional racial and ethnic minorities have become the new majority in America. The lack of acknowledging and addressing the new diversity seriously challenges the integrity and survival of these institutions. An important question is whether historically white theological institutions can continue in their historical and traditional practices. Or, will they become irrelevant in the new reality? Is there a role for theological schools that maintain racial and ethnic practices of the past? A vision of a culturally diverse and racially just world suggests that such is not the case. It is no longer only a matter of civil rights; it has become a matter of institutional survival. Historically white theological schools need a major transformation in order to be relevant in today's realities. What do they need to do? Who will lead them?

A key element in addressing these struggles is the character and will of institutional leadership. This chapter proposes that institutional leadership needs to reflect the demographic changes in the environment, as well as dynamics in the nature of religious denominations and institutions. It is important to explore potential leadership among the new participants in theological education such as minority faculty, minority members on boards of trustees, leaders in historically black schools and Bible institutes, the emerging denominations, and racial and ethnic clergy. However, the answer is not simply to select leaders based on their race or ethnicity. Rather, it will be important to select leadership that brings competence, insights, and commitment to the new cultural realities and norm. This chapter suggests that ethnic persons are ready to step up to the plate.

As institutions look to the future in redefining leadership in the new day of minority majority populations and white denominational struggles and decline, it is important to learn from recent history of the experience of racial and ethnic minority persons serving in leadership positions within historically white theological institutions. Their experiences can offer insights and helpful lessons as these institutions move toward a more inclusive and just future.

PROVEN RACIAL/ETHNIC LEADERSHIP

A rich history of leadership provided by persons of racial and ethnic backgrounds exists among historically Black institutions as well as among Hispanic Bible institutes. Schools serving African American Communities, especially theological schools related to historic Black denominations, have provided ample opportunity for ethnic administrative and trustee leadership to emerge and lead theological institutions in ways that reflect leadership ability, commitment to quality theological education, and faithfulness to values of a diverse society that take into consideration the racial and ethnic communities. Such commitment and faithfulness have not diminished leadership or institutional competence and effectiveness; on the contrary, they have prospered in providing a valuable service to the church and community. They have successfully overcome challenging dynamics in the history of race relations in this country.

Within the Hispanic/Latino communities, theologically trained individuals have been produced by the highly successful Hispanic Theological Initiative and other efforts by progressive institutions. Many of these Latinas/os are ready to take leadership positions and have indeed begun to do so in a limited way. Proven leadership has been in place among some significant Bible institutes, especially among the schools offering baccalaureate degrees. Latino leaders have emerged in leading their institutions in the development of pastors for the hundreds of Hispanic congregations throughout the nation.

HISTORICALLY WHITE THEOLOGICAL INSTITUTIONS

Historically white theological institutions refer to those seminaries whose primary constituency, ownership, and leadership have been mainly white. Many of these institutions were established during the expansion era and early years of the last century, most during the pre-civil rights era of segregation. It is not surprising that these institutions emerged as segregated institutions by the very nature of the broader environment and the denominations that owned and supported them. Their purpose was that of providing a learned and theologically trained clergy for denominations whose membership was primarily white. It was an era of denominational energy, growth, and expansion. The graduates of these seminaries came from and returned to the white congregations and denominations that sent them. Most of the graduates were male. There was a clear connection between financial support from denominations, their wealthy laity, and the graduates produced by these schools. Schools prospered. Boards of trustees reflected denominational leadership, wealthy supporters, and leaders of the community. As expected, such leadership was also overwhelmingly white and reflected white denominations and structures of a strong middle class and wealth in American communities. They also reflected the social and racial realities of the day. These institutions were established by white denominations during periods of segregation and thus were influenced by values, norms, and practices of the period. Whatever diversity within and among these institutions existed, it related more to theological, denominational, and regional differences. Racial and ethnic diversity in their composition and programming were not a founding principle or social force at the time of institutional formation.

The history of institutional life and governance of historically white institutions reflects the dynamics of their formative years before the civil rights era. Not surprisingly, institutional leadership among white theological schools historically has been white to the exclusion of racial and ethnic minorities. For many years, the leadership was also heavily male and wealthy. This is the case even among denominational schools whose denominations included racial and ethnic persons within their membership. Why? One given explanation was that a critical mass of racial and ethnic educators within historically white institutions was small and thus extremely limited. Thus, upon selection of leadership, theological institutions justified the lack of minority leadership on the basis of a limited pool in numbers and experience. In other words, the reason for the lack of racial or ethnic leadership in these institutions resided in the condition of minority populations. Supposedly, it had nothing to do with the institutional culture, values, and nature of institutional leadership in place. A vicious cycle was in place and operated against the possibility of selecting racial minority leadership. These institutions did not produce racial or ethnic graduates who could provide leadership. Thus, a pool of potential leaders was not available. Such a cycle was blindly perpetuated and produced a self-fulfilling prophecy. There were no acceptable candidates for institutional leadership among the racial and ethnic populations.

However, the critical mass of racial and ethnic theological educators has changed and an increasing number of racial and ethnic persons fill academic positions within historically white theological institutions. Historically black institutions and Bible institutes are populated by well-trained persons. The traditional justification of selecting only white persons no longer is viable or acceptable. It has not been until recent history, and especially since the civil rights movement, that a limited number of persons of non-white background have been selected to lead such institutions. Most common are appointments to decanal positions. Appointments to presidencies are more limited and reflect early efforts.

GOVERNING BOARDS

Racial and ethnic minority representation in institutional governance of historically white schools has emerged to a limited extent among the various boards of directors. Appointment to boards of trustees has been the first step in the invitation of racial and ethnic persons to the leadership table. Unfortunately, this too has been quite limited and many times one racial or ethnic person is used to cover the overall expectation of minority presence at the table. For example, an African American is supposed to represent Asian as a well as Hispanic communities. The same is applicable for members of any ethnic/racial group: a person who is Hispanic is expected to represent the Hispanic population, one who is Asian is expected to represent all of Asia, and so on. In other words, one racial or ethnic person on the Board of Directors has been a common practice.

As the demographic change moves toward an increase of the people of color and the proportional decrease of the white population, historically white theological institutions can no longer defend the practice of inviting one minority person to represent all minority groups. The practice of maintaining the people of color in the minority within the boards continues the institutional practice of marginalizing minority populations. The practice of white exclusivity and dominance among their boards of directors is not a viable option in today's realities. This is especially true as mainline denominations struggle and lose white membership as well as keep white churches in operation. Yet, too many boards continue with board profiles that do not reflect the changing times for the church and theological schools. Racial and ethnic trustees continue to play the minority role.

For racial or ethnic persons to serve on a dominant white board can be a challenging experience. After the celebration of "achieving diversity" by inviting a person of color to serve on the board, reality sets in as the individual notices the agendas, policies, and reports on student enrollment, financial aid, faculty hiring, academic program, and staff profiles. Boards tend to be conservatively cautious, committed to the tradition of the school, supportive of the president, and many times in awe of the faculty. For many board members, nothing is more important than the bottom line and financial strength of the school. While this is an important concern and responsibility for boards of trustees, a bottom line perspective fails to raise broader and different concerns, such as the direction of the school and its relations and service to racial and ethnic communities. For example, academic programs and financial aid geared towards serving racial and ethnic populations may be perceived as too expensive and not generating financial income. When financial aid is tied to the traditional constituencies such as congregations and denominational structures, or other criteria, it is difficult for racial and ethnic minorities to qualify. Trustees can easily see their hands tied in their effort to make a difference in pushing for increased minority enrollment and support. In other words, the school might not be able to afford minority students or compete for ethnic faculty. The minority trustees face traditional agendas that ignore or deny an agenda that seriously incorporates concerns and needs of the minority communities and churches.

Issues related to budget matters are another example of the conservative mentality among board members and challenges to minority trustees. These concerns center on financial stability for the institution and are an important responsibility for trustees. However, budget challenges can be more than simply controlling expenses and increasing income. For the ethnic board member, the bottom line mentality and conservative posture leads to frustration and disappointment when other options and needs are not explored. Budget challenges can open new ways of looking at school programming and staffing. Minority students could be a growth area!

Commitment to the tradition of the school can also contribute to a conservative approach to institutional mission and direction. To tie institutional mission to historic institutional roles can lead to isolation from new realities and a defensive posture toward change. Relations with historic partners such as denominations, church leaders, large congregations and especially significant financial donors, while important, can limit explorations of new directions, new constituencies, new partners, and critical examination of institutional mission. The celebration of achieving diversity in the invitation of the racial/ethnic board member can quickly result in more frustration for the new board member if what follows is business as usual. Commitment to historic tradition becomes the status quo. Racial and ethnic board members are many times expected to submit to and support the tradition. To include an ethnic person on the board may not necessarily mean that the board leadership expects to move in new directions. It may simply be a matter of reporting diversity on the board.

Membership on the board of directors is normally a process of board self-selection. Boards invite persons to join the board. The identification and selection may well reflect whom they know through their social or business networks. Thus, it may reflect a limited circle of social friends or business associates. If a new name is proposed, trustee visits and interviews might be conducted to screen out persons who might not "fit" or screen in those who are perceived to fit with the nature and expectations of the board. As might be expected, the selection of a minority person to join the board can be a sensitive matter. The board may well desire the new trustee to be able to speak to minority issues, but certainly do not want the new trustee to become a "troublemaker." This might not be a spoken concern, but it can be important to the new trustee and influence her or his approach to serving. Why were they selected? Are expectations related to their racial or ethnic background?

Many times the president plays a very important role in identifying, selecting and inviting new board members. Thus, it is not surprising that board members develop a sense of loyalty to the president. The president may be identified as a key person for their being on the board. Supporting the president is a natural outcome of the invitation process. Normally, such support is very important for developing strong and stable administrative leadership in the president's office. However, if racial and ethnic board members are to represent and articulate the concerns of their communities, loyalty to the president may limit their advocacy for new and even challenging positions. Developing a voice that faithfully reflects the concerns and needs of the minority churches and communities can be a challenging situation for racial and ethnic persons serving on boards of trustees. To do so may affect their relationship with the president, access to informal information, and the whole issue of trust.

Probably one of the most subtle and often difficult situations for board members is their relationship with the faculty, staff, and students. Board members are normally encouraged to participate in the life of the school. Usually, this involves invitations to chapel, public lectures, school-wide celebrations, and other public events. This can be a healthy and important way for the trustees to have a sense of the school, its students, activities, and especially the faculty. However, their roles as members of the board call for careful and sensitive management of confidential and trusting relations with the faculty and students. For racial and ethnic board members, one challenge is in their relations with ethnic faculty, staff, and students. Minority faculty, staff, and students may well articulate minority concerns or bring issues to the attention of the minority trustee. The minority trustee may possess a natural affinity to their concerns. Minority faculty, staff, and students may have high expectations that the new minority trustee is able to address these issues and will them bring to the board table. Likewise, there might well be an expectation from the board that minority members of the board will now address and correct the many issues and concerns that minority students and faculty have. Minority students and faculty might also share more information than the trustee may want and often the trustee may not know what to do with the information. Thus, simply by being a racial or ethnic person, the trustee may be in very difficult situations in relating to minority faculty, staff, and students, and her/his role on the board.

Another dynamic between trustees and faculty is a sense of awe that may develop among the trustees toward to the faculty. As laypersons and probably members of congregations, trustees may develop a sense of awe that may affect their roles as policy makers. Faculty are perceived, and rightly so, as the experts in the field of theological studies. The faculty are the professors and teachers. In other words, the faculty represents the expertise of the core technology of the institution. The faculty represents the core of what seminaries are about. The board members may develop a sense that they are the non-experts while the faculty members are the experts. This is especially true with senior and tenured faculty members who have been with the school for a long time. As a result, many trustees find it difficult to challenge faculty recommendations and action. As laity, trustees are called upon to oversee an institution in which they have no expertise. For the minority trustee, they may face a challenging power dynamic that includes both race and expertise.

Although many would suggest that commitment to institutional tradition, support of the president, conservative financial management, and respect for the faculty are important for boards if they are to serve the institutional well-being of the school and protect its integrity, it is also important to recognize that such postures can be quite challenging to racial and ethnic board members who seek to make a difference and impact the school. As the church and society struggle with the huge demographic changes with respect to both ethnicity and race, as well as with age, minority trustees face a challenge in representing and addressing such realities at the table of boards of trustees. This is especially true when the minority trustee is the only minority person on the board of a historically white institution. It can be a lonely role to play with many challenging obstacles and pitfalls.

THE PRESIDENT

Persons leading historically white theological schools traditionally have been white and male. This is no surprise. Board members and constituencies are used to generations of white presidents. The pictures and portraits of past presidents on the heritage walls are visual reminders of who has led the school. Their pictures reflect a historic continuity and sense of stability as to the nature of institutional leadership. The gallery of former presidents reflects an exclusive club and offers a clear reminder of the tradition and the nature of its leadership.

In addition to their administrative responsibilities, presidents are also the public face of the school. They represent the school wherever they go, such as public events, as well as private and informal settings and conversations. Their names are associated with the school. Mention of their names in local and regional media is usually followed by their position as president of the school. There seems to be a consistency between the public face and the character of the school. There is a sense of institutional comfort with a president that reflects the historical and traditional profile. Only when there is a perceived disconnect between the historically white nature of the institution and the president is attention given to the fact that the president has a Spanish or Asian surname, or is African American. In historically white institutions, the norm is a white president with a European surname. Minority presidents are considered new or exceptional to the tradition.

THE PRESIDENTIAL SEARCH

Presidential searches offer insights into commitments of the schools with regard to their traditions, levels of comfort with their current situation, and expectations for the type of presidential leadership desired. A strong commitment to tradition, and a high level of comfort with the institutional situation, will likely lead to presidential searches that follow traditional norms and profiles. Trustees basically will seek a status quo in presidential leadership. There is no need to seek new direction or a new type of leadership.

Presidential searches also provide insight into the school's relations with historic constituencies and especially with donors. When searches reflect a status quo, the school seems to be comfortable with its institutional position and direction. There is no call or pressure to consider new possibilities. Historic constituencies do not perceive a need to change the nature of leadership and seek new directions. Emphasis is on maintaining institutional stability and staying the course. In these cases, presidential searches normally follow past approaches and are run internally by the board. This will involve the usual postings and public announcements. It may well include private word of mouth explorations. A directed or targeted search may be conducted on an informal basis in order to avoid legal problems. This is especially true when a certain individual is identified as a desirable candidate or is already in a comparable position in another institution. Such a search is perceived as a safe search for the type of leader desired to maintain the status quo. Contracting with a "headhunter" is not part of this situation because trustees desire more control of the search. Traditional searches promise to find another leader similar to the ones of the past. Donors and constituencies are happy.

A presidential search that is truly open and would seriously consider a candidate with a different racial or ethnic background is a big step for many boards of trustees. Such a step can risk support among traditional donors, trust from denominational leaders, members of the board, and criticism from some members of the faculty. Internal resistance may develop among such stake holders. A racial or ethnic candidate could be perceived as an unknown entity and maybe too radical a change from the past. Questions on how having an ethnic minority president might impact the public image, on the impact to institutional direction, and on priorities will probably arise. How would a minority president change the public image of the school? Could a minority president raise funds from a basically white donor base? Will a minority president bring in a minority agenda? How committed would she or he be to the traditional priorities of the school? Uncertainty on what having a minority president means for a basically white faculty and staff may be raised. Would the minority president know how to supervise white staff and faculty?

Given the historic nature and reputation of white institutions among many racial and ethnic scholars and leaders, many potential minority candidates might not apply. The reputation of the school as a white institution might well be an obstacle in its sincere efforts to move in a new direction. Minorities might wonder if minority candidates would not be taken seriously and would be used only for statistical purposes in documenting non-discrimination. Thus, both internal and external dynamics and perceptions can work against moving toward a diverse and just future in presidential searches.

Racial and ethnic persons who might be potential presidential candidates need to be persuaded to apply. How serious is the school in its stated invitation that ethnic and minority candidates are welcome to apply? Minorities have heard this before only to see white persons selected as usual. Who wants to be a candidate in order for the school to document that it did not discriminate? No candidate wants to be simply a statistic in the search report. Minority candidates will want to know who is on the search committee. Are there persons of color and from the broader community on the committee? How does the announcement articulate a sincere invitation and commitment to diversity? Who chairs the search and what is the experience and history of the committee membership in relating to or working with minority communities and constituencies? Are announcements posted in minority networks? What conversations have been held with minority groups so they will encourage minority candidates to apply?

THE PRESIDENTIAL CANDIDATE INTERVIEW

If the minority candidate makes it through the initial screenings and to the list of potential finalists, an informal visit off campus is usually conducted. That it is an informal conversation does not make it any less critical and full of challenges for both the minority candidate and for the interviewers representing the institution. Sizing up the candidate and exploring questions held by trustees and faculty, as well as testing the candidates on sensitive issues, are done with care. Issues such as competence, scholarship, and administrative experience are normally already addressed via formal applications, resumes, and background checks. Informal interviews normally address issues such as how the person comes across, public presentation of self, articulation, maturity, and leadership potential. Behind much of the informal conversation is the basic question, "How would this candidate fit with the institution, with its traditions, its personnel, and in leading the school?" Does the racial or ethnic factor play a dominant role in the character of the person? How would these factors affect his/her leadership? Given the nature of the institution's history and tradition as a white institution, the racial and ethnic question cannot be avoided and should be addressed. However, as might be expected, these questions are not usually addressed openly or directly. They are behind the traditional and normal examination of the minority candidate.

The formal campus visit and interview of the minority presidential candidate can be more complex and intense. Going in, the candidate knows the history and reputation of the school. Its history as a white institution is a given. He or she has some questions and maybe even concerns with regard to that history. Yet, she/he might feel uncomfortable raising those questions directly. To do so might give the impression that minority issues are high in the person's mind and agenda. To not do so could make the candidate feel dishonest. The faculty might be quite concerned with regard to minority issues but also feel uncomfortable in raising those issues. As a result, both parties dance around the issues, without really addressing this issue openly, and draw conclusions about the other.

The faculty can be expected to be committed to the academic and value traditions it has built over the years. They are concerned that the minority candidate might bring in other priorities and values, especially with regard to racial and ethnic issues. For some faculties, minority issues and programming are associated with lower academic standards. Thus, it is not surprising that much conversation centers on academic and programming issues. Code words become critical. However, other concerns of the faculty may also focus on the ability of the candidate to raise funds to support the faculty and its priorities. Can this minority candidate raise funds from wealthy white donors? Does the candidate fully understand the priorities of the faculty and is this person committed to raising funds in its support? The faculty is also concerned about its public image and recruitment. Would having a minority president impact the profile of the student body? Would we become a minority school? The faculty has much invested in who is selected as the new president and will engage the candidate directly and indirectly in issues related to minority concerns about which they have not had to be concerned with regard to who sits in the presidential office. The minority president will also have power affecting faculty matters such as hiring, terminations, and tenure. All of a sudden there is the possibility that they might have a minority president with power. A totally new set of concerns can be frightening.

APPOINTMENT OF A MINORITY PRESIDENT

The selection and appointment of a racial or ethnic minority person to the presidency of a historically white institution is a monumental step. For the institution it is a historic step and it may also be for the denomination. The public announcement can be a moment of celebration. Announcements in local press, national denominational media, and other venues celebrate the event not simply because an institution has appointed a new president. What is especially newsworthy is the fact that the new president is a racial or ethnic minority and that such an appointment is made for the very first time. It is celebrated as a new day for diversity.

However, the announcement calls attention not only to the new president, but also to the institution. All of a sudden, the school draws wide attention to its courageous action in appointing a minority president. High expectations are created for the institution. The denomination, other theological schools, donors, and other peers will be looking at the school and its experience with the new president. To be in the spotlight is not always the most comfortable position. Members of other faculties will be curious and will ask the school faculty about the new president and the new reality. Trustees from other schools will also be intrigued and wonder what is happening. Donors will pay close attention to how the school responds to the new president. The spotlight can put all players in positions that not only are unprecedented, but also somewhat experimental. There may be nervous expectations. Let's see how it works.

MOVING INTO THE OFFICE

Moving into the presidential office will be a new reality for the minority president. She or he has probably been a member of a theological faculty and maybe even a dean. But, being the president is a new situation. She/he is now responsible for the whole institution. It is no longer simply academics or student life. The president's desk is now the final stop for issues and questions related to all aspects of institutional life. From the buildings and facilities to tenure decisions and fundraising, all key decisions come to this desk. Clearly, the president cannot do it all. He/she will have to rely on key faculty and staff administrators in place. This is the first line of relations that need attention. Most likely, persons serving as administrators are white. They might never have had a minority person as their supervisor. This is also a new experience for them. They too may be nervous and wonder how it will be to have a minority supervisor. How different will it be from previous white presidents? The minority president will have to walk a careful line in creating trust and confidence, and settling fears that may be there simply because she/he is a racial or ethnic person.

There is also the question of anticipated expectations from the institution. Although the informal and formal interviews addressed many issues and conversations centered on the school and the presidency, what the trustees and faculty really expect from the new president might not necessarily have been articulated in a clear and coherent voice. The new president probably heard many voices and expectations. Some of the expectations were not in total agreement, but rather were competing expectations. Trustee expectations may be very different from those of the faculty. Sorting out the expectations and stake holders is an early challenge for the new president. This is especially true with regard to minority issues. To what extent and how early should minority issues be addressed by the new minority president?

A somewhat more personal matter, and yet a very important matter, is that of the president's ethnic self-identity and cultural lifestyle. While quite aware that he/she is serving as president of a historically white institution in which the vast majority of persons are also white, the new minority president will have to find ways to affirm who she/he is and celebrate his/her culture, as well as nourish it through friendships, symbols, and other forms of cultural life. For many racial or ethnic persons, one's race and ethnicity has been a significant part of self-identity, worldview, and cultural style. It has been part of his/her personal and social life. It is part of one's life that is not easily left behind because of a new job. To deny it or leave it behind would be to live a culturally lonely life, isolated from an important part of one's life and community.

Racial and ethnic topics may have been important topics in his/her scholarship and research. It may be an area of high importance intellectually that draws his/her attention and interest. It has been part of his/her intellectual and even social conversation. As a scholar the ethnic minority president would like to continue that interest and those conversations. However, it is a topic that will require careful attention, especially in addressing issues such as white racism, discrimination, and segregation. To do so may draw the critique that this person may have a chip on her shoulder or even be biased. Does the minority president have to sacrifice her/his research and intellectual interest in order not to offend?

A related situation is just the opposite of the two issues identified above. If the new president does not demonstrate any interest or competence on matters related to minority topics, there may be some disappointment within the faculty, students, and trustees. They were hoping that the new president would bring new insights, expertise, and leadership on minority issues. To not articulate such interest or concerns can be a letdown for those who had advocated for the new president. Thus, the minority president is caught between being too ethnic or not ethnic enough, having too much interest in ethnic issues or not enough. The new president is caught between two opposing expectations and hopes.

DIVERSITY HIRE?

A question that may not be articulated publicly is the quiet concern among some stake holders that the new president was hired because he or she is an ethnic minority. In other words, they see the appointment as a diversity hire. The suspicion that the minority factor was a major driving force behind the appointment suggests that competence might have been a lower standard. Such suspicion can easily lead to expectations of failure. A self-fulfilling prophecy of incompetence settles in. Quickly, the minority president is under the microscope of suspicion. Any hesitation, questionable word, or action is construed to suggest the incompetence of the president. A minority president may receive a short honeymoon in such cases. He or she has to be super good and make no mistakes in order to survive the eyes of self-fulfilling suspicion.

RELATION WITH THE MINORITY COMMUNITY

The appointment of the minority president generates a celebration among her/his ethnic community as well as among the other minority communities. It is a great day for them and one that raises many expressions of hope and expectation. The minority community has been waiting a long time for this day and their laundry list of criticisms and frustrations with the school can be quite extensive. Now that the minority president is in office, the hope and expectation is that this person will be able to address their concerns satisfactorily. The criticisms of past experiences with the institution are not held back. On the contrary, they are shared with the new president as he/she is educated and lobbied about past community issues with the school. At last the community feels that it has a direct line to the president. And it does. The president wants to relate to his/her ethnic community and there is an affinity. However, the new president quickly finds him/herself caught between the expectations of the community and the course of the institutional ship that she is called to correct. Moving too quickly raises concern within the institution. Moving too slowly can result in disappointment and a new set of issues with the minority community.

RELATIONS WITH DENOMINATIONS

As a theological school, the primary mission is to produce future clergy for the denominations that relate to the school. Among a large number of schools, multiple denominations are involved, each with its own set of expectations for what constitutes theological education and clergy formation. Each denomination also has its own set of historical issues relating to racial and ethnic minority populations. In some cases, the school may also have students from historically minority denominations, such as historically Black denominations or Hispanic Pentecostal groups. These denominations also bring their issues to the president's table and want them addressed. The issues may include theological concerns as well as matters dealing with admission, curriculum, and preparation for ministry within the racial and ethnic communities. A traditional curriculum that addresses primarily the needs and assumptions of the white church and its constituencies can develop a pent up frustration among the minority denominations and students. The new president thus finds himself dealing with multiple sets of theological and academic issues relating to multiple denominations and their issues connected to racial and ethnic matters.

RELATION WITH HISTORIC WHITE CONSTITUENCIES.

As president of a historically white institution, the new president must learn quickly how to deal across racial and cultural differences. Not that the president has not already learned to do so throughout her professional career. Most likely, cross-cultural competencies have been perfected during her professional career. However, the vast majority of her constituencies are now white. The microscope includes sensitivity toward anything that the minority president might say or do can could be construed as biased. If the president socializes with the few racial and ethnic minorities on the faculty and staff more than with the white, she can be accused of being biased. For a Hispanic president to speak Spanish with subordinates can be construed as suspicious. Thus, the president must learn to be very careful in social and informal interactions as well as in public and settings. For certain, ethnic jokes are out. Even tolerating ethnic jokes by others can lead to suspicion.

SHAPING THE INSTITUTION AND LEADERSHIP

Having been appointed as the new president and being quite aware of the racial and ethnic dynamics that he brings into the picture simply by being the person he is, nonetheless, the minority president is eventually going to make critical decisions that may open the many issues and questions about his competence, cultural perspective, ethnic bias, and even his theological orientation. Not all of his critical decisions will be popular. Routine decisions are one matter. But decisions that affect institutional policy, direction, and personnel are critical and can be perceived as changing the nature of the faculty and institution. This is a matter that can reveal previously unstated concerns, fears, and assumptions with regard to the minority president. The minority president will have to be careful in processing and articulating his decision in a way that assures the school that his decision is not a culturally biased decision, but is based on the best interests of the school.

CONCLUDING REMARKS

To apply for and, especially, to accept the position of president of a historically white theological school takes courage and a willingness to enter uncharted waters. Each school is different and presents its own set of challenges for the minority president. It can be a lonely job with few true peers who understand the many complexities of serving in such a position as a minority executive. No maps exist to guide the newcomers. A very few have entered. Others are in the process of learning to navigate the waters. Important lessons can be learned in reflecting upon their experiences. Both minority individuals and historically white institutions are encouraged to do such reflection. It is an important step for racial and ethnic minority persons to take if we are to reach the certain future of a diverse society and the hope for a just world. It is essential for historically white institutions if they are to be relevant and effective in the transformed society.

12

Angle of Vision from a Companion/Ally in Teaching for a Culturally Diverse and Racially Just World

PAUL O. MYHRE

INTRODUCTION

The curious thing about vision is that it is something most of us share and yet we don't see anything in quite the same way as anyone else. Scientists have claimed recently through a variety of studies that females distinguish a wider range of colors than males, especially in their peripheral visual perception.[1] The scientists' findings suggest that females tend to be able to see more of the green-yellow spectrum of color than males.

Although the capacity of sight is generally a given for humans, the range of perception related to sight varies widely. For example, the capacity to see things as they actually exist in space is a challenge for most beginning artists. I have found in working with art students in North America that there is a shared tendency to look at singular objects isolated from the environments in which they are situated. Whether this is a learned behavior in K-12 instruction, fostered by contemporary advertising schemes, or something else, the propensity toward looking at things in a certain way is

---

1. Murray et al., "Sex-related differences," 1.

common. For example, if I were to ask a student to draw a still life of objects set on a table before them, they would choose a portion of the still life to concentrate on rather than the entire composition of objects in space. In addition, they would resist the impulse or not even recognize an impulse to include, as background for the still life set up, the students on the other side of the room who are also in the artists' line of vision and as such form part of the larger still life environment. So vision is a matter of physical and cognitive perception rooted in social and cultural experience.

Cognitive perception of strands involved in any issue or topic can be complicated to recognize or discern. I am a product of my cultural conditioning, my age development, my intellectual development, my social location, and so on. My capacity to discern how to work within any given environment in which I find myself is conditioned by my core epistemic framework, through which I filter data. Hence, when it comes to the topic of the interlocking systems of racism in the United States and within theological education in particular, I find that I am either blind or I lack a perceptive capacity to see my involvement within the systemic dimensions of racism itself; thereby I am complicit at times even when I don't think I am. This recognition is a small step in my journey toward facing my own deficiencies and capacities for engaging racism and white privilege. That said, I am committed to staying engaged with the topic and conversation. I am committed to remaining in the room even though the exit door to leave the conversation at any time is available to me as a white male. I am committed to attempting to deal with the interlocking system of privilege in which I am embedded. I welcome others showing me where my perception about any given topic is off so that I might see more clearly what the issues might really entail. And I am committed to working as an ally with others in facing the hard work of dismantling racism in personal, interpersonal, institutional and systemic contexts.

For over a decade I have served as an associate director for the Wabash Center for Teaching and Learning in Theology and Religion. Prior to that I taught in Fiji and Missouri, served as a minister in Alaska and the Midwestern United States, and I have had career experience as a professional artist and musician. These administrative, teaching, ministerial, and vocational positions have provided me with host of vantage points from which to discern the realities of racism. My current position as associate director for the Wabash Center has also given me a wealth of opportunities to lobby for and participate in specific racial-ethnic conversations about what it means to live and teach in North America as faculty of color. It also has provided me the honor of working alongside others in crafting conversations around anti-racism pedagogy and addressing cultural diversity concerns. The

Wabash Center has been and continues to be an ally and advocate for work in anti-racism and racial-ethnic cultural diversity issues. The Center's commitment to this work has eventuated in a host of faculty grants for projects that directly address anti-racism at their institutions and within their own teaching practices. It is from this vantage point that I offer my reflections and perspectives as one who is committed to serving as an ally working toward the development of teaching capacities for a culturally diverse and racially just world.[2]

RACISM AND ANTI-RACISM WORK

I contend that racism has not ceased to exist in the United States and that it is prevalent in every sphere of American life. It morphs into different forms in various regions of the country, it situates itself in diverse strata of business and education, it threads its way through congregational and interpersonal relationships, and it finds expression in any number of ways in any given context. It is ubiquitous and may be so pervasive because it is essentially an interlocking system of privilege or lack of privilege based on the construction of race itself.

Division along racial-ethnic lines is woven into United States history. From the beginning of subjugation and ethnic cleansing of first nations people living in North America, to the forced migration of Africans to the North American continent as slaves, to the Mexican-American War and dislocation of people from historic homelands in the Southwestern U.S., to the labor camps of Chinese workers in the Western U.S., to World War II Japanese internment camps, to the civil rights campaigns of the 1950s and 1960s, to the present, the United States has a variegated history of racism and racist practices that have leveraged privilege and power for European Americans and diminished, decreased, and dismantled privilege and power for any other racial-ethnic group living in North America. It is a history in which the Christian church was and is a willing participant, engaged social activist, and unknowing advocate for racist practices. Theological education itself is intimately connected with the histories of diverse people living in North America and racism itself in both positive and negative ways.

The history and experience of racism affects theological higher educational institutions and Christian congregations in overt and covert ways.

2. For more information about what the Wabash Center has supported in anti-racism, social justice, and cultural diversity projects, see the Wabash Center website: www.wabashcenter.wabash.edu.

It is subtle and often subdued in its expressions. It presents itself in everything from Christian education curriculum and stained glass windows in American congregations that picture European Americans as disciples and Christ-like figures to hymnals that feature poetic imagery that is laden with racially charged images—white equals good, black equals bad. Christianity prides itself on working toward social justice because the gospel message itself is one of social justice. Yet, when it comes to questions of participation in institutionalized racism and the prevalence of white privilege, the Christian church as a whole, along with theological institutions, has been largely silent.

The concept of "race" itself is a social construction for maintaining power by a select group—European Americans—over other groups of people: people of color. Citing the work of Allen, Ignatiev, and Roediger, Nora Hyland claims that, "The construction of an in-group, or dominant group, necessitates the construction of one or more subordinate out-groups, which have been configured in different ways throughout history but have always included people of African descent."[3] Furthermore she claims, "Racism relies on institutional power and the mask of normalcy to subordinate people of color. Analyzing Whiteness is inseparable from a critique of racism because racism is built upon the preservation of Whiteness."[4]

The experience of racism perhaps is most evident to those who are racialized. It also seems to be least evident to those who have the power and privilege to exercise racist behaviors. Consider the Christian who flies a Confederate flag from the bed of their truck or raises it on a flagpole in their yard next to a United States flag. In my conversations with these people the refrain has been a desire for a more conservative government that allows for greater personal freedom of expression. They don't care if the behavior might be regarded as offensive or racist. They see it as an exercise of their freedom of expression and privilege rather than any kind of ethical offense.

Racism is a phenomenon that is experienced by everyone living in the U.S. and it affects every dimension of human experience—economic, political, religious, social, health, business, education, etc. Definitions for racism abound. It can be defined as race prejudice + power.[5] It can be defined as something that is latticed with beliefs and stereotypes about different racial ethnic groups. David Wellman claims, "The essential feature of racism is not hostility or misperception, but rather the defense of a system from which

3. Hyland, "Being a Good Teacher," 431.

4. Ibid.

5. The Center for the Study of White American Culture, Inc., "Definitions of Racism."

advantage is derived on the basis of race . . . [I]t insures the continuation of a privileged relationship. Thus it is necessary to broaden the definition of racism beyond prejudice to include sentiments that in their consequence, if not in their intent, support the racial status quo."[6]

The problem of racism is its systemic capacity to maintain itself within structures and systems, even when people would like it to be dismantled. The work is constant and will not cease until the last vestiges of privileging or de-privileging on the basis of racial-ethnic identity are removed. Students, administrators, and teachers in North American theological education are embedded in interlocking systems of racism and as such require means for unlocking the doors that keep the system in place. This is particularly problematic for European American or "white" faculty and students who suffer from degrees of blindness due to their racial-ethnicity and social status, white privilege, and historic connections with interlocking systems of racism.

Nora Hyland in her essay "Being a Good Teacher of Black Students? White Teachers and Unintentional Racism," sketches some of the difficulties for European American teachers as they endeavor to teach with social justice in mind. She claims,

> The research in this field generally points to the idea that successful teachers of students of color identify the public school system as racist and see themselves as part of a larger political struggle for racial justice . . . A shared history, culture racial identification, or experience has often soldered these connections between teachers and historically marginalized communities. Moreover, culturally or politically relevant teachers see their connection to the community as integral to their identities as teachers. The roles and practices adopted by teachers identified as culturally relevant are not determined by the teacher's race, but these teachers do actively identify and resist racism in schools.[7]

The question of success in social justice concerns and pedagogy is directly tied to an aggressive stance toward addressing systemic racism.

Karyn D. McKinney provides another angle of vision on the issue of anti-racism work in her essay, "Whiteness on a White Canvas: Teaching Race in a Predominantly White University." She claims,

> Teaching race and ethnicity courses has been one of the most rewarding and challenging experiences in my academic career . . .

6. Ibid.

7. Hyland, "Being a Good Teacher," 430.

> I find teaching about race in a predominantly white university
> to be . . . difficult. Most white students come to college with only
> the faintest outlined knowledge of who they are racially . . . They
> have no real substance with which to fill in their racial identity
> or to decipher where they fit into this country's racial hierarchy.
> It is a singular challenge to reveal the contours of whiteness on
> the white canvas of a predominantly white university.[8]

She also claims that it is common for her students to deny the existence of racism or the fact that white people benefit from it. This is a common refrain among white students and faculty. Some would rather avoid the question altogether and indeed do so through course selection, text choices, and pedagogical decisions related to the structure of a given course. Diverse voices in text selection can be seen as an add-on rather than an infused component for teaching by European American faculty. Their formation involved a specific canon of their discipline that often excluded non-European voices.

Anti-racism work is arduous and slow. It can involve one step forward and three steps backward. It is deeply personal and gut-wrenching because of complicity in not addressing it head on. It is soul-searching and soul-rending because of theological and Christological commitments that can be interwoven with systems that are racist. Even the dimensions of a theological school curriculum that is founded and guided by anti-racist principles and aspiring toward a holy ground of truth and social justice can be mired in systems that keep privilege in the hands of a few who will not relinquish power or privilege easily or allow the canons of a curriculum to change swiftly—even if those canons reify racist beliefs and practices.

Citing the work of *The National Dialogues on Anti-Racism*, Sheryl Kujawa-Holbrook identifies a need for cultural competence capacity building for theological school students, staff, and faculty. It is this that may offer some hope and a way forward toward activism. She recounts that cultural competence includes:

1. Students knowing the difference between race, ethnicity, and culture; that culture is more than race and ethnicity, and can apply this competency within theological contexts;

2. Students getting in touch with their own issues of prejudice and stereotypes;

---

8. TuSmith and Reddy, *Race in the College Classroom*, 126–28.

3. Students challenging the myth of color blindness, and are aware of the reality of color consciousness as it pertains to race and theological institutions;

4. Students understanding that race, ethnicity, gender, economic class, sexual identity, age, ability, religion, etc. are organizing principles for good or ill in everything they do;

5. Students recognizing that there are multiple centers of truth, whose legitimacy is often determined by the amount of power any given perspective may have in a particular context.[9]

Perhaps one of the most profound issues facing theological education today is this: that the realities of racism and white privilege are quite adept in speeding away from the spotlight so as to remain undetected or unnoticed; yet, at the same time, they reinforce patterns and habits of mind that keep them in place.

ALLIES AND WHITE PRIVILEGE/RACISM

So what are allies and why might they be important for this work? Being an ally requires courage to face our own complicity in the interlocking systems of racism and to endeavor to address these systems by some tangible means. Each institutional context requires approaches unique to the institution since each has a unique history and institutional culture. Teaching and learning environments require careful attention to the contours at play in a learning space. Who is present, what histories they bring, what epistemic frameworks are evident, what is missing, whose voices are privileged and whose are silenced, and so on are relevant questions for teacher and student reflection and for lifting up conversations about the racialized traps into which many find themselves.

According to the Anti-Racist Alliance website, allies can

- Help foster environments where inclusivity is the norm and exclusivity is exposed;

- Engage and address white privilege;

- Speak to issues of injustice in systems and practices;

- Work toward dismantling unjust systems of oppression;

- Align themselves with the needs of culturally diverse faculty, staff, and students;

9. Kujawa-Holbrook, "Beyond Diversity," 143–44.

- Name issues and practices that are racist and offer alternatives that are less or not at all racist.[10]

As a Norwegian-American I am identified as "white" in the United States. However, I think the colorization of people based on ethnic identity is odd. It is a social construction meant to privilege some and diminish power and privilege among others. When I was a practicing artist, I had an array of tubes of oil paint. They went by such names as: "Naples Yellow," "Cerulean Blue," and "Cadmium Red Light." They also had such labels as: "Flesh" and "Indian Red." As a young adult growing up in the upper Midwest, I didn't pay much attention to the names on the tubes. However, when a college classmate of mine asked me about the label name on a tube of paint—I had an "aha" moment. The color inside the tube of "flesh" paint roughly matched my own pinkish, yellow, white skin pigmentation. It did not match the skin pigmentation of my friend. This was one of my many awakenings to the subtle ways by which racism infuses American culture. Why couldn't the tube color for "dark brown" or "saffron light" be called "flesh"? I would guess that the paint producers were unaware of the racism associated with naming colors of paint and may have been catering to a mostly "white" flesh-toned buyers who also didn't find the names problematic. This unnamed racism went unexamined by me—the art student who prided myself on keen observational capacities—until it was brought to my attention in an awakening moment. I think this is now part of my work as an ally: naming the obvious that goes unnoticed until it is pointed out.

White racism is threaded through American culture and is as common as affinities for apple pie and vanilla ice cream. Sheryl Kujawa-Holbrook in her essay, "Beyond Diversity: Cultural Competence, White Racism Awareness, and European-American Theology Students," asserts ". . . the need for a greater awareness of cultural and racial differences is a challenge facing theology students who live and work within changing contexts. For European American students this challenge includes an understanding of the power dynamics inherent in 'whiteness' and how the resultant social power affects persons of other races and cultures."[11] In this essay she names well the presenting problem for European American students and, I would add, faculty and staff located in theological school contexts.

White privilege is something that European Americans share regardless of their social, educational, or regional backgrounds. It is not confined to a particular religious or political affiliation. It is a given reality that affects

---

10. For more ideas about how to engage in anti-racism work and confront white privilege, see the Anti-Racist Alliance website at http://www.antiracistalliance.com.

11. Kujawa-Holbrook, "Beyond Diversity," 141.

the psyches and behaviors of people who would be labeled as "white" and those who would be identified as something other than white. This division in itself exposes part of the problem. White is regarded as the base from which comparisons are made. Peggy McIntosh in her foundational study, "White Privilege: Unpacking the Invisible Knapsack," articulates well the nature of the problem. European Americans suffer from a socialized construction that sees their values, perspectives, and so on as ". . .mentally neutral, normative, and average, and also ideal, so that when . . . [they] work to benefit others, this is seen as work that will allow them to be more like us."[12]

A helpful chapter for teaching about racism and engaging in ally work can be found in the book *Teaching for Diversity and Social Justice: A Sourcebook*, edited by Maurianne Adams, Lee Anne Bell, and Pat Griffin. The chapter is co-authored by Charmaine L. Wijeyesinghe, Pat Griffin, and Barbara Love and is entitled "Racism Curriculum Design." The chapter provides a helpful checklist of characteristics for those who would strive to be allies in anti-racism work. The characteristics of an ally are provided in an appendix and include:

- Feels good about own social group membership; is comfortable and proud of own identity;

- Takes responsibility for learning about own and target group heritage, culture, and experience, and how oppression works in everyday life;

- Listens to and respects the perspectives and experiences of target group audiences;

- Acknowledges unearned privileges received as a result of agent status and works to eliminate or change privileges into rights that target group members also enjoy;

- Recognizes that unlearning oppressive beliefs and actions is a lifelong process, not a single event, and welcomes each learning opportunity;

- Is willing to take risks, try new behaviors, act in spite of own fear and resistance from other agents;

- Takes care of self to avoid burnout;

- Acts against social injustice out of a belief that it is in her/his own self-interest to do so;

- Is willing to make mistakes, learn from them, and try again;

- Is willing to be confronted about own behavior and attitudes and to consider change;

12. Ibid., 142.

- Is committed to taking action against social injustice in own sphere of influence;

- Understands own growth and response patterns and when she/he is on a learning edge;

- Understands the connections among all forms of social injustice;

- Believes she/he can make a difference by acting and speaking out against social injustice;

- Knows how to cultivate support from other allies.[13]

The chapter includes a helpful appendix entitled "Action Continuum." This could provide an excellent piece for faculty conversations around the topic of ally work in their teaching and service to the institution.

ALLIES AND TWENTY-FIRST-CENTURY THEOLOGICAL EDUCATION

The issues facing North American theological higher education are manifold and no one solution will respond to them all. For allies the work of dismantling structures that reinforce racist practices is unfinished business. A quick read of theological institution websites in the United States and Canada would yield important insights about the ongoing stratification of those institutions. Many still favor privileging white leadership in the positions of president and dean. Although some important steps have been taken in recent years toward diversifying the administrations of many schools, much remains to be accomplished to better reflect the racial-ethnic diversity that makes up the North American continent and theological student demographics. Perhaps theological educational institutions could benefit from the use of anti-racism consultants who could work with trustees, administrators, staff, faculty, and students. Institutions could apply for one through the Wabash Center's consultant program.[14]

Racism embedded in institutional systems could remain unaddressed until those with the power and privilege in the institution decide to tackle it head on. In my opinion it will remain a sizeable impediment for sustained and significant growth for any theological institution in the twenty-first century. The North American continent is becoming more and more diverse. Theological education, to be relevant and committed to social justice, ought

13. Adams et al., *Teaching for Diversity*, 2nd ed., 108.

14. See the Wabash Center website for details about the consultants program: http://www.wabashcenter.wabash.edu/consultants/default.aspx.

to reflect something of that same diversity at all strata within the ecology of theological institutions themselves. At the time of this writing, of the over 250 or so ATS accredited schools, most are served by white presidents and deans (roughly 75 percent), and are largely served by white faculty.[15]

At the heart of theological education is the study of God. Any approach to theology generally takes into account the great love of God for diversity and complexity. This great variety of life that populates the planet gives testimony to this propensity of God toward multiple variations on the overarching theme of life. If theological educational systems could be reframed to reflect this more in the various dimensions of their institutional life, one has to wonder what kind of formation might be evident. In addition, it also causes one to wonder what formation is present in contexts where leadership and faculty profiles remain relatively monochromatic.

Those who would be counted as privileged in theological institutional systems are especially entrusted with the task of facing squarely what privilege means and how it might be realigned so as to provide more space for power and privilege to be shared by those who historically have had neither experience in theological education. This examination and realignment cannot be a patronizing move, however, since by so doing one would only reify unjust systems of oppression latticed within any racist framework.

I think part of the hard work of addressing racism is to face squarely one's own place within the interlocking systems of oppression that have hundreds of years of expression in North America. What does it mean to be part of the problem? More than that, what does it mean to be one who may not only be part of the problem, but also one who perpetuates the problem without addressing it? Those who were born white in North America were born into a privileged status. From the poorest to the most wealthy, to be white in North America means that you will enjoy a host of unearned privileges that racial-ethnic people will not by the very nature of their biological and social location. Those who would consider themselves to be other than white have to struggle, fight, earn, or receive benevolent gifts for the same or greater privilege to be experienced.

This interlocking system of racism extends and threads its way through institutional systems in ways that can be discerned. In some cases it is relatively easy to denote how a system has selected against diverse leadership or diverse faculty and staff. It is a bit more complicated when it comes to

15. For more precise details about theological institutions located in North America, see the Association of Theological Schools or the Auburn Institute websites: http://www.ats.edu/Pages/default.aspx, and http://www.auburnseminary.org/research; and http://www.auburnseminary.org/research?par=838.

curricular decisions and the actual canon of material that might make up a given course. Discerning which texts are privileged and which are not is often a faculty decision. If the faculty is unconcerned or disconnected from issues of privilege in the classroom, then it may be that the selections will represent a particular bias toward Western European scholarly texts from the late nineteenth and early twentieth centuries, or Western European texts from the Middle Ages onward to the present. A quick perusal of syllabi from theological school curriculums will find an abundance of required readings representing a common twentieth-century European-bias curriculum that largely ignores the voices on the margins of this European canon. However, when looking from a global perspective, one might quickly see that the European canon comprises only a small slice of the overall intellectual canon that is available for theological education. Sometimes it takes a faculty member or faculty members occupying privileged positions in an institution to call attention to this reality and encourage a wholesale reevaluation of the overall curriculum and its aims at a theological school.

If theology students are to embrace an anti-racist curriculum it will require theological institutions to offer one. A quick read of syllabi in any given theological institution located in North America will reveal much about the commitments of that school toward privileging certain voices above others. It will demonstrate how the school has or has not faced issues of white privilege and ongoing systems of racism oriented toward maintaining the status quo. For example, a common core course in theology will show much about which epistemic frameworks are privileged and which are diminished or sidelined. It causes me to wonder what a theological school curriculum would look like if it fully embraced anti-racist practices.

Consider a multiplicity of voices from a diversity of racial-ethnic positions woven into a theological school curriculum. No one perspective or type of writing is privileged over another. Latino/a scholarly texts written in Convivencia are set alongside European texts written in the nineteenth and twentieth centuries as equally valid and important. The work of James Cone is set alongside the work of Friedrich Schleirmacher or Karl Barth as equal in sharing approaches to writing about theology. This pairing and coupling of various theologically rich scholarly works could perhaps move the writings that are often lodged at the periphery or margins of a course to be resituated as central and not as alternatives to the main or "authoritative" work on a given topic.

Students could be moved toward new perspectives in theological imagination as they encounter in more robust ways a diversity of perspectives and voices on any given subject. The voices of scholars on the margins would be centralized and coupled with voices that had been regarded as central. In the orbit of reflection on theological ideas would be the students themselves as they move around a diverse curriculum core, rather than moving around a heavily European-centered curriculum that is regarded as normative. The normative center would be shifted to one of a diversity of racial-ethnic voices addressing core themes and ideas. For example, Christology would be set within a frame of multiple epistemological approaches rather than a singularity rooted in classic texts drawn from a European intellectual tradition.

A diverse curriculum that infuses diversity from start to finish as the core of the theological school curriculum may enable students to begin to see how ministry is also diverse in construction, expression and practice. It could help students to complexify their understanding of theology, ethics, biblical studies, and so on so as to be more flexibly responsive to a diversity of people and contexts with which they will be engaged in their ministerial practice.

Given the current state of North America and North American theological institutions, one might quickly conclude that the work of allies is never fully accomplished. The task of facing one's own white privilege in North America is never over. If you have been born to be a white, male, heterosexual adult that finds yourself in theological education, then it is incumbent on you to daily work toward dismantling the systems of racism that both oppress minorities and keep you locked in positions of privilege.

The reality of living in a racialized and prejudiced society is part of the fabric of living in the United States. Theological education cannot proceed forward effectively in my estimation until it has adequately addressed these issues. A recent Mellon-funded grant project involving six college campuses reached a similar conclusion. Kathleen Skubikowski in her article "Beyond Diversity: Social Justice Education Across the Curriculum" asserted that the Mellon grant organizers found "that pedagogical change, curricular change, and institutional change go necessarily together: The socially just classroom needs a socially just academy in order to flourish. Faculty will take pedagogical risks in supportive environments. Thus the kinds of collaborations . . . might best be horizontal (among faculty across the curriculum) and vertical (among faculty, administrators, students, staff, alumni) to create such socially just educational environments."[16]

16. Skubikowski et al., *Social Justice Education*, 97.

TEACHING STRATEGIES FOR ANTI-RACISM

There is no shortage of possibilities for teaching strategies that can actively address anti-racism in theological education. Vijay Prashad's article "On Commitment: Considerations on Political Activism on a Shocked Planet" indicates four principles that could undergird teaching strategies. His four principles are:

1. Celebrate differences but also put each cultural world into the other. Never allow anyone to become complacent about his or her culture.

2. Always seek the grounds of solidarity or interconnection, and then seek the barriers that need to be overcome. We have tensions we should talk about and push before our adversaries exploit them.

3. Solidarity should be based on a scrupulous attention to the interests of different pan-ethnic formations in the rat race of bureaucratic multiculturalism.

4. Always put the spotlight on White supremacy.[17]

Since theological schools are interested in issues pertaining to social justice and adherence to the gospel, I think these modest principles could be utilized as support for teaching practices within theological school contexts across North America. Four models/approaches for teaching from an anti-racism ally position are provided below for reflection and consideration.

Five-step Model

Sheryl Kujawa-Holbrook offers a five-step model for engaging students in the work of anti-racism. This model could be utilized among faculty and staff also as both an awareness developing set of practices and a set of topics for a faculty retreat. Kujawa-Holbrook suggests that these stages include: "1. Appreciating Diversity—Deconstruction; 2. Prejudice Reduction—Behavior Analysis; 3. Power Analysis—Social Constructivism; 4. Visioning—Anti-Oppression; and 5. Reconstruction—Institutional Racism."[18] Each one of these topics could comprise an entire retreat or semester of engagement by students. It causes me to wonder how a theological school curriculum could embrace the five steps in a systematic way. I wonder how a curriculum would look if, each semester, one topic served as a focal point that would be examined by all courses in that given term. What would the ministerial formation of graduates look like at the end of three years? I suspect a group of

17. Ibid., 125.

18. Kujawa-Holbrook, "Beyond Diversity," 145–47.

graduates would be better equipped to engage the diverse ministerial needs of their congregations in the twenty-first century.

Risking Conflict

In a collection of essays published in *Teaching Theology & Religion,* one essay, "Beyond Black and White: How to Handle Conflict," expresses well some of the risks associated with raising the topic of racism and anti-racism work in a classroom space. Clearly the issue of establishing racial conversations as a binary conversation about "white and black" is not sufficient. The questions at the conclusion of the essay provide a set of questions that faculty might employ when considering teaching about racism in America. These questions include: "1. In a multiracial classroom, how can teachers and students go beyond a binary construction of race (in terms of black and white) to understand the many cultural and pedagogical assumptions shaping the classroom? 2. How can teachers turn potential racial conflicts in the classroom into teachable moments? 3. What kinds of skills must racial and ethnic minority teachers acquire to handle an increasingly diverse student body? What kind of support do these teachers need?"[19]

Since theological schools are in general committed to ministerial formation, it strikes me that the importance of understanding how to handle conflict effectively is a vital ingredient for ministerial development. Although this is handled in some manner within the pastoral care course requirement, it seems to me that topics sure to raise conflict within the classroom ought not be avoided in all cases. Clearly, when the topics pertain to the types of issues that ministers will face in congregational and ministerial contexts, constructive conversations could help in any number of ways. Faculty who structure classroom teaching such that difficult conversations in the classroom about any given topic could occur may see significant learning outcomes and ministerial formational development. Such conversations about the topic of anti-racism and white privilege could aid in the development of student capacities to foster similar conversations in the ministerial contexts they will serve in twenty-first-century ministry, and could enhance their own capacities to know what may be difficult about the conversations for themselves and for the other.

---

19. Kwok et al., "Taken with Surprise," 35–46.

Redefining Whiteness

Karyn D. McKinney offers an approach to dismantling racism by focusing on the problem of "whiteness." For her, teaching about racism in America among white students in particular requires careful attention to the multiple layers in which racist attitudes and practices prevail. "In order to challenge structural racism, whites must relearn what it means to be white . . . Antiracist instructors should place U.S. and global relations in a historical context so that the fiction of whiteness as a liability is disrupted. We must . . . suggest how whites may become antiracist allies to people of color . . . Facing student fears of social awkwardness or racial tension [ought to be central to any approach]."[20] Although McKinney doesn't offer a particular strategy for doing this other than naming and defining what it means to be white, perhaps that could be a significant place for the conversation and the work of anti-racism to begin. It provides a place for an honest dialogue about one of the most elusive components of anti-racism pedagogy—facing squarely the problem of white privilege. Jane Bolgatz's book, *Talking Race in the Classroom*, provides another way by which to raise conversations around whiteness and for understanding and challenging racism in the classroom. For heightening conversations about and inquiry into the dynamics of racism and privilege in the classroom, she suggests that it can be fostered by teachers' attentiveness to social dynamics and relationships in the classroom. For her it is a matter of asking poignant questions that sing to the heart of the issue. She suggests asking, "Who has more influence in discussions? How do teaching styles accommodate or alienate particular learners? How do teachers share or maintain their authority? . . . How do race, class, gender, geography, and history affect one's position in the world and one's view of others? What institutional forces are at play? How does language shape our understanding? How do race and racism intersect with other aspects of identity and forms of oppression? What is the problem?"[21] Bolganz also suggests the use of case studies as a means toward getting at the various threads involved with racism and white privilege.

In addition, George Lipsitz's "The Possessive Investment in Whiteness" provides good fuel for conversation about the pervasive power of white privilege. He claims, "Whiteness is everywhere in U.S. culture, but it is very hard to see . . . As the unmarked category against which difference is constructed whiteness never has to speak its name, never has to acknowledge its role as an organizing principle in social and cultural relations. To identify,

---

20. TuSmith and Reddy, *Race in the College Classroom*, 138.

21. Bolgatz, *Talking Race*, 34–35.

analyze, and oppose the destructive consequences of whiteness . . . requires an understanding of the existence and the destructive consequences of the possessive investment in whiteness that surreptitiously shapes so much of our public and private lives."[22] This sometimes slippery reality of "whiteness" is difficult to grasp and yet at the same time easier to name once faculty and students begin to see the traces of it in images, texts, television, film, advertising, and so on. Hence, an approach to shining a black light on whiteness will begin to show the contours of what had been previously hidden to the eyes of those unable to discern "whiteness."[23]

Problem-Based Learning Approaches

Perhaps tackling subjects such as institutional racism and white privilege could be accomplished through a problem-based learning approach. Two clear advantages in this pedagogical approach are discerned through power as diversified and learning as contextualized. Students work collaboratively with other students and teachers in determining what needs to be discovered about a given problem or learning question. Instead of the teacher maintaining a privilege over knowledge distribution, students are empowered to discover sources for knowledge acquisition and development. Some teachers have employed this approach by first providing students with a thought-provoking question or scenario that cannot be easily answered and requires a substantial amount of research in order to begin to construct an answer or answers that could begin to address the question. For example, one might ask, "Are American congregations in our community or region racist? Do American congregations in our community or region exhibit elements of white privilege and how are they addressing it? Are American congregations in our community or region engaged in anti-racism training and activism?" Students could then be charged with the responsibility of uncovering the answers through interviews of congregations, congregational leaders, and so on with a host of survey questions that the teacher and students would have constructed together. Students engaged in PBL activities quickly discover that they need to perform research associated with each particular piece of a question. In this case, such work may involve analyzing systems of racism, identifying marks of institutional racism, and becoming acquainted with definitions for and expressions of white privilege.[24]

22. Lipsitz, "The Possessive Investment in Whiteness," 79.

23. See also Hill, "Fighting," 3–23.

24. For additional information about Problem-Based Learning, see these resources: Knowlton and Chart, eds., *Problem-based Learning*; Lee, *Teaching & Learning*; Amador

Goal Setting for Classroom Design

One of the first things to consider when developing courses or modules that will directly address racism is that of goal setting. Charmaine L. Wijeyesinghe, Pat Griffin, and Barbara Love co-authored a helpful chapter for thinking about how to engage in ally work through course and curriculum design. In their chapter, "Racism Curriculum Design," for the book *Teaching for Diversity and Social Justice: A Sourcebook*, edited by Maurianne Adams, Lee Anne Bell, and Pat Griffin, they provide an overview of specific modules for racism that could be adaptable for theological school classrooms. The list of goals that are embedded in module designs include: identification of racial and ethnic heritages; discerning socialization into a racist culture; discovering definitions for assumptions about race and racism in America; developing awareness of racism's various manifestations; exploring white privilege, collusion, internalized racism, and empowerment; widening perceptions about different racial heritages and experiences; reflection about what it takes to end racism; and activism against racism in whatever form it is discovered.[25] The *Sourcebook* would make an excellent addition to any faculty member's library and could serve as a source for faculty retreat conversations around the topic of teaching for diversity and social justice.

CONCLUSION

The need for theological school faculty, students, and ministerial professional practioners (who possess keen abilities for seeing the landscape of racism, diversity, and needs for anti-racism work in America) cannot be overstressed. The twenty-first century will show growth in racial-ethnic diversity and interaction. The need for anti-racism work is ongoing in theological schools, parish contexts, and ministerial locations and shows no sign of lessening. On the contrary, as the Latina/o population grows over the next decade or two there will come a point at which there will be no dominant racial-ethnic group in the United States.

Perhaps as more people become cognizant of injustices caused by racism and white privilege, they will seek to become allies and agents in the work of anti-racism. The call for faculty, theological school administrators, and ministerial professionals to effectively engage issues of racism and diversity in the next few decades will grow with each successive year. As diversity increases and the historic majority of European Americans decreases

---

et al., *The Practice of Problem-Based Learning*; and Barrett and Moore, *New Approaches*.

25. Adams et al., *Teaching for Diversity*, 86.

there will be opportunities for new conversations about racism, anti-racism work, and dismantling white privilege. It is incumbent on each theological institution in the present to take proactive steps to address racism, work toward social justice in anti-racism efforts, and promote diversity awareness in its life and mission to meet the present and forthcoming needs and justice concerns.

Racism will not cease to be a reality with which to contend. It will continue to find expression in a host of contexts and ways. Calls for anti-racism actions for social justice will only increase as historic positions of power and privilege will be pressured to change to reflect the growing realities of diverse needs and voices. It has taken hundreds of years for racism to embed itself within systemic frameworks latticed through North America. It will take time and diligent effort to dismantle it piece by piece.

The need for allies is as prevalent as it has ever been. One of the roles that Caucasian faculty in theological institutions can embrace is that of serving as allies for their racial-ethnic colleagues, staff, and students. Such alliance includes a willingness to assert that whiteness is a problem within a racism systemic structure. As such, it can be addressed through classroom teaching practices, faculty meetings, institutional decision-making, and so on. To risk not serving as an ally is to be complicit in a potentially racist system. The risk of claiming that white privilege doesn't exist only will serve to reify unjust systems of racism. There is no exit door for those who would actively seek to work toward anti-racism in all sectors of life.

Twenty-first century theological education is in turmoil and may benefit from discernment of future directions for forming ministers. Clearly pressing issues that could be taken up at present are associated with anti-racism and cultural diversity. Anti-racism requires a close self-examination of the present institutional contours of racism, power, privilege, etc. that exist not only at the school, but also in the immediate ecclesial and social environments in which the seminary serves. I think building capacity for engaging cultural diversity across the curriculum and in subsequent parish contexts is paramount to a theological institution's relevance for the twenty-first century. There are a number of theological schools that have been actively working on anti-racism for at least a decade and many others that have recently begun to work on the multiple issues associated with racism in their institutional contexts. From my angle of vision, I have hope for a future in which a more culturally diverse and racially just world will be realized.

13

Faculty Colleagues as Allies in Resisting Racism

NANCY RAMSAY

. . . I have been unwilling until now to open in myself what I have known all along to be a wound—a historical wound, prepared centuries ago to come alive in me at my birth like a hereditary disease, and to be augmented and deepened by my life. If I had thought it was only the black people who have suffered from the years of slavery and racism, then I could have dealt with the matter long ago; I could have filled myself with pity for them, and would no doubt have enjoyed it a great deal and thought highly of myself. But I am sure it is not so simple as that. If white people have suffered less obviously from racism than black people, they have nevertheless suffered greatly; the cost has been greater perhaps than we can yet know. If the white man has inflicted the wound of racism upon black men, the cost has been that he would receive the mirror image of that wound into himself. As the master, or as a member of the dominant race, he has felt little compulsion to acknowledge it or speak of it. . . . But the wound is there, and it is a profound disorder, as great a damage in his mind as it is in his society. . . . I want to be cured; I want to be free of the wound myself, and I do not want to pass it on to my children. . . . [I]f I fail to make at least the attempt I

forfeit any right to hope that the world will become better than
it is now.[1]

INTRODUCTION

White supremacy is the context that shapes the lifelong work of becoming
an ally in higher education for those of us on faculties who identify racially
with the dominant culture. When racism is recognized as an interlocking
system of advantage based on race arising in and sustained at personal,
group, institutional, and cultural symbolic levels, the focus for allies is clearly on confronting issues of power and white privilege that are insinuated
throughout academic institutions, such as in classrooms, departmental
and shared governance contexts, administrative practices, and policy and
procedural levels.[2] For allies, the goal of this intentional use of ourselves in
our institutional contexts is to enact our commitment to deconstructing the
effects of white supremacy, because we have come to understand that apart
from this very intentional engagement we otherwise are contributing to the
reproduction of white privilege and the inequalities it perpetuates. In other
words, the work of becoming an ally involves developing a self-interested,
political intentionality and willingness to use one's self to help effect practices that support racial justice and institutional transformation. Such opportunities arise in myriad ways and often outside the awareness of those
of us who enjoy the benefits of white privilege so pervasive in the dominant
culture. A few examples noted below may help inform our imaginations.

Classroom Contexts

Diane, a white, married faculty member at a theological seminary finds
herself sitting across from two angry students who are enrolled in her class
on pastoral care. They self-identify as African American and Latina, and requested an appointment after witnessing an unsettling classroom exchange
between Diane and two other students who identify as White or European-
American. Diane had assigned readings that pointed to the importance of
pastors being aware of the effects of racial and cultural oppression in the
practice of care in church and culture. A white student had complained that
this reading was too political and that it distorted how similar suffering is for
us all, adding that we create our own situations. Another had complained

1. Berry, *Hidden Wound*, 3–4.
2. Wellman, *White Racism*.

that these issues are too isolated to warrant an entire class session, especially because we are a post-racial culture now. Diane had been surprised by the two comments. She had responded to the first by asserting that while there are a variety of ways persons experience oppression, racial oppression was real and enduring. It would be important for pastors to be alert to ways to assist those who experience such oppression. She had responded to the second that she realized some had asserted that the election of an African American president had signaled the end of racism, but that hate crime statistics signaled the opposite. She suggested racism was an ongoing issue in the church as well as the culture. Questions and conversation then focused only on particular aspects of the reading rather than the larger political and ethical issue of racism. The two students now in her office complain that Diane failed to demonstrate knowledge of and a readiness to advocate for racial justice in church and culture during the class discussion. They are angry at their classmates and especially at her for failing to stand up for the importance of this issue. And, they want to know why that one class session is the only place in the syllabus where race is located for discussion.

Curricular Issues

The faculty of a seminary associated with a Mainline Protestant tradition is in the midst of a curriculum revision process. The faculty agreed to discuss in departmental conversations prior to the next faculty meeting how their new curriculum will deal with literature beyond those resources associated with Northern Europe, such as African American, Latina/o, Asian, Feminist, and LGBTQ scholarship. The faculty of twenty presently includes an Asian American, Sam, an assistant professor in the Bible department, and an African American Womanist scholar, Carol, an assistant professor in the theology and ethics department. In the theology and ethics department, there are four faculty members. In addition to Carol, a married mother of two children, the department includes Sharon, a married, white feminist scholar who is an associate professor; Charles, a married white man who is an associate professor; and Ted, a married white man and full professor who is the senior member of the faculty.

Ted chairs the meeting and begins the discussion by indicating that he cannot imagine supporting "watering down" the limited amount of reading he can assign to teach the Tradition by having to include ideological resources. Sharon, wanting to support Carol, says that she believes the "body of knowledge" now presumed by the required courses in the department is too limiting, and she turns to Carol saying, "Carol, we welcome the insights you bring to this discussion as an African American scholar." She is stunned when Carol replies that she thinks Ted raised a good point about how carefully changes would need to be made, and that Sharon is right to suggest that they review the current body of knowledge. She looks forward to more conversation about how they might make those proposals. Sharon feels betrayed by Carol, a junior colleague she had thought would be her ally after her years as the only woman in the department.

Recruiting and Retaining Faculty of Color

A search committee in a religious studies department gathered to review the applications for an assistant professor position in biblical literature. The department chair began the meeting by reminding them of the faculty's commitment in every search to look for opportunities to widen the diversity of the faculty. Currently there are no faculty "of color" teaching Bible in the department. There were many applicants whose racial identity would add diversity. The senior member of the Bible department, Tom, spoke first, indicating that he found the pool uninspiring and suggested that, reluctantly, he could only support a candidate who happened to be a white man. The chair invited other members of the committee to share their preferences. No one challenged Tom's assessment. A relatively new assistant professor in the Bible department wondered if the chair felt there were any ways to widen the pool, given the committee's concerns.

Tenure and Promotion Issues

The tenure and promotion committee of a theological seminary met to review materials for Carol, a Womanist ethicist, the only African American on the faculty of fifteen, who was now in her third year in a tenure track position. Ted, the senior member of the theology and ethics faculty, indicated that his primary concern was that Carol's publications and teaching continued to be so narrowly ideological. Sally, a senior member of the biblical studies faculty pointed out that Carol's classes were full and that her publications were aligned with her appointment in Womanist ethics. She also noted that Carol's publications were well-reviewed and more numerous than those of her peers in this stage of their careers. Sally expressed concern that so many students whose racial identity is under-represented in the student body were asking for Carol's time.

Institutional Practices and Policies

The president of a theological seminary sent out the semi-annual report of the actions of the Board which included new appointments to the Board of Trustees. Jim, a white professor in the history faculty, noticed that once again the Board of thirty included only two persons of color, which was far below the representation of students of color in the student body. Further, he noticed that the request for additional funds for recruiting and retaining students of color, recommended to the faculty by the admissions committee, was not funded despite the urgent request of the faculty. He knew from conversations with his junior colleague, an Asian American man, that his colleague agreed these were important indicators for institutional integrity; but how could he move forward with this issue?

RESOURCES FOR FACULTY ALLIES

The vignettes that begin this essay point to the many politically complex situations in educational institutions that call for allies to exercise the leverage that accompanies white privilege in a context of white supremacy. In every case, the vignettes point to the importance of developing skills and collegial networks for engaging in the highly political work of being an ally for racial justice. These vignettes also demonstrate that whether in classrooms, student life, or shared governance, the telos of the practice of being white allies is institutional transformation, because at stake is the integrity of institutional and communal life and practices. This also means allies engage in this work because it is in our own interests to do so; our goals ought not be to relieve guilt or to receive thanks. I hope it is also clear in these vignettes that one cannot be neutral about racial justice. We are either committed to increasing our skills as allies, or we are entangled in reproducing and enjoying the privileges that accompany being White in this dominant culture. In the pages that follow we will use these vignettes to review a range of resources and strategies that support the practice of becoming racial justice allies.

The work of allies for classroom contexts includes a range of pedagogical and student issues, as well as faculty members' intentional preparation to expand their self-awareness about the way racial privilege may function to distort teaching and learning experiences. In the vignette focused on a classroom context we can identify concerns in all three of these areas. Diane considers herself an ally in racial justice. And, in the aftermath of this painful classroom event, she realizes that she has nonetheless constructed a syllabus that apparently compartmentalizes attention to racial difference to one class session, thus normalizing the privileges of white identity. This pedagogical error undermines her intention to support the importance of addressing racism as a systemic issue of justice. As the white students' comments reflect, her syllabus unwittingly reproduces an understanding of racism as a system of disadvantage that Whites of good will should address, rather than disclosing how the distortions of privilege as systemic advantage are insinuated in church and culture.[3] Unfortunately her responses to those students, while heartfelt, also unwittingly reproduce racism, because her comments suggest that information about racism is important in order to support those it disadvantages rather than to deconstruct the asymmetries of power in structures and systems that reproduce white students' unearned privileges and subordinate others' opportunities unjustly.

The two questions by the white students reflect common distortions that avoid responsibility for asymmetries of power that reproduce racism. The first suggests there is no difference in suffering, a version of "we're all alike." The second suggests the problem is past. Hindsight is always easier; however, in these exchanges Diane missed an opportunity to speak directly to issues of privilege and to clearly define why understanding racism as a system of advantage matters for effective ministry. Her responses were at once partially accurate and inadequate. She could have used her authority in the classroom to invite the class to recognize the way racism distorts their identities, imaginations, and context.

Because her responses did not clarify this political and theological claim about race and privilege, the two students of color came to share their anger and disappointment in her. In this vignette, the courage of the two students of color to share their concerns gives Diane another opportunity. Always being ready to repair mistakes and relationships is one of the important aspects of being an ally. Imagine what it could mean to the students if Diane acknowledges her mistake both in the syllabus and in the classroom discussion. Imagine further what could happen if she returns to class and reopens the conversation differently. If she chooses to return to the subject in class, there are excellent resources to assist her in shaping a presentation that introduces the way in which racism is learned and internalized as stigma or privilege; how it arose; how it is reproduced as privilege; and ways in which it represents important theological issues for ministry.[4] White persons who model antiracism make an important statement to those who enjoy privilege as well as to those who experience marginalization. This

---

3. Stanley et al., "Multicultural Course Transformation," 566–84.
4. Adams et al., *Teaching for Diversity*.

vignette underscores the political dimensions of even the construction of a syllabus and the implications for developing a highly reflective self-awareness about who our students are and what and how we teach students across a range of disciplines.[5]

Ally work also arises regularly in faculty discussions about curriculum. In this vignette we find other predictable, complicating dynamics arising in the ongoing politics that pervade faculty and institutional life. For example, even before race is foregrounded, we find here a theology department with a lone, white feminist, Sharon, who is eager for support from her new African American colleague, Carol, in deconstructing a traditional construction of teaching Christian theological tradition as championed by Ted. This vignette illustrates at least three important practices in being an ally: an ability skillfully to articulate the way white privilege limits our imaginations regarding the consequences of racism for real cognitive and material losses; the importance of self-aware intentionality in building strategic networks for deconstructing privilege; and a commitment on the part of allies always to protect the more vulnerable colleague of color when engaging in faculty political processes.

It is easy to imagine that Sharon has lost count of the times she and Ted have had one version or another of the conversation this vignette describes, in which Ted's response normalizes one way of conceptualizing an intellectual tradition that includes a corresponding trivialization of critical perspectives on that tradition and feminism in particular. His defense of his point of view illustrates painfully well how racism and privilege distort persons' imaginations in ways that reflect the hegemonic effects of privilege.[6] Whether a more substantial engagement with Ted's ideas on Sharon's part will be effective in this context is uncertain; however, her response is an isolated, simple assertion of a point of view he will dismiss out of hand. Since the agenda for the meeting was well known in advance, Sharon had time to explore conversation with Carol, Jim, and other faculty colleagues as well as with her dean, who appears to realize the need to revise this aspect of the curriculum. Thinking in this way would have helped Sharon avoid simply re-entering an ineffective, familiar, circular process with Ted, and would have enlarged her and others' imaginations about how to raise this important issue about deconstructing any notion of a singular way of understanding an intellectual tradition and welcoming previously marginalized points of view. We find no indication that Sharon has thought strategically about this conversation or the larger change process the curricular revision may

5. Adams and Love, "A Social Justice Education," 3–25.
6. Matsuoka, *The Color of Faith*.

make possible. This sort of strategic intentionality and networking is a very important aspect of effective ally practice as institutional change agents.[7]

It is also the case that it is not Carol's responsibility to articulate the rationale for the value of any additional points of view as Sharon asks her to do. Sharon's other misstep lies in her failure to consider Carol's political vulnerability in the departmental meeting. It is critical for allies to maintain mindfulness about ways to leverage our own social capital in a system in ways that protect the more vulnerable colleagues of color. The work of being an ally is based in our own self-interested recognition of the importance of institutional transformation rather than some sacrificial act that requires Carol's thanks or indebtedness. It will be very important for Sharon to approach Carol with apologies: first, for failing to take responsibility herself to articulate the value of a revised, wider understanding of the Tradition and second, for putting Carol at risk politically. Then, she should invite Carol to join her to build a relationship that reflects Sharon's clear commitment to building a racially just institution.

Recruiting and retaining faculty of color is a central commitment for transformation toward a racially just institution. As this vignette suggests, it is also fraught with complexity. There are several important positives in this vignette. Certainly one of those is the chair's opening statement that indicates the faculty has gone on record that a goal in every search is to add racial diversity to the faculty. It is also encouraging to learn that there are many applicants whose racial identity would help the faculty achieve this goal. Finally, the fact that the search is for an entry level position also increases the possibility of achieving the goal for bringing a colleague of color to the faculty because there are fewer limiting factors in considering all the applicants. Of course there is no way to guarantee a positive outcome.

What options are available to this department chair and to the committee and faculty? Once again themes of strategic networking and intentionality arise. Given the vote of the faculty for this priority we may well wonder how informed the faculty has become about the ways in which faculties that embody various forms of diversity enjoy wider conceptual richness of instruction, research, and scholarship; an enhanced institutional profile; and stronger possibilities in recruiting and retaining students. We do not know how actively the chair worked to recruit a diverse pool. There are networks in the academy that help locate and support young faculty who identify with racial groups that are minoritized in the academy. We can expect the intentionality of the chair around recruiting a pool that supports an institutional goal. She has not signaled that here. If she did do that work

7. Kendall, *Understanding White Privilege*, 141.

in advance, it would be well to rehearse what other well-regarded faculty indicated to her about applicants.

Tom's immediate response to the department chair's opening question dismissing the pool may also suggest that the chair did not use opportunities to discuss the pool with members of the committee in advance. Of course if she did do that, it would be well to share what she learned with all the members so as to support transparency. Such preliminary discussion could be quite useful and appropriate because the chair would have particular responsibility for recruiting the pool and enhancing it. It would also allow her to know ways to support committee members who may feel wary of the possible politics. Given Tom's seniority, it might be appropriate for the department chair to have taken time in advance to invite Tom's impressions of the field and engage him in conversation so as to assess his commitment to seeking a colleague who would add diversity to the Bible faculty. If she had heard any comment that implied different standards of evaluation, she would have had an opportunity to engage it. Also, given the asymmetries of power in the committee composition, the chair might exercise strategies that help mitigate those asymmetries by inviting members to offer their ideas in a rotation that does not allow the senior person to begin the conversation and possibly foreclose other discussion. Further, the department chair could be useful to the process by following up with references, especially for the applicants who add diversity, to have deeper information about their readiness at the time of the initial meeting. These strategies reflect strategic intentionality that supports both an institutional commitment and also faculty development around the importance of the goal of widening diversity.

Since the meeting began with Tom's dismissal of the applicants of color, the department chair can certainly use the assistant professor's idea to allow a later reconsideration of the pool with wider information and possibly a wider pool of applicants. That interim period would allow for further discussion, again with transparency, among the search committee members. In a faculty meeting, the chair might also report challenges in the search committee's progress on the institutional goal. These reflections demonstrate that there is no simple or guaranteed process for success with recruiting colleagues of color. They also suggest the importance of strategic intentionality and the value of advance faculty discussion to lay the foundation for a common commitment in searches and in supporting new colleagues who do add diversity.

Tenure and promotion policies and practices are critically important in every instance, and certainly so regarding faculty colleagues who may understandably imagine that their experience and evaluation will be colored by the fact of white supremacy as a pervasive influence in institutional and communal life, especially in institutions shaped by the dominant culture. In this vignette we overhear two colleagues who are part of a committee charged with reviewing a pre-tenure faculty member's progress toward tenure. We can immediately identify that there are asymmetries of power in the room because we know Sally is an associate professor and Ted is a full professor. Ordinarily such committees would be composed of tenured faculty. We know that as a tenured colleague Sally would be safe to comment. We can imagine that she also may feel some pressure since Ted's approval may someday matter when she seeks status as a full professor. We do not know whether other colleagues are willing to venture in, nor do we know how this committee will report to the faculty as a whole.

Sally is clearly seeking to function as an ally and does so with skill. We have met Ted and Carol in an earlier vignette so we know that Ted is consistent in his concern about "ideological scholarship." A critical factor in review processes is that evaluations be aligned with stated expectations, including those for teaching assignments. Sally responds well in noting that Carol's publications and teaching align with the position in which she was hired. Further, she also supports the quality of those publications, noting they are well-placed and reviewed by faculty peers. She goes further to indicate Carol's level of productivity is exceptional relative to her earlier peers in this rank. She notes that Carol's classes are fully enrolled. In each of these statements she is making strategic contributions to Carol's review.

Sally also raises important indicators for faculty and administration to consider: the response of students of color to Carol's presence and the unacknowledged considerable time and energy Carol is giving as well as the way in which this action by the students may well be an institutional indicator requiring further attention. In her conversation with Carol following the review, it will be important for the dean to inquire further about Sally's observation of a heavy informal student "advising" load. It is quite possible that Carol has accepted this informal advising load because she wants to be helpful to these students, and she is aware the students of color who are minoritized in that student body are uniquely comfortable sharing some concerns with her. Together the dean and Carol may discuss ways the institution can support Carol in the short term with the time constraints the advising creates; they may also begin to identify ways the institution can be responsive to the concerns of the students of color so as to relieve Carol and better support the students.

In this situation, we see how faculty of color may bear burdens directly related to inattention to practices and policies needed to support and retain students of color in institutions shaped by the dominant culture. Further, their experience is a particularly helpful resource for administration and faculty in the important work of recruiting and retaining students in minoritized populations.[8] It will be critically important that Carol experience confidence in the dean and assurance that any observations about ways the institution could be more responsive will not circle back around as injurious to her or to the students who shared concerns with her. Rather, the dean and other administrative and faculty colleagues need to convey appreciation for her contribution to enlarging their imaginations about ways to strengthen student services in particular and institutional integrity more broadly.

Institutional practices and policies as described in the vignette above may seem far removed from syllabi and classroom instruction or departmental conversations about curriculum, but they are a critical link in the overall process of transformation toward a truly multicultural institution. In this vignette, Jim, a full professor who is White, recognizes that it is time to be more direct in challenging an administrative pattern of inaction on two interrelated institutional practices: racial diversity as a priority in recruiting members of the Board, and institutional support for students whose minoritized racial identity in an institution shaped by the dominant culture requires additional practices and policies that recognize what such students are likely to need in order to complete their degree programs successfully. Once again we encounter a situation that points to important themes for effective allies: effective leveraging of the power that privileged faculty allies have and strategic intentionality regarding initiatives toward institutional change. Jim knows that his disappointment about the president's report on recent elections to the Board of Trustees is shared by at least one other colleague, Sam, whose Asian American racial identity is minoritized on the faculty and whose pre-tenured rank also indicates vulnerability. Jim needs to take the lead and protect Sam while expressing the losses for the institution that a pattern of underrepresentation of diversity represents. On the other hand, Jim knows that many faculty colleagues share his concern for the priority of funding better efforts to recruit and retain students of color. He can seek others to stand with him in raising the issue.

Less clear from the vignette is whether he would have similar faculty support for widening the diversity of the membership of the Board so that it better reflects the level of diversity in the student body. Jim is correct to recognize the political implications for the Board if there are few voices of color to speak to such issues, and in the vignette it is plausible to imagine that the need has been raised with the president before. The president of the

8. Reason et al., eds., *New Directions*.

school is the primary point of contact for Jim and colleagues who wish to engage these two issues.

For the purposes of this essay, let's imagine that Jim knows from earlier faculty meetings that the president supports efforts to move the institution toward practices and policies that enhance racial justice in its life and mission. However, the president does not have experience in leading this sort of institutional change process. What resources and strategies can Jim and other faculty and administrative allies offer to help the president succeed at the Board level in building support for this larger institutional effort? Important first steps include the critical recognition that racism develops in persons as socialized, learned behavior, and effective change begins with education and conversation rather than pronouncements of guilt.[9] This realization is an important strategic reminder to begin a change process invitationally, assuming the concern of others and opening with informed conversation, evidences of institutional self-interest in such action, and indications of resources and energy to support change. Some describe this as a process of building capacity for engaging issues that will no doubt challenge the institutional community. Strategically, persons such as Jim will realize that if the president recognizes there is a core group of colleagues prepared to help articulate the need for change, she is in a stronger position to engage the Board and the institution. In educational institutions, allies may well find that efforts to prompt institutional change begin by building an awareness of what racism is; how it undermines the integrity of the educational mission of the school; and what resources are available to support change. There are certainly ample resources for posing such questions.[10]

Colleagues in the area of critical pedagogy and social justice education have refined multicultural organizational development (MCOD) resources in ways that may be of use for a process of change in this institution.[11] MCOD theory provides resources for a community-wide process of assessment or an audit of institutional policies and practices to identify strategic points for change. It presumes the importance of wide, confidential input across the organizational structure of the school and then the development of a benchmarked strategic engagement in change. The approach recognizes that institutional change toward a fully multicultural organization will not be linear or uniform. It is more likely to be uneven and experienced as a spiral of increasing recognition of the effects of privilege deeply insinuated in practices as diverse as shared governance, Board membership, curricu-

9. Harro, "Cycle of Socialization."
10. Adams et al., *Teaching for Diversity.*
11. Jackson, "Multicultural Organization Development," 3–20.

lum, student services, recruitment and retention of students and faculty, and financial aid and institutional financial development strategies. It will also require a critical engagement with the insinuations of racial privilege and rearticulation of more just values and assumptions informing the ethos, worldview, and patterns of power sharing. Such engagements are not for the fainthearted. The process requires the full authorization of the leadership of the institution. The leadership team that oversees the process also will need to enjoy the trust of faculty and staff. This description underscores the earlier emphasis on wide, careful conversation that builds capacity and commitment with awareness that change of this sort will inevitably include challenging moments personally and institutionally.

On the other hand, it is also important to bear witness to the increase in freedom and hope that may emerge personally and institutionally from such a process. As Wendell Berry's comments at the outset of this essay note, the "wound" of racism is a profound disorder for those who identify with the dominant racial group as well as for the marginalized groups for whom it is even more invidious. It is at once a personal and social or corporate disorder that distorts the contexts into which we are born, and we in the dominant racial group reinscribe and augment its death-dealing ways. The MCOD process provides racially marginalized and privileged persons a structure and context for difficult and potentially life- and institution-changing conversations and actions. As changes begin, a certain momentum builds that, in my experience, helps deepen honesty and a corresponding hope and freedom. Such outcomes are not inevitable, but they are far more likely in an authorized, widely embraced, and closely monitored process.

A further aspect of such change processes lies in the inevitable recognition of the social construction of our identities that incorporate multiple, intersecting aspects of difference simultaneously.[12] Race, gender, sexuality, class, and other forms of identity intersect and mutually constitute and inform one another through a person's subjective sense of identity and in social structures.[13] Similarly the patterns of oppression and privilege accompanying these forms of difference are interwoven and dynamically related, i.e., asymmetrical patterns of power are insinuated in these intersections. Consider for example the curricular revision vignette in which Sharon, a white feminist, feels betrayed by Carol, an African American pre-tenure colleague who does not immediately support Sharon's feminist challenge to a critique of "ideological literatures" as peripheral to "the Tradition" in Christian theology. These two women colleagues are experiencing the complexity and

12. Holvino, "Simultaneity."

13. Ibid., 166–69.

multiplicity of their identities in which both may experience constraints related to gender, but for Carol, racism has more salience in the particular moment. For white allies who promote institutional transformation toward racial justice, it will be important to avoid construing a hierarchy of oppressions, and rather to develop an ability to discern the fluid ways asymmetries of power complicate such intersections as Carol and Sharon experienced in that departmental meeting. This is necessarily at once a subjective awareness and a capacity to observe such intersections in the life of an institution. Allies for racial justice should be wary of any construction that implies a hierarchy of oppressions.[14] Allies do need to become fluent in understanding distinctive aspects as well as similarities in how differences such as race and gender, when treated oppressively, arise and are reproduced in subjective and institutional life. Similarly, allies need to become self-aware of the diverse ways their experience incorporates the complexity and multiplicity of privilege and possibly stigma.

CONCLUSION

This essay began by acknowledging that the work of white allies on behalf of racial justice in educational institutions begins with an acceptance of the pervasive influence of white supremacy and the recognition of the self-interested imperative for allies to leverage our privilege on behalf of institutional transformation. The vignettes we have engaged demonstrate the complexity and the interconnection of such change. Successful retention and recruitment of faculty and students who widen the racial diversity of an institution, for example, rely on corresponding changes in syllabi and pedagogies, curricula that value broad intellectual traditions, and revised patterns of shared governance that resist the asymmetries of power accompanying racism.

The collection of vignettes included in this essay helps to disclose the complexity of the work of a white ally and the range of skills and sorts of intentionality, as well as resources, available to allies. In particular, white allies are persons who continue to sharpen our sensibilities about the pervasive asymmetries of power insinuated in personal, group, institutional, and cultural experience related to racial difference. We come to "own" our privileged position in relation to such power. That is, we embrace the connection between privilege and accountability. We learn to think strategically and collaboratively. We are eager to recruit others as allies.

14 Young, *Justice*, 39–65.

Allies also necessarily embrace this work because of our own self-interest in the ongoing deconstruction of the distortions of racism in our own lives and in the institutions and cultural contexts in which we work and live, as well as our desire to enhance our experience of freedom from these distortions. We recognize that our freedom and well-being is inevitably linked with the freedom and well-being of others whose lives, relationships, and opportunities are distorted by racism. As Wendell Berry suggested, we want to do our part to heal the wound of racism and not pass it on to the next generation.

Bibliography

Adams, Maurianne, and Barbara J. Love. "A Social Justice Education Faculty Development Framework for a Post-*Grutter* Era." In *Social Justice Education: Inviting Faculty to Transform Their Institutions*, edited by Kathleen Skubikowski, et al., 3–25. Sterling, VA: Stylus, 2009.

Adams, Maurianne, et al., eds. *Teaching for Diversity and Social Justice: A Sourcebook*. New York: Routledge, 1997.

———. *Teaching for Diversity and Social Justice*. 2nd ed. New York: Routledge, 2007.

Aguinis, Herman, et al. "Effects of Nonverbal Behavior on Perception of Power Bases." *Journal of Social Psychology* 138 (August 1998) 455–69.

Aleshire, Daniel O. "Gifts Differing: Race and Ethnicity in Theological Education." Paper presented at the ATS Chief Academic Officers Society Seminar, June 2008.

———. "Gifts Differing: The Educational Value of Race and Ethnicity." *Theological Education* 45 (2009) 1–18.

———. "The Future Has Arrived: Changing Theological Education in a Changed World." *Theological Education* 46 (January 2011) 69–80.

Alfred, Mary V. "Challenging Racism through Postcolonial Discourse: A Critical Approach to Adult Education Pedagogy." In *The Handbook of Race and Adult Education: A Resource for Dialogue on Racism*, edited by Vanessa Sheared, et al. San Francisco: Jossey-Bass, 2010. http://bridges.searchmobius.org:80/record=b1854202~S9.

Allan, Elizabeth J. "Bringing Voice to the Silences of Privilege: Strategies for Faculty Development and Curricular Change." Paper presented at the annual meeting of the American Educational Research Association, Chicago, April 2003.

Althaus-Reid, Marcella. *Indecent Theology: Theological Perversions in Sex, Gender, and Politics*. London: Routledge, 2000.

Amador, Jose A., et al. *The Practice of Problem-Based Learning: A Guide to Implementing PBL in the College Classroom*. Bolton, MA: Anker, 2006.

American Council on Education. "Leading Demographic Portrait of College Presidents Reveals Ongoing Challenges of Diversity, Aging." http://www.acenet.edu/newsroom/Pages/ACPS-Release-2012.aspx.

The American Heritage College Dictionary, 4th ed. Boston: Houghton Mifflin Co., 2004.

Anderson, Benedict R. *Imagined Communities: Reflections on the Origin and Spread of Nationalism*. London: Verso, 1983.

Anderson, Herbert. "Seeing the Other Whole: A Habitus for Globalisation." In *Globalisation and Difference: Practical Theology in a World Context*, edited by

Paul Ballard and Pam Couture, 3–17. Fairwater, Cardiff, Great Britain: Cardiff Academic Press, 1999.

Andraos, Michel Elias. "Engaging Diversity in Teaching Religion and Theology: An Intercultural, De-colonial Epistemic Perspective." *Teaching Theology and Religion* 15 (January 2012) 3–15.

Anonymous. "Black Faculty at the Nation's Highest-Ranked Colleges and Universities." *The Journal of Blacks in Higher Education* 48 (2005) 78–84.

———. "Black Students Show Solid Progress in Graduation Rates at Highly Selective Colleges and Universities." *The Journal of Blacks in Higher Education* 66 (September 2009) 46–56.

———. "Nearly 3 Million Black Students Are Enrolled in Higher Education." *The Journal of Blacks in Higher Education,* October 2012. http://www.jbhe. com/2012/10/nearly-3-million-black-students-are-enrolled-in-higher-education.

The Anti-Racist Alliance: http://www.antiracistalliance.com.

Asian Women United of California, ed. *Making Waves: An Anthology of Writings By and About Asian American Women.* Boston: Beacon, 1989.

Association for the Study of Higher Education. "Status of Ethnic and Racial Diversity in College and University Administration." *ASHE Higher Education Report* 35 (September 2009) 11–30.

The Association of Theological Schools. Association of Theological Schools. http://www.ats.edu/Pages/default.aspx, and http://www.auburnseminary.org/research. http://www.auburnseminary.org/research?par=838.

———. "2011–2012 Annual Data Tables." http://www.ats.edu/ResourcesPublications Presentations/Documents/AnnualDataTables/2011–12AnnualDataTables.pdf.

———. "Issue: Tenure and 'What is Academic.'" In *Folio: Diversity in Theological Education,* no publication date available, 29. (Some material included in this issue paper was extracted from table conversations at the ATS Seminar for Racial/ Ethnic Faculty Members at Predominantly White ATS Institutions, October 5–7, 2001.) http://www.ats.edu/LeadershipEducation/Documents/DiversityFolio.pdf.

———. "White and Combined Racial/Ethnic Faculty as Percentage of Full-Time Faculty in All Member Schools." http://www.ats.edu/Resources/PublicationsPresentations/ Documents/AnnualDataTables/2011–12AnnualDataTables.pdf.

The Auburn Institute. http://www.auburnseminary.org/research?par=838

Barndt, Joseph. *Understanding and Dismantling Racism: The Twenty-First Century Challenge to White America.* Minneapolis: Fortress, 2007.

Barrett, Terry, and Sarah Moore. *New Approaches to Problem-based Learning: Revitalising Your Practice in Higher Education.* New York: Routledge, 2011.

Bass, Dorothy C., and Craig Dykstra, eds. *For Life Abundant: Practical Theology, Theological Education, and Christian Ministry.* Grand Rapids: Eerdmans, 2008.

Bennett, Christine. *Comprehensive Multicultural Education: Theory and Practice.* Boston: Allyn and Bacon, 1991.

Bennett, John B. *Academic Life: Hospitality, Ethics, and Spirituality.* Boston: Anker, 2003.

Bernstein, Basil. *Class, Codes and Control: The Structuring of Pedagogic Discourse.* New York: Routledge, 1990.

Berry, Wendell. *The Hidden Wound.* New York: North Point, 1989.

Bessler, Joseph A. "Seminaries as Endangered Habitats in a Fragile Ecosystem: A New Ecology Model." In *Revitalizing Practice: Collaborative Models for Theological Faculties*, edited by Malcom L. Warford, 1–31. New York: Peter Lang, 2008.

Bhabha, Homi K. *The Location of Culture*. New York: Routledge, 1994.

Boff, Leonardo. *Trinity and Society*. Translated by Paul Burns. Maryknoll, NY: Orbis, 1988.

Bolgatz, Jane. *Talking Race in the Classroom*. New York: Teachers College Press, 2005.

Brookfield, Stephen D. *Becoming a Critically Reflective Teacher*. San Francisco: Jossey-Bass, 1995.

———. *The Skillful Teacher: On Technique, Trust, and Responsiveness in the Classroom*. 2nd ed. Jossey-Bass Higher and Adult Education Series. San Francisco: Jossey-Bass, 2006.

Brookfield, Stephen D., and John D. Holst. *Radicalizing Learning: Adult Education for a Just World*. 1st ed. The Jossey-Bass Higher and Adult Education Series. San Francisco: John Wiley, 2011.

Cahalan, Kathleen A. "Integration in Theological Education." In *Wiley-Blackwell Companion to Practical Theology*, edited by Bonnie J. Miller-McLemore, 386–95. The Atrium, UK: Wiley-Blackwell, 2012.

———. *Introducing the Practice of Ministry*. Collegeville: Liturgical, 2010.

Campbell, Bruce. "Multiple Intelligences in the Classroom." *In Context* (Winter 1991) 12.

Cannon, Katie G. "Structured Academic Amnesia: As If This True Womanist Story Never Happened." In *Deeper Shade of Purple: Womanism in Religion and Society*, edited by Stacey Floyd-Thomas, 19–28. New York: New York University Press, 2006.

———. "Unctuousness as Virtue, According to the Life of Zora Neal Hurston." In *Katie's Canon: Womanism and the Soul of the Black Community*, by Katie Cannon, 91–100. New York: Continuum, 1995.

Carbado, Devon W., and Mitu Gulati. "Working Identity." *Cornell Law Review* 85 (2000) 1259–1307.

Carrette, Jeremy, and Richard King. *Selling Spirituality: The Silent Takeover of Religion*. London: Routledge, 2005.

Carroll, Jackson W., et al. *Being There: Culture and Formation in Two Theological Schools*. New York: Oxford University Press, 1997.

Case, Karen A. "Claiming White Social Location as a Site of Resistance to White Supremacy." In *Disrupting White Supremacy from Within: White People on What We Need to Do*, edited by Jennifer Harvey, et al., 63–90. Cleveland: Pilgrim, 2004.

The Center for the Study of White American Culture, Inc. "Definitions of Racism." http://www.euroamerican.org/Library/Definitions_Racism.asp.

Cha, Peter. "Student Learning and Formation: An Improvisational Model." In *Revitalizing Practice: Collaborative Models for Theological Faculties*, edited by Malcolm L. Warford, 33–66. New York: Peter Lang, 2008.

Chopp, Rebecca S. *Saving Work: Feminist Practices of Theological Education*. Louisville: Westminster John Knox, 1995.

Clarke, Matthew. "The Ethico-politics of Teacher Identity." *Educational Philosophy and Theory* 41 (April 1, 2009) 185–200.

Coates, Rodney D. "Covert Racism in the USA and Globally." *Sociology Compass* 2 (January 2008) 208–31.

Conde-Frazier, Elizabeth. "From Hospitality to Shalom." In *A Many Colored Kingdom: Multicultural Dynamics for Spiritual Formation*, edited by Elizabeth Conde-Frazier, et al., 169–210. Grand Rapids: Baker Academic, 2004.

———. *Hispanic Bible Institutes: A Community of Theological Construction*. Scranton, PA: Scranton University Press, 2004.

———. "Prejudice and Conversion." In *A Many Colored Kingdom: Multicultural Dynamics for Spiritual Formation*, edited by Elizabeth Conde-Frazier, et al., 105–20. Grand Rapids: Baker Academic, 2004.

Copeland, M. Shawn. *Enfleshing Freedom: Body, Race, and Being*. Minneapolis: Fortress, 2009.

Cornell, Stephen. *The Return of the Native: American Indian Political Resurgence*. New York: Oxford University Press, 1988.

Costas, Orlando E. *Christ Outside the Gate: Mission Beyond Christendom*. Maryknoll, NY: Orbis, 1982.

de Botton, Alain. *The Architecture of Happiness*. London: Penguin, 2006.

de Gruchy, John W. *Theology and Ministry in Context and Crisis: A South African Perspective*. London: Collins Liturgical Publications, 1986.

De La Torre, Miguel and Stacey M. Floyd-Thomas, eds. *Beyond the Pale: Reading Ethics from the Margins*. Louisville: Westminster John Knox Press, 2011.

Delgado, Richard. *Critical Race Theory: The Cutting Edge*. Philadelphia: Temple University Press, 1995.

DeVos, George A. "Dimensions of the Self in Japanese Culture." In *Culture and Self: Asian and Western Perspectives*, edited by Anthony J. Marsella, et al., 141–84. New York: Tavistock, 1985.

Douglas, Kelly Brown. "Twenty Years a Womanist: An Affirming Challenge." In *Deeper Shade of Purple: Womanism in Religion and Society*, edited by Stacey Floyd-Thomas, 19–28. New York: New York University Press, 2006.

Du Bois, W. E. B. *The Souls of Black Folk*. New York: Bantam Classics, 2005.

Dunbar, Paul Lawrence. "We Wear the Masks." http://www.potw.org/archive/potw8.html. (Originally published in Dunbar, Paul Lawrence. *Lyrics of Lowly Life*. New York: Dodd, Mead, and Company, 1896.)

Duncan, Carol B. "Visible/Invisible: Teaching Popular Culture and Vulgar Body in Black Religious Studies." In *Being Black, Teaching Black: Politics and Pedagogy in Religious Studies*, edited by Nancy Lynne Westfield, 3–15. Nashville: Abingdon, 2008.

Dykstra, Craig R. "The Pastoral Imagination." *Initiatives in Religion* 9 (2001) 1–11.

Eisner, Elliot W. *The Educational Imagination: On the Design and Evaluation of School Programs*. 3rd ed. New York: Pearson, 2001.

Elbaz-Luwisch, Freema. "How Is Education Possible When There's a Body in the Middle of the Room?" *Curriculum Inquiry* 34 (2004) 9–27.

Ellison, Ralph. *The Invisible Man*. New York: Random House, 1980.

Emerson, Michael O. *People of the Dream: Multiracial Congregations in the United States*. Princeton, NJ: Princeton University Press, 2006.

Emerson, Michael O., and Christian Smith. *Divided by Faith: Evangelical Religion and The Problem of Race in America*. New York: Oxford University Press, 2000.

Espiritu, Yen Le. *Asian-American Panethnicity: Bridging Institutions and Identities*. Philadelphia: Temple University Press, 1992.

————. *Asian American Women and Men: Labor, Laws and Love*. Thousand Oaks, CA: Sage, 1997.

Evans, Kathy M., and Edwin L. Herr. "The Influence of Racism and Sexism in the Career Development of African American Women." *Journal of Multicultural Counseling & Development* 19 (July 1991) 130–35.

Fernandez, Eleazar S. "Global Hegemonic Power, Democracy, and the Theological Praxis of the Subaltern Multitude." In *Wading through Many Voices: Toward a Theology of Public Conversation*, edited by Harold Recinos, 53–67. New York: Rowman & Littlefield, 2011.

————. *Reimagining the Human: Theological Anthropology in Response to Systemic Evil*. St. Louis: Chalice, 2003.

Floyd-Thomas, Juan M., and Stacey M. Floyd-Thomas. "Emancipatory Historiography as Pedagogical Praxis: The Blessing and the Curse of Theological Education." In *Being Black, Teaching Black*, edited by Nancy Lynne Westfield, 95–106. Nashville: Abingdon, 2008.

Floyd-Thomas, Stacey M. "Writing for Our Lives: Womanism as an Epistemological Revolution." In *Deeper Shades of Purple: Womanism in Religion and Society*, edited by Stacey M. Floyd-Thomas, 1–16. New York: New York University Press, 2006.

Ford, Terry. *Becoming Multicultural: Personal and Social Construction Through Critical Teaching*. New York: Falmer, 1999.

Foss-Snowden, Michele S. "Standpoint Theory and Discontinuing Denial of Racism, Sexism, and Ageism." In *Still Searching for Our Mothers' Gardens: Experiences of New, Tenure-Track Women of Color at 'Majority' Institutions*, edited by Marnel N. Niles and Nickesia S. Gordon, 79–91. Lanham, MD: University Press of America, 2011.

Foster, Charles R. "Diversity in Theological Education." *Theological Education* 38 (2002) 15–37.

Foster, Charles R., et al. *Educating Clergy: Teaching Practices and the Pastoral Imagination*. San Francisco: Jossey Bass, 2006.

Frankenberg, Ruth. *White Women, Race Matters: The Social Construction of Race*. Minneapolis: University of Minnesota Press, 1993.

Freire, Paolo. *Education for Critical Consciousness*. New York: Seabury Press, 1973.

————. "Letter to North-American Teachers." Translated by Carman Hunter. In *Freire for the Classroom: A Sourcebook for Liberatory Teaching*, edited by Ira Shor, 211–14. Portsmouth, NH: Boynton/Cook, 1987.

————. *Pedagogy of Freedom: Ethics, Democracy, and Civic Courage*. Translated by Patrick Clarke. Critical Perspectives Series. Lanham, MD: Rowman & Littlefield, 1998.

————. *Pedagogy of the Oppressed*. New York: Herder and Herder, 1970.

————. *The Politics of Education: Culture, Power, and Liberation*. South Hadley, MA: Bergin & Garvey, 1985.

————. *Teachers as Cultural Workers: Letters to Those Who Dare Teach*. Translated by Donaldo Macedo, Dale Koike and Alexandre Oliveira. The Edge, Critical Studies in Educational Theory. Boulder, CO: Westview, 1998.

Frey, William H. "The Census Projects Minority Surge." Washington DC: The Brookings Institution, August 18, 2008. http://www.brookings.edu/research/opinions/2008/08/18-census-frey.

Friedland, Roger, and Richard D. Hecht. "The Powers of Place." In *Religion, Violence, Memory, and Place*, edited by Oren Baruch Stier and J. Shawn Landres, 17–36. Bloomington: Indiana University Press, 2006.

Gadoti, Moacir. *Reading Paulo Friere: His Life and His Work*. Albany: State University of New York, 1994.

Gans, Herbert J. "Symbolic Ethnicity and Symbolic Religiosity: Towards a Comparison of Ethnic and Religious Acculturation." *Ethnic and Racial Studies* 17 (1994) 577–92.

Gardner, Howard. *Frames of Mind: The Theory of Multiple Intelligences*. New York: Basic, 1983.

Gatison, Annette Madlock. "Playing the Game: Communicative Practices for Negotiating Politics and Preparing for Tenure." In *Still Searching for Our Mothers' Gardens: Experiences of New, Tenure-Track Women of Color at 'Majority' Institutions*, edited by Marnel N. Niles and Nickesia S. Gordon, 3–20. Lanham, MD: University Press of America, 2011.

Geertz, Clifford. *The Interpretation of Cultures*. New York: Basic Books, 1973.

Gibson, Linda S. "Teaching as an Encounter with the Self: Unraveling the Mix of Personal Beliefs, Education Ideologies, and Pedagogical Practices." *Anthropology and Education Quarterly* 29 (1998) 360–71.

Giddings, Paula. *When and Where I Enter: The Impact of Black Women on Sex and Race in America*. New York: Harper Collins, 1984.

Gillborn, David. "Critical Race Theory and Education: Racism and Anti-Racism in Educational Theory and Praxis." *Discourse: Studies in the Cultural Politics of Education* 27 (March 1, 2006) 11–32.

Giroux, Henry A. *Pedagogy and the Politics of Hope: Theory, Culture, and Schooling*. The Edge, Critical Studies in Educational Theory. Boulder, CO: Westview, 1997.

———. *Curriculum & Instruction: Alternatives in Education*. Berkeley, CA: McCutchan, 1981.

Glascock, Jack, and Thomas E. Ruggiero. "The Relationship of Ethnicity and Sex to Professor Credibility at a Culturally Diverse University." *Communication Education* 55 (April 2006) 197–207.

Gordon, Nickesia S. "Watching My B/Lack: The Not So Colorblind World of Academia." In *Still Searching for Our Mothers' Gardens: Experiences of New, Tenure-Track Women of Color at 'Majority' Institutions*, edited by Marnel N. Niles and Nickesia S. Gordon, 3–20. Lanham, MD: University Press of America, 2011.

Gorsline, Robin Harvey. "Shaking the Foundations: White Supremacy in the Theological Academy." In *Disrupting White Supremacy from Within: White People on What We Need to Do*, edited by Jennifer Harvey, et al., 33–62. Cleveland: Pilgrim, 2004.

Graham, Elaine. "Towards a Practical Theology of Embodiment." In *Globalisation and Difference: Practical Theology in a World Context*, edited by Paul Ballard and Pam Couture, 79–84. Fairwater, Cardiff, Great Britain: Cardiff Academic Press, 1999.

Greenwood, David A. "Education in a Culture of Violence: A Critical Pedagogy of Place in Wartime." *Cultural Studies of Science Education* 5 (June 2010) 351–59.

Groody, Daniel G. *Globalization, Spirituality, and Justice*. Maryknoll, NY: Orbis, 2007.

Groome, Thomas H. *Christian Religious Education: Sharing Our Story and Vision*. San Francisco: Jossey-Bass, 1999.

Grossman, Bart. "Online College—a matter of class." *San Francisco Chronicle* (March 15, 2013).

Gupta, Kavita, et al., eds. *A Practical Guide to Needs Assessment*. 2nd ed. San Francisco: Pfeiffer, 2007.

Gutiérrez y Muhs, Gabriella. *Presumed Incompetent: The Intersections of Race and Class for Women in Academia*. Boulder: University Press of Colorado, 2012.

Hall, Douglas John. *Lighten Our Darkness: Toward an Indigenous Theology of the Cross*. Philadelphia: Westminster, 1976.

Harding, Sandra. "Gendered Ways of Knowing and the 'Epistemological Crisis' of the West." In *Knowledge, Difference, and Power: Essays Inspired by Women's Ways of Knowing*, edited by Nancy Rule Goldberger, et al., 431–54. New York: Basic, 1996.

Harris, Maria. *Fashion Me a People: Curriculum in the Church*. Louisville: Westminster John Knox, 1989.

Harro, Bobbi. "The Cycle of Socialization." In *Readings for Diversity and Social Justice*, 2nd ed., edited by Maurianne Adams et al., 45–51. New York: Routledge, 2010.

Harvey, Joan C. "The Impostor Phenomenon and Achievement: Issues of Sex, Race, and Self-Perceived Atypicality." Paper presented at The Annual Convention of the American Psychological Association, Los Angeles, August 24–26, 1981.

Hayes, Diana. *Hagar's Daughters: Womanist Ways of Being in the World*. Notre Dame, IN: Saint Mary's College, 1995.

Heggins III, Wille J., and Jerlano F. L. Jackson. "Understanding the Collegiate Experience for Asian International Students at a Midwestern Research University." *College Student Journal* 37 (2003) 134–44.

Heschel, Abraham Joshua. *The Insecurity of Freedom: Essays on Human Existence*. New York: Farrar, Straus & Giroux, 1966.

Hessel, Dieter. *Social Ministry*. Rev. ed. Louisville: Westminster John Knox, 1992.

Hill, Jack. "Fighting the Elephant in the Room: Ethical Reflections on White Privilege and Other Systems of Advantage in the Teaching of Religion." *Teaching Theology & Religion* 12 (January 2009) 3–23.

Hinton, Mary. "In Need of a Newer Model." *Diverse Issues in Higher Education* 27 (October 2010) 43.

Hobgood, Mary Elizabeth. *Dismantling Privilege: An Ethics of Accountability*. Rev. ed. Cleveland: Pilgrim, 2009.

Hoggart, Simon. *On the House*. London: Robson, 1981.

Holvino, Evangelina. "The 'Simultaneity' of Identities." In *New Perspectives on Racial Identity Development: Integrating Emerging Frameworks*, 2nd ed., edited by Charmayne Wijeyesinghe and Bailey Jackson III, 161–91. New York: New York University Press, 2012.

hooks, bell. "Engaged Pedagogy." In *Teaching to Transgress: Education as the Practice of Freedom*, by bell hooks, 13–22. New York: Routledge, 1994.

———. *Talking Back: Thinking Feminist, Thinking Black*. Boston: South End, 1989.

———. *Teaching Community: A Pedagogy of Hope*. New York: Routledge, 2003.

———. *Teaching Critical Thinking: Practical Wisdom*. New York: Routledge, 2010.

———. *Teaching to Transgress: Education as the Practice of Freedom*. New York: Routledge, 1994.

Hui, C. Harry, and Harry Trandis. "Individualism-Collectivism: A Study of Cross-Cultural Researchers." *The Journal of Cross-Cultural Psychology* 17 (June 1998) 225–48.

Humphreys, Debra. "Faculty Recruitment in Higher Education: Research Findings on Diversity and Affirmative Action." http://www.diversityweb.org/diversity_

innovations/faculty_staff_development/recruitment_tenure_promotion/faculty_recruitment.cfm.

Hyland, Nora E. "Being a Good Teacher of Black Students? White Teachers and Unintentional Racism." *Curriculum Inquiry* 35 (Winter 2005) 429–59.

Jackson, Bailey W. "The Theory and Practice of Multicultural Organization Development in Education." In *Teaching Inclusively: Resources for Course, Department & Institutional Change in Higher Education*, edited by Mathew Ouellett, 3–20. Stillwater, OK: New Forums, 2005.

Jinkins, Michael. "The Professor's Vocations: Reflections on the Teacher as Writer." *Teaching Theology & Religion* 7 (April 2004) 64–70.

Jones, Charisse, and Kumea Shorter-Gooden. *Shifting: The Double Lives of Black Women in America*. New York: Harper Perennial, 2004.

Jones, L. Gregory, and Stephanie Paulsell, eds. *The Scope of Our Art: The Vocation of a Theological Teacher*. Grand Rapids: Eerdmans, 2002.

Kegan, Robert. *The Evolving Self: Problem and Process in Human Development*. Cambridge, MA: Harvard University Press, 1982.

Kendall, Frances. *Understanding White Privilege: Creating Pathways to Authentic Relationships Across Race*. New York: Routledge, 2006.

Kerner, Otto, et al. *The Kerner Commission Report*. Washington, D.C.: The President's National Advisory Commission on Civil Disorders, 1968.

Kingston, Maxine Hong. *The Woman Warrior: Memoirs of a Girlhood Among Ghosts*. New York: Vintage International, 1989.

Klimoski, Victor. "Evolving Dynamics of Formation." In *Practical Wisdom: On Theological Teaching and Learning*, edited by Malcolm L. Warford, 29–47. New York: Peter Lang, 2004.

Klimoski, Victor, et al. *Educating Leaders for Ministry*. Collegeville, MN: Liturgical, 2005.

Knowlton, Dave S., and David C. Chart, eds. *Problem-Based Learning in the Information Age*. San Francisco: Jossey-Bass, 2003.

Kong, Luis. "Immigration, Racial Identity, and Adult Education: Reflections on a Transnational Paradigm of Resistance." In *The Handbook of Race and Adult Education,* edited by Vanessa Sheared, et al. San Francisco: Jossey-Bass, 2010. http://bridges.searchmobius.org:80/record=b1854202~S9.

Kress, Robert. "Unity in Diversity and Diversity in Unity: Toward an Ecumenical Perichoresic Kenotic Trinitarian Ontology." *Dialogue and Alliance* 4 (Fall 1990) 66–70.

Krueger, Richard A., and Mary Anne Casey. *Focus Groups: A Practical Guide for Applied Research*. 4th ed. Thousand Oaks, CA: Sage, 2009.

Kujawa-Holbrook, Sheryl. "Beyond Diversity: Cultural Competence, White Racism Awareness, and European-American Theology Students." *Teaching Theology and Religion* 5 (July 2002) 141–48.

Kumashiro, Kevin K. *Troubling Intersections of Race and Sexuality: Queer Students of Color and Anti-Oppressive Education*. Curriculum, Cultures, and (Homo) Sexualities. Lanham, MD: Rowman & Littlefield, 2001.

Kuruvila, Matthia. "'Enough is enough.' Black pastors emerge as strong voice pushing city to combat violent crime." *San Francisco Chronicle* (February 17, 2013).

Kwok, Pui-lan. "Fishing the Asia Pacific: Transnationalism and Feminist Theology." In *Off the Menu: Asian and Asian North American Women's Religion and Theology*, edited by Rita Nakashima Brock, et al., 3–22. Louisville: Westminster John Knox, 2007.

Kwok, Pui-lan, et al. "Taken with Surprise: Critical Incidents in Teaching." *Teaching Theology & Religion* 8 (2005) 35–46.

LaCugna, Catherine Mowry. *God for Us: The Trinity and Christian Life*. New York: HarperCollins, 1991.

Ladson-Billings, Gloria. "Racialized Discourses and Ethnic Epistemologies." In *Handbook of Qualitative Research*, 2nd ed., edited by Normat K. Denzin and Yvonne S. Lincoln, 257–77. Thousand Oaks, CA: Sage, 2000.

Lawson, Erica. "Feminist Pedagogies: The Textuality of the Racialized Body in the Feminist Classroom," 107–17. http://journals.msvu.ca/index.php/atlantis/article/view/923/919.

Lee, Boyung. "Broadening the Boundary of 'Textbooks' for Intercultural Communication in Religious Education." *Religious Education* 105 (2010) 249–52.

Lee, Virginia S., ed. *Teaching & Learning Through Inquiry: A Guidebook for Institutions*. Sterling, VA: Stylus, 2004.

Liew, Tat-siong Benny. *What Is Asian American Biblical Hermeneutics? Reading the New Testament*. Intersections: Asian and Pacific American Transcultural Studies. Honolulu: University of Hawai'i Press, 2008.

Lines, Timothy Arthur. *Functional Images of the Religious Educator*. Birmingham, AL: Religious Education Press, 1992.

Lipsitz, George. "The Possessive Investment in Whiteness." In *Readings for Diversity and Social Justice*, 2nd ed., edited by Maurianne Adams, et al., 79–87. New York: Routledge, 2010.

Littlejohn, Stephen W., and Karen A. Foss. *Theories of Human Communication*. 10th ed. Long Grove, IL: Waveland, 2011.

Lorde, Audre. *Sister Outsider: Essays and Speeches by Audre Lorde*. Freedom, CA: The Crossing, 1984.

———. *Sister Outsider: Essays and Speeches by Audre Lorde*. 2nd ed. Berkeley: Crossing, 2007.

Loughlin, Gerard. "What Is Queer? Theology after Identity." *Theology & Sexuality* 14 (January 1 2008) 143–52.

Lowe, Lisa. *Immigrant Acts: On Asian American Cultural Politics*. Durham, NC: Duke University Press, 1996.

Machado, Daisy L. "Voices from *Nepantla*: Latinas in U.S. Religious History." In *Feminist Intercultural Theology: Latina Explorations for a Just World*, edited by María Pilar Aquino and María José Rosado-Nunes, 89–108. Maryknoll, NY: Orbis, 2007.

Maldonado Pérez, Zaida, et al. "Dancing with the Wild Child: *Evangélicas* and the Holy Spirit." In *Latinas Evangélicas: A Theological Survey from the Margins*, by Loida I. Martell-Otero et al., no pages. Eugene, OR: Cascade, forthcoming.

Marable, Manning. "Losing Ground? Recent Trends in Black Higher Education Along the Color Line." *The Black Commentator* 270 (March 27, 2008). http:// www.blackcommentator.com.

Marchesani, Linda S., and Maurianne Adams. "Dynamics of Diversity in the Teaching-Learning Process: A Faculty Development Model for Analysis and Action." *New Directions for Teaching and Learning* 52 (1992) 9–19.

Martell-Otero, Loida I. "From *Satas* to *Santas*: *Sobrajas* No More—Salvation in the Spaces of the Everyday." In *Latinas Evangélicas: A Theological Survey from the Margins*, by Loida I. Martell-Otero et al., no pages. Eugene, OR: Cascade, forthcoming.

"Masks." *The Encyclopedia of World Art* 9 (1964) 520–70.

Matsuoka, Fumitaka. *The Color of Faith: Building Community in a Multicultural Society.* Cleveland: United Church Press, 1998.

Mays, Benjamin E. Response to Sydney E. Ahlstrom. In *American Religious Values and the Future of America*, edited by Rodger van Allen. Philadelphia: Fortress, 1978.

McAdams, Dan P. *The Stories We Live By: Personal Myths and the Making of the Self.* New York: William Morrow, 1993.

Mills, David, and Mette Louise Berg. "Gender, Disembodiment and Vocation: Exploring the Unmentionables of British Academic Life." *Critique of Anthropology* 30 (December 2010) 331–53.

Misawa, Mitsunori. "Musings on Controversial Intersections of Positionality: A Queer Crit Perspective in Adult and Continuing Education." In *The Handbook of Race and Adult Education*, edited by Vanessa Sheared, et al. San Francisco: Jossey-Bass, 2010. http://bridges.searchmobius.org:80/record=b1854202~S9.

Mitchell, Jacquelyn. "Visible, Vulnerable, and Viable: Emerging Perspectives of a Minority Professor." In *Teaching Minority Students*, New Directions for Teaching and Learning 16, edited by James H. Cones, et al. , 17–28. San Francisco: Jossey-Bass, 1983.

Mohanty, Chandra Talpade. *Feminism Without Borders: Decolonizing Theory, Practicing Solidarity*. Durham, NC: Duke University Press, 2003.

Moore, Mary Elizabeth Mullino. "Stories of Vocation: Education for Vocational Discernment." *Religious Education* 103 (April 2008) 218–39.

Murray, Ian J., et al. "Sex-related differences in peripheral human color vision: A color matching study." *Journal of Vision: A Journal of Scientific Research on Biological Vision* 12 (January 23, 2012) 1–10. http://www.journalofvision.org/content/12/1/18.full.

Museus, Samuel D., ed. *Conducting Research on Asian Americans in Higher Education.* New Directions for Institutional Research 142. San Francisco: Jossey-Bass, 2009.

Museus, Samuel D., and Peter N. Kiang. "Deconstructing the Model Minority Myth and How It Contributes to the Invisible Minority Reality in Higher Education Research." In *Conducting Research on Asian Americans in Higher Education*, New Directions for Institutional Research, issue 142, edited by Samuel D. Museus, 5–15. San Francisco: Jossey-Bass, 2009.

Nagel, Joane. *American Indian Ethnic Renewal: Red Power and the Resurgence of Identity and Culture.* New York: Oxford University Press, 1996.

Nakanishi, Don T., and Tina Yamano Nishida, eds. *The Asian American Educational Experience: A Source Book for Teachers and Students.* New York: Routledge, 1995.

Niebuhr, H. Richard. *The Purpose of the Church and Its Ministry.* New York: Harper and Brothers, 1957.

Niles, Marnel N., and Nickesia S. Gordon, eds. *Still Searching for Our Mothers' Gardens: Experiences of New, Tenure-Track Women of Color at 'Majority' Institutions.* Lanham, MD: University Press of America, 2011.

Oliver, Kelley. *The Colonization of Psychic Space: A Psychoanalytic Social Theory of Oppression.* Minneapolis: University of Minnesota Press, 2004.

Omi, Michael, and Howard Winant. *Racial Formation in the United States: From the 1960s to the 1980s*. Critical Social Thought, edited by Michael W. Apple. London: Routledge & Kegan Paul, 1986.

————. *Racial Formation in the United States from the 1960s to the 1990s*. 2nd ed. Critical Social Thought, edited by Michael W. Apple. New York: Routledge, 1994.

Ong, Aihwa. *Flexible Citizenship: The Cultural Logics of Transnationality*. Durham, NC: Duke University Press, 1999.

Pacific School of Religion. Direction Statement, from http://www.psr.edu/direction-statement.

Palmer, Parker J. *The Courage to Teach: Exploring the Inner Landscape of a Teacher*. San Francisco: Jossey-Bass, 1998.

————. "A Life Lived Whole." http://www.yesmagazine.org/issues/healing-resistance/a-life-lived-whole. 2004.

————. *To Know as We are Known: Education as a Spiritual Journey*. New York: HarperCollins, 1993.

Palumbo-Liu, David. *Asian/American: Historical Crossings of a Racial Frontier*. Stanford, CA: Stanford University Press, 1999.

Patitu, Carl Logan, and Kandace G. Hinton. "The experiences of African American women faculty and administrators in higher education: Has anything changed?" In *Meeting the Needs of African American Women: New Directions for Student Services*, edited by Mary F. Howard-Hamilton, 104 (Winter 2003) 79–93.

Patterson, Orlando. "Race Unbound." Review of *Who's Afraid of Post-Blackness?: What It Means to Be Black Now*, by Touré. *The New York Times*, September 25, 2011.

Pazmiño, Robert W. *Foundational Issues in Christian Education: An Introduction in Evangelical Perspective*. 4th ed. Grand Rapids: Baker Academic, 2008.

Pederson, Ann Milliken. "The Nature of Embodiment: Religion and Science in Dialogue." *Zygon* 45 (March 2010) 264–72.

Pinar, William F. "Notes on Understanding Curriculum as Racial Text." In *Race, Identity, and Representation in Education*, edited by Cameron McCarthy and Warren Crichlow, 60–70. Critical Social Thought. New York: Routledge, 1993.

Pinn, Anthony. "Reading the Signs: The Body as Non-Written Text." In *Being Black, Teaching Black: Politics and Pedagogy in Religious Studies*, edited by Nancy Lynne Westfield, 79–94. Nashville: Abingdon, 2008.

Prater, Angela, et al. "Disclose and Demystify: The Discrepancy between the Concept of Diversity and the Action of Diversity in the Face of 'Stubborn Faculty, Wary Students, and Unsupportive Administrators.'" In *Still Searching for Our Mothers' Gardens: Experiences of New, Tenure-Track Women of Color at 'Majority' Institutions*, edited by Marnel N. Niles and Nickesia S. Gordon, 3–20. Lanham, MD: University Press of America, 2011.

Quiñones Rivera, Maritza. "From Trigueñita to Afro-Puerto Rican: Intersection of the Racialized, Gendered, and Sexualized Body in Puerto Rico and the U.S. Mainland." *Meridians: Feminism, Race, Transnationalis* 7 (2006) 162–82.

Ramsey, Nancy J. "Teaching Effectively in Racially and Culturally Diverse Classrooms." *Teaching Theology and Religion* 8 (2005) 18–23.

Reason, Robert D., et al., eds. *New Directions in Student Services* 110 (Summer 2005). San Francisco: Jossey Bass, 2005.

Rendón, Laura I. *Sentipensante Pedagogy (Sensing/Thinking): Education for Wholeness, Social Justice and Liberation*. Sterling, VA: Stylus, 2009.

Ridderbos, Herman. *Paul: An Outline of His Theology*. Translated by John Richard de Witt. Grand Rapids: Eerdmans, 1975.

Ropers-Huilman, Becky, ed. *Gendered Futures in Higher Education: Critical Perspectives for Change*. Albany: State University of New York, 2003.

Rumbaut, Rubén G. "Vietnamese, Laotian, and Cambodian Americans." In *Contemporary Asian America: A Multidisciplinary Reader*, edited by Min Zhou and James V. Gatewood, 175–206. New York: New York University Press, 2000.

Russell, Letty M. *Just Hospitality: God's Welcome in a World of Difference*. Louisville: Westminster John Knox, 2009.

Said, Edward. *Culture and Imperialism*. New York: Vintage, 1994.

———. *Reflections on Exile and Other Essays*. Cambridge, MA: Harvard University Press, 2002.

Schein, Edgar. *Organizational Culture and Leadership*. 4th ed. San Francisco: Jossey Bass, 2010.

Schiro, Michael. *Curriculum for Better Schools: The Great Ideological Debate*. Englewood Cliffs, NJ: Educational Technology Publications, 1978.

Schüssler Fiorenza, Elisabeth. *But She Said: Feminist Practices of Biblical Interpretation*. Boston: Beacon, 1992.

Sealey-Ruiz, Yolanda. "Reading, Writing, and Racism: Developing Racial Literacy in the Adult Education English Classroom." In *The Handbook of Race and Adult Education,* edited by Vanessa Sheared, et al. San Francisco: Jossey-Bass, 2010. http://bridges.searchmobius.org:80/record=b1854202~S9.

Shah, Sonia, ed. *Dragon Ladies: Asian American Feminists Breathe Fire*. Boston: South End, 1997.

Shor, Ira, and Paulo Freire. *A Pedagogy for Education: Dialogues on Transforming Education*. South Hadley MA: Bergin & Garvey, 1987.

Shrewsbury, Carolyn M. "What is Feminist Pedagogy?" *Women's Studies Quarterly* 15 (1993) 8–16.

Shriver, Jr., Donald W. "The Pain and Promise of Pluralism." *The Christian Century* 97 (March 26, 1980) 345–50.

Skubikowski, Kathleen, et al., eds. *Social Justice Education: Inviting Faculty to Transform Their Institutions*. Sterling, VA: Stylus, 2009.

Smith, William A., et al., eds. *The Racial Crisis in American Higher Education: Continuing Challenges for the Twenty-First Century*. Albany: State University of New York, 2002.

Snow, Richard F. "The Smile Above the Tragedy." *American Legacy* 2 (Summer 1996) 8–9.

Soja, Edward W. *Postmodern Geographies: The Reassertion of Space in Critical Social Theory*. London: Verso, 1989.

Spelman, Elizabeth V. *Inessential Woman: Problems of Exclusion in Feminist Thought*. Boston: Beacon, 1988.

Stanley, Christine, et al. "Multicultural Course Transformation." In *Teaching Inclusively: Resources for Course, Department & Institutional Change in Higher Education,* edited by Mathew L. Ouellett, 566–84. Stillwater, OK: New Forums, 2005.

Swidler, Ann. "Culture in Action: Symbols and Strategies." *American Sociological Review* 51 (1986) 273–86.

Takaki, Ronald T. *Iron Cages: Race and Culture in 19th-Century America*. Rev. ed. New York: Oxford University Press, 2000.

———. *Strangers from a Different Shore: A History of Asian Americans.* Updated and rev. ed. Boston: Little Brown, 1998.

Toll, Robert C. *Blacking Up: The Minstrel Show in Nineteenth Century America.* New York: Oxford University Press, 1974.

Trinh, T. Minh-ha. "Cotton and Iron." In *Out There: Marginalization and Contemporary Cultures,* edited by Russell Ferguson, et al. Documentary Sources in Contemporary Art, 327–36. Cambridge: MIT Press, 1990.

Turner, Caroline Sotello Viernes. "Women of Color in Academe: Living with Multiple Marginality." *The Journal of Higher Education* 73 (January/February 2002) 74–93.

Turner, Caroline Sotello Viernes, and Samuel L. Myers Jr. *Faculty of Color in Academe: Bittersweet Success.* Boston: Allyn and Bacon, 2000.

TuSmith, Bonnie, and Maureen T. Reddy, eds. *Race in the College Classroom: Pedagogy and Politics.* New Brunswick, NJ: Rutgers University Press. 2002.

U.S. Census Bureau News. "Population," released on August 24, 2008. www.census.gov/Press-Release/www/releases/archives/population.

van den Blink, A. J. "Empathy Amid Diversity: Problems and Possibilities." *Journal of Pastoral Theology* 3 (Summer 1993) 1–14.

van Gennep, Arnold. *The Rites of Passage.* Chicago: University of Chicago Press, 1960.

Vella, Jane Kathryn. *Learning to Listen, Learning to Teach: The Power of Dialogue in Educating Adults.* San Francisco: Jossey-Bass, 1994.

Volf, Miroslav. *Exclusion and Embrace: A Theological Exploration of Identity, Otherness, and Reconciliation.* Nashville: Abingdon, 1996.

The Wabash Center. www.wabashcenter.wabash.edu.

The Wabash Center, Consultants Program. http://www.wabashcenter.wabash.edu/consultants/default.aspx.

Walker, Alice. *In Search of Our Mothers' Gardens: Womanist Prose.* 1st ed. San Diego: Harcourt Brace Jovanovich, 1983.

Warford, Malcom, ed. *Practical Wisdom: On Theological Teaching and Learning.* New York: Peter Lang, 2004.

Waters, Mary C. *Ethnic Options: Choosing Identities in America.* Berkeley, CA: University of California Press, 1990.

Watt, John. *Individualism and Educational Theory.* Boston: Kluwer Academic, 1989.

Weber, Max. *The Protestant Ethic and the Spirit of Capitalism.* New York: Scribner, 1958.

Wellman, David. *Portraits of White Racism.* Cambridge: Cambridge University Press, 1977.

Westerhoff III, John H. *Will Our Children Have Faith?* New York: Seabury, 1976.

Westfield, Nancy Lynne, ed. *Being Black, Teaching Black: Politics and Pedagogy in Religious Studies.* Nashville: Abingdon, 2008.

———. "Called Out My Name, or Had I Known You Were Somebody: The Pain of Fending Off Stereotypes." In *Being Black, Teaching Black,* edited by Nancy Lynne Westfield, 61–78. Nashville: Abingdon, 2008.

Wildman, Stephanie M., and Adrienne D. Davis. "Language and Silence: Making Systems of Privilege Visible." In *Readings for Diversity and Social Justice,* edited by Maurianne Adams et al., 50–60. New York: Routledge, 2000.

Williams, Rowan. *Writing in the Dust: After September 11.* Grand Rapids: Eerdmans, 2002.

Wilmore, Gayraud S. "Introduction." In *Black Pastors/White Professors: An Experiment in Dialogic Education,* edited by Gayraud S. Wilmore. *Theological Education: Special Issue* 16, (Winter 1980) 85–97.

Wilson, Elvinet S. "Strangers in the Ivory Tower: Framing International Female Faculty Identity Negotiations in a 'Majority' Academic Institution." In *Still Searching for Our Mothers' Gardens: Experiences of New, Tenure-Track Women of Color at 'Majority' Institutions,* edited by Marnel N. Niles and Nickesia S. Gordon, 153–74. Lanham, MD: University Press of America, 2011.

Wolff, Hans Walter. *Anthropology of the Old Testament.* Translated by Margaret Kohl. Philadelphia: Fortress, 1974.

Yamato, Gloria. "Something About the Subject Makes It Hard to Name." In *Experiencing Race, Class, and Gender in the United States,* edited by Virginia Cyrus, 206–9. Mountain View, CA: Mayfield, 1993.

Young, Iris Marion. *Justice and the Politics of Difference.* Princeton, NJ: Princeton University Press, 1990.

Zamudio, Margaret. *Critical Race Theory Matters: Education and Ideology.* New York: Routledge, 2010. http://bridges.searchmobius.org:80/record=b1854152~S9.

Zizioulas, John. "Communion and Otherness." *St. Vladimir's Theological Quarterly* 38 (1994) 347–61.

☆ Liberation/ist: pp. 3, 5, 29, 93, 133, 179,

☆ justice: pp. 15, 16, 29, 48, 68, 70, 98, 135, 139, 145, 148,
149, 150, 152-3ff, 160, 163, 184ff, 193, 199, 200,
201, 203, 228, 232, 237, 239, 249

☆ Common Good: pp. 14, 92,

☆ incarnation(al), pp. 64